SUCCESS OVER SIXTY

Albert Myers and Christopher P. Andersen

SUMMIT BOOKS · NEW YORK

Published by SUMMIT BOOKS
A Division of Simon & Schuster, Inc.
Simon & Schuster Building
1230 Avenue of the Americas
New York, New York 10020
SUMMIT BOOKS and colophon are trademarks of Simon & Schuster, Inc.
Designed by Eve Kirch
Manufactured in the United States of America

10 9 8 7 6 5 4 3 2 1

Library of Congress Cataloging in Publication Data
Myers, Albert.
   Success over sixty.
   Bibliography: p.
   Includes index.
   1. Retirement—United States.   2. Aged—Employment—
United States.   3. Success.   I. Anderson, Christopher P.
II. Title.
HQ1062.M93   1984   646.7'9   84-8703
ISBN 0-671-49460-0

ACKNOWLEDGMENTS

In our search for the key to Success Over Sixty, we were fortunate to have the encouragement and cooperation of hundreds of men and women. First, we owe a special debt of gratitude to Jim Silberman, editor-in-chief of Summit Books, our editor Ileene Smith, Summit publicity director Wendy Nicholson and our agent, Ellen Levine, who is simply the best in the business. We must also thank Shirley and Richard Clurman and William Friedman for bringing us together in the first place—without them, there might never have been a *Success Over Sixty*.

Our special thanks to Dr. Alex Comfort, Richard Bolles, Senator Charles Percy, William Dooner, Sylvia Porter, J. K. Jamieson, Donald Kendall, Edgar Stern, Dr. Lawrence Morehouse, Jack Holtz, Ron Gross, Frank Pace, Gerald Peale, Carson Conrad, Barbara Hildeband, Corrine Willing, George Becker, Stanley Marcus, Robert Rubenstein, B. A. Hyde, Dr. Emerson Ward, Dr. Bruno Balke, William Alley, Larry Phillips, Henry Henley, Marion Jeffreys, Marion Heiskell, Mort Heller, William Arnold, William Gingold, Charles Israel, Clarence Parker, Joseph Perkins, Stuart Watson, Kaylan Pickford, Polly Myers, Wilton and Jean Jaffee, Stanley and Jim Myers, Marilyn Silver, Sam Dorman, Len Berman, Dr. Bernard Haldane, Gunnar Wennerstrom, Fritz Benedict, Thomas Larkin, William Hersey and the late Ray Kroc.

Valerie and Katharine Andersen, Shirlee Kay and the rest of the Myers and Andersen families were pillars of support and patience; the demands on them matched the demands we made on ourselves.

To the important people in our lives

CONTENTS

FOREWORD

When the day came for him to retire, after more than forty years spent with the company his father started, Albert M. Myers was accorded the usual farewell banquet. After all the speeches and the toasts had been made, Myers was presented with an impressive-looking, Swiss-made gold clock. It wasn't until later that night that he noticed that his name was engraved on the clock's base. The only trouble: it was misspelled—"Meyers" instead of "Myers." How soon they forget!

But if Myers, who was not only the president of Myers Brothers Department Stores but also one of the company's namesakes, could so easily and callously be shunted aside, what chance is there for the average man or woman facing retirement? What can be done for those growing numbers of working people unwilling to pull over to the side of the road just because they have reached a particular age?

Plenty of books have been written by psychologists, sociologists and financial planners on how to adjust emotionally and make the most out of a pension, Medicare and Social Security. *But not one has been written by a successful businessman over sixty—until now. Success Over Sixty* spells out in plain English what is out there for you in the way of second careers, business and volunteer opportunities—and how to make the most of these opportunities. *Success Over Sixty* is also intended to help corporate executives make the most of one of their most valuable resources, the experienced employee. By formulating policies that take the graying of the

American workforce into account, corporations can add to their productivity and profits while enhancing the lives of the men and women who are not ready to drop out of the mainstream just because there are more candles on the cake.

We have also consulted the experts: sociologists, gerontologists, psychologists, attorneys, and authorities on finance, fitness and family relations. Most important, we went to hundreds of "retired" people who are anything but retired in the conventional sense—successes over sixty (many of them heads of *Fortune 500* companies, but mostly middle-management executives) who point the way for those of us who are truly coming of age in the 1980s.

Success Over Sixty is more than a book. It is a national movement, a program for coping with all the problems of adjustment confronted by millions of Americans unwilling to lie down and die because they have gray hair. Certainly, if your idea of bliss is retiring at sixty or sixty-five to a life of golf or fishing, then *Success Over Sixty* is not for you.

If, however, you are a few years from retirement and you want to begin planning for that second career, a business of your own, or just ways to hold on to the job you've got, *Success Over Sixty* is the key. Perhaps you are already retired and have grown bored and disillusioned, or maybe you are a homemaker who wants to try her wings in the business world, or one who is simply being driven crazy by a retired husband always under foot. *Success Over Sixty* can be your passport to a brighter future. In addition, it shows you where the volunteer and educational opportunities are and how to lead a healthier, sexier life.

All these years, you have been working for other people—your boss, your spouse, your children, your company, your country. Now you have the chance to start doing what *you* have always wanted to do.

At last it's your turn!

1 Success Over Sixty

*Of course I believe in the future. I intend to spend the
rest of my life there.*

—Charles Kettering

*Will you still need me,
will you still feed me,
when I'm 64?*

—The Beatles

You are over fifty or you care about someone who is. *Now*—
not next month or next year—is the time to start thinking
about what life will be like for you after sixty. Society is not
likely to make it easy for you. Even though 60 million Americans—more than a quarter of the population—are now fifty
or over, and current projections indicate that figure will climb
to one-third the total by the end of the century, ours is likely
to remain a nation of youth worshipers. And yet today's sixty-
five-year-old male can expect to live to seventy-nine and today's sixty-five-year-old female is likely to live to eighty-four.
Men now in their forties have an even chance of making it
past eighty-five, and women will live even longer: past ninety.

What we do with this precious gift of time is up to us. Now
that science and medicine have added years to our lives we
are left with a more formidable task—adding life to our years.
If we fail to look out for ourselves; if we refuse to act now to
make our sixties and beyond as productive and rewarding as
they can be, we have only ourselves to blame.

Ironically, the executive who takes great care in drafting five-year projections for his department or company almost never does the same for himself. The consequences of such career myopia are often calamitous. Larry Wilding joined a major West Coast liquor distributorship when he was discharged from the navy in 1948. He soon distinguished himself as a brilliant manager of inventory, and by the time he turned forty-five in 1965, Wilding was named a vice-president. But Wilding had reached a plateau; it was clear that he had risen as high as he could in the company and that he would go no farther. Not that it bothered him. After all, Larry had always prided himself on two things: being a company man and a realist.

What he had not bargained for, however, was that his company would be gobbled up by a New York-based conglomerate. At the age of fifty-seven, after twenty-nine years with the same employer, Larry was made an early retirement offer he couldn't refuse.

Financially, Larry and his wife had no worries. They bought a two-bedroom condominium in a suburban adult community and settled in for a life of golf and puttering. But for a man like Larry, it was not enough. Soon he gave up his golf game entirely, and despite urging from his wife to pursue a hobby or another sport, such as tennis or fishing, he did nothing but sit in front of the television set. When we met Larry, he was already sleeping twelve to fourteen hours a day, and his wife admitted to us that their life together—the "golden years" she had so been looking forward to—had turned into a nightmare. She had even urged him to go back to work, and in desperation had gone through the want ads herself, circling the possibilities and leaving them next to his coffee cup in the morning. Larry was enraged. Wasn't he *retired* now? Wasn't it his turn to relax, he would ask his wife angrily? Didn't he *deserve* it? Within two years of his retirement, Larry, who had never exhibited any signs of coronary disease, developed congestive heart failure. The following year, shortly after his sixtieth birthday, he died.

Or was it suicide, a sort of corporate hara-kiri. He did not understand that he owed it to himself to remain a productive human being—that *he had a right to keep working,* regardless of what his employer and society told him. Had he recognized that right earlier in life, he might have made the turn-off to a second career without experiencing as much as a bump in the road. Even if he had not come to his senses until the golfing began to wear thin, there was still time to rediscover the work that had made his life worth living, if only he had given himself the chance—the way Bob Marinero had.

Straight out of college, at the age of twenty-two, Marinero signed on as a trainee in the operations division of the Chase Manhattan Bank. For the next thirty years, he worked his way up the banking ladder, eventually becoming a vice-president. Though he was one of a hundred or so v.p.'s at the bank, Marinero came to depend on the salary, the security and—most important—the same sense of accomplishment he derived from his job. When it came time for him to retire at sixty-five, the loss of a sense of purposefulness came as no less a shock to Bob Marinero than it had to Larry Wilding. But there was a difference: Bob did not deny the obvious; he did not attempt to convince himself that the pension and a home overlooking the fairway were enough. Even though he was eight years older than Larry Wilding when he retired, Marinero sat down with his wife, a part-time department store salesperson, and tried to figure out what he wanted to get out of the next twenty years. Bob cast an eye over his past, thinking back to his aspirations of forty years before, when he was just getting out of college. He weighed his strengths and weaknesses, his marketable talents and skills. And he came up with an answer that worked.

At the bank, Bob had been a specialist in the home mortgage field, and much of his personal satisfaction came from finding ways for would-be homeowners to obtain financing. He remembered that a real estate agent involved in one of the deals he had handled for Chase had told him that if he ever left the bank, his services and expertise would be much in demand by realtors. Two months after he retired, Marinero called the real estate agent and went to work in his office, arranging mortgages with local banks and expediting closings. Five years later, at the age of seventy, Bob Marinero is one of the real estate agency's key employees. The head of the agency vows Marinero will have a job as long as he wants it, and Bob intends to stay put for "at least another five years." What then? "Oh, I'll move on to something else—the sales end of real estate is beginning to intrigue me."

Bob Marinero is just one of thousands of men and women across the country who are redefining what it means to be "retired" in America in the 1980s. There is no reason to resign yourself to a life of staring at the tube just because you have reached a certain age. In fact, there is every reason *not* to.

SINK THE BISMARCK: OTTO'S LOUSY LEGACY

It is one of history's not-so-small ironies that German Chancellor Otto von Bismarck, who remained a force to be reckoned with on the European scene well into his seventies, picked sixty-five as the age at which German citizens would be entitled to a pension, when he set up the world's first social security system in 1881. Bismarck chose sixty-five because, according to actuarial tables, toward the end of the nineteenth century few Germans lived much longer than that. Unfortunately, the sixty-five-and-out mentality prevailed, and America fell into line when Franklin Delano Roosevelt signed the U.S. Social Security system into law in 1934. As a result, Larry Wilding, like the overwhelming majority of us, was programmed to accept the notion that the calendar tells us when we are old, that around sixty or sixty-five something happens to us—some mystical physical and mental change—that limits our ability to make sound decisions, take on responsibility or continue to function in the working world. The fact is that there is no biological event that diminishes the mental or physical capacity of people in their late fifties (sixties, seventies or eighties, for that matter). Nearly everyone who reaches sixty-five can and should go on working.

SUCCESS OVER SIXTY: NOT FOR MEN ONLY

Success Over Sixty is meant to apply equally to both sexes. It must be noted, however, that there can be differences in the nature of problems confronting men and women in this age group. And the magnitude of the special difficulties facing women, as well as the implications these issues have for society as a whole, cannot be overemphasized.

Women over sixty-five constitute the fastest growing portion of the population. This is also the poorest group in the United States, with an average retirement income of just half that of men. Says Tish Sommers, president of the Oakland, California-based Older Women's League: "Retirement has always been a man's problem. Now it's a woman's issue, too." Concludes a recent George Washington University study: "By every economic measure, women are more deprived in their later years than men." For men retirement is usually a one-time thing; for many women it occurs in multiple stages —she retires at various stages, not only as an employee, but also as wife and mother. A century ago, a woman might have been nearly sixty (if she survived that long) when the last of her five or six children (the average then) was grown. Today, she may be only forty-five when the last of her two or three children packs for college. That leaves a yawning span of time that she, unlike her grandmother, must now fill.

One woman who took full advantage of the opportunities offered her later in life was Ethel Gingold, an Illinois mother of three who actively participated in a wide variety of community affairs. Her volunteer activities paid off when, after serving on the state's Department of Corrections Advisory Board, Gingold was appointed to a salaried position on the Illinois Prison Review Board at age sixty.

Josephine Oblinger is another case in point, although she was a practicing lawyer, teacher and administrator, as well as a housewife and mother. "Boring" is the word she used to describe her view of retirement, so—at age sixty-six—she shifted careers and ran for the Illinois state legislature. She won. Now in her seventies, Oblinger also serves on the boards of fifty-six organizations and still finds the time to play golf and bridge.

Working men and women often confront Success Over Sixty issues at different times. "Even men's and women's retirement clocks are out of synch," wrote Marilyn Gardner of the *Christian Science Monitor*. "While women in the 45–60 groups are entering the work force in record numbers, men of the same age are leaving." As Elaine Brody, director of the Department of Human Resources at the Philadelphia Geriatric Center explains: "Women may be working uphill on careers as men are winding down."

Many women apparently settle for much the same retirement situation as their male counterparts. Despite the fact that they are creating what Gardner calls a "last-in, first-out pattern," these women do retire, and frequently early, 70 percent at sixty-two. "The prospects for retirement are not pleasant," says Maggie Kuhn of the Gray Panthers. "Women are survivors, outliving men by anywhere from eight to thirteen years. It's desperately needed for women, if they can accept this, that they should continue to be gainfully and usefully employed."

Togetherness may not be for everyone. We are all familiar with complaints from wives who suddenly find Dad under foot. "He was driving me absolutely stark raving *mad,*" one New York woman told us in no uncertain terms. "All of a sudden he was asking to come along to the supermarket, taking out the vacuum cleaner and cleaning spots on the rug he thought I'd missed, looking over my shoulder in the kitchen." Her solution? "Well it was either get a job or get a divorce. So when he wouldn't go back to work, I took some real estate courses and landed a job with Merrill Lynch Realty. Now he's running the house, and I don't think he minds one bit. I know I don't."

It should not be overlooked that too much togetherness can be a serious burden on the marriage of retirees. "After spending 70 percent of their time apart during their working years, now couples are spending 80 percent of it together," says Gerard Svendsen, vice-president of the Del Webb Corporation in Sun City, Arizona. "Couples should enjoy doing things together and separately. They need separate spaces." Indeed, one informal survey of Sun City residents found "too much time together" ranked fourth behind "absence of work excitement," "being away from friends" and "too much time" (translation: dead time) as retirees' biggest headaches.

Maggie Kuhn suggests that "Marriage vows have to be rethought and recast at retirement." Divorce has increasingly become a solution. "We know three couples," says one sixty-four-year-old woman, "where the wife just couldn't take his retirement. One left, another is thinking about it. The third couple, they just go their separate ways."

Anne Firor Scott, professor of history at Duke University, offers a few solutions in her "Perspectives of Aging" lecture series: "The importance of being an independent woman is obvious. If a woman has always been defined as somebody's wife and/or somebody's mother, she is not in very good shape at age 60 to become a person in her own right. Furthermore, if one is likely to live until 80 or 90, it is exceedingly important to have a great deal of unfinished work on hand to make it worth getting up in the morning. While some few of us are designed for the contemplative life, many more are most alive when most involved with real problems beyond our daily existence." The same doors that are open to older men are open to older women, though it may often take considerably more pounding to open them. Above all, women—be they single, married, divorced, widowed—should continually remind themselves that it is their lives they are leading, not their husbands' or their children's. Again nothing can be accomplished without some measure of risk. Take that gamble with your spouse, or take it alone. But take it.

THE PARENT TRAP

If retirement thrusts wives and husbands too close together, often forcing a domestic confrontation, it can also foster an undue dependence on children for emotional support. We found that in an alarming number of cases, parents in their fifties and sixties are now far less willing to cut the economic ties that bind their grown children to them. For other than financial reasons, more and more parents are buying homes for their adult children, providing them with significant financial support, and in many cases using their influence and business connections to get their sons and daughters jobs. "Even if your children are in their forties," one sixty-four-year-old grandmother of six told us, "you never stop looking for signs of improvement."

Why do so many parents of grown children seem less willing than their forebears to let go? Perhaps this is the logical outgrowth of being raised in the depths of the Depression and coming of age during World War II. Just as this desire to "give our children the things we never had" led to the permissiveness of the 1960s, it seems also to have led to the dependence of the 1980s. It is one thing always to love one's children; quite another never to let them grow up. And in failing to let them take a risk by being responsible for their own lives, we cheat ourselves by never laying our love on the line. So long as they owe us something, we feel we deserve their allegiance. The only real way for us to know if we have done a good job as parents is to snip those financial ties and see if our children still love us—only this time for all the right reasons.

There are other, more tangible rewards if we manage to extricate ourselves from undue involvement in our children's finances. Once they are on their own, we can concentrate on making our own lives more productive, enjoyable and rewarding—and in the end this can only benefit our children.

FIVE WAYS TO FULFILLMENT

"Retirement." The word by its very nature implies letting go, dropping out, giving up. Some people legitimately want to spend their later years relaxing, true. But according to studies done at Harvard and Johns Hopkins universities, the vast majority of retired people list boredom as their primary complaint. "Two weeks," says noted gerontologist Alex Comfort, "is about the ideal length of time to retire."

The successful over-sixties we spoke to offer living proof

that boredom need not play any role at all in "postretirement" life. Indeed, each has cultivated a state of mind that makes each day more stimulating than the last. It won't just *happen* to you. *You must make it happen.* At the heart of Success Over Sixty is what we call "the Five Cs":

Change. Even if it is only for its own sake, a change of scene, profession, hobby, sport, what you read, wear, eat or drink, can jolt you back to the reality that no matter how long you've lived, there is always something new and interesting that you have not done or experienced.

Curiosity. Maintain and nurture this important natural instinct. A sense of wonder staves off cynicism and defeatism. Nothing is more important than wanting to learn, and no reward greater than the feeling of satisfaction that accompanies each new discovery.

Communication. It may be through volunteer work, or through breaking down a wall of silence between you and your neighbors. Such overtures can redound to your benefit in a hundred ways, from broadening your information network (a significant number of job-seekers learn of new opportunities through social contacts) to reminding you of your stake in the welfare of your fellow human beings.

Confidence. In yourself—you have much to offer prospective employers, lovers and friends by virtue of your long experience. Remember: you are not as good as a younger person, all other factors being equal, you are better!

Commitment. To yourself, your goals and ideals. There will still be setbacks, disappointments and frustrations. This is all part of the Sisyphean reality of life. Having suffered this and more a thousand times over a long lifetime on this planet, you should be better prepared than most for such difficulties. But there is no reason why you cannot meet whatever challenge comes your way. Even over sixty, you must be ready to hang tough.

THE FIRST C: CHANGE

As Alvin Toffler so brilliantly pointed out in *Future Shock,* each of us risks being overwhelmed by the sudden, sweeping technological and social changes of the final third of the twentieth century. The standard response, however, particularly among older people, is to deny *change.* Understandably, an individual tends to feel safe and secure in familiar surroundings, doing familiar things with familiar people. But the inevitable result is mental stagnation.

If it is stress we are seeking to avoid, we could not be making a bigger mistake. Dr. Hans Selye, head of the University of Montreal's Institute of Experimental Medicine and Surgery since 1945, published a pioneering paper on the subject of stress in 1950. In his thirtieth book, *Stress Without Distress,* he outlined a code of behavior designed for coping with everyday anxiety, but he also pointed out that stress was a natural, necessary part of life. Now aged seventy-seven, Selye rises at 4 A.M., hops on his bicycle and pedals up Montreal's Mount Royal on the way to his laboratory. "Surplus energy can't simply be discarded," he told us. "We must put it to work somehow." Selye has put his seemingly inexhaustible supply to work with a grueling schedule of writing, teaching and research, though he makes a point of easing tensions by working with his feet up on his desk at every opportunity. "When I was a medical student," he says, "I studied fourteen hours a day. My mother warned me that I'd have a nervous breakdown, but those are the hours I still work. I suppose the inventor of the race car," he adds with a wink, "is not always the best driver."

When Art Jason was retired by his company at sixty-five, he headed west for the retirement home he had purchased for himself and his wife in Sun City, Arizona. "Like most of my friends," Jason said, "I could hardly wait to live the American retirement dream—lazing in the sun, playing golf and tennis, no meetings, no having to answer to anyone, no stress. Boy, I didn't know what stress was until I retired."

Now Jason is scrambling to return to the real world, to recapture the active life he once had. The trouble is, nearly two years after his relocation in Sun City, Jason has lost much of the sharp edge he once had. The Five Cs will help him regain that edge, but Jason must write off those years in limbo.

William M. Marlin, a former vice-president of Prudential-Bache Securities, was luckier. He had spent twenty-eight years at Bache, and like Jason was eager to get out of the rat race. "I spent a few weeks loafing around playing golf in Florida, but after getting bored I decided I had to get back into the business." Marlin accepted an appointment as president and a director of Matthews & Wright Inc., a Wall Street firm specializing in municipal securities. His first task at his new company: to launch a government bond department. It's a formidable assignment but, says Marlin, "I'm up to it."

None of the successful over-sixties we interviewed avoided change, nor did they merely accept it: they actually sought it out. They realized that unless one keeps pace with new ideas, life-styles, technologies and businesses one will be literally buried under an avalanche called "progress." Coping with a changing world starts at a very early age for many, but the motivation for change can come at any point in one's life.

Bill Barnaby had spent the better part of his sixty years making gold inlays and bridges as a dental technician when he suddenly decided to devote half of his time to his other love —Chinese art and antiques. He soon qualified as an expert appraiser of jade, cloisonné and cinnabar. That led to another career as a jewelry designer. Barnaby now spends six months each year in Florida making gold jewelry and six months at his dental lab in Illinois.

After a career in retailing, Edgar Stern bought a ranch near Aspen, Colorado, and developed it into Starwood, one of the country's leading mountain resort communities. Well into his sixties, Stern then embarked on an equally ambitious plan to build a world-class ski resort on 7,000 acres, less than 30 miles from Salt Lake City. The result: Deer Valley, one of the country's top-rated winter playgrounds. Meantime, Stern also got into the business of building hotels. His Stanford Court Hotel on Nob Hill in San Francisco is considered one of the finest in the world.

Another advocate of change for the sake of it was Dr. Joel H. Hildebrand, a professor of chemistry at the University of California's Berkeley campus, who was still publishing scientific papers in his hundredth year. He was perhaps best known in academic circles for his pathfinding research into "the bends," the often-fatal formation of nitrogen bubbles in the blood of deep-sea divers.

Hildebrand taught freshman chemistry students until he was retired from the faculty in 1952 at the age of seventy and given the title "Professor Emeritus." He published nearly 300 papers (43 percent of which were written, by Hildebrand's own tally, after he retired) and taught more than 40,000 students. But he was also an avid outdoorsman. Hildebrand wrote several books on camping, skiing (he strapped on his first pair of skis at forty) and hiking. Not long after winning the Priestly Medal, which, next to the Nobel prize, is the highest honor that can be bestowed on a chemist, Hildebrand marked his seventy-seventh birthday by swimming half a mile in twenty-two minutes. He attributed his productive longevity to "good health" and a worry-free mind. "I've never had a headache in my whole life," he said. "I never fret." Hildebrand also abstains from smoking, large doses of television, and eyeglasses "because that way you don't have to clean them." He was eighty-four when the university named a chemistry building in his honor. "They have a rule never to name a building after a living person," he smiles, "but they got tired of waiting for me to die."

The Doctor and the Diamond Dealer

An Aspen ski instructor, seventy-eight-year-old Jack Holtz, told us of a week spent teaching two men to ski. One was forty, a diamond merchant from New York. The other was a sixty-year-old Florida brain surgeon. The diamond merchant worked in a cramped cubicle on 47th Street—the heart of Manhattan's diamond district—and kept a revolver under his pillow at night. He was in Aspen on a one-week vacation. The ski instructor was amazed to discover that the diamond merchant was actually a poorer skier on his last day than he had been on his first. The reason he was so preoccupied with his diamond business was that he could not cope with life outside of his cubicle.

The surgeon, on the other hand, emerged from his week of instruction a competent skier. The dramatic difference between the two did not relate to their athletic abilities; in fact, the diamond dealer appeared to be considerably stronger and more flexible than the older physician. But the surgeon, who always took off at least a month a year to travel, was simply more able to adjust quickly to new situations. If you are sufficiently accustomed to it, change can be made to work for you.

That proved doubly true for Wayman Presley. When Presley retired as a rural mail carrier at the age of sixty-one, he had $1,000 in his savings account and a strong desire to transform his life. He did just that. During his twenty-two years as a postman near the Missouri-Illinois border, Presley would often take local youngsters on walking tours of the hills and regale them with tales of the area. Their parents began to tag along, and by the time he reached his mid-fifties, Presley was spending his weekends and vacations taking trainloads of people from central Illinois and St. Louis on tours of the hill country at $6 a head.

Then, seven years after Presley started giving tours, one Midwesterner offhandedly remarked to Presley that he'd never seen the ocean. With that, Presley organized a tour to Miami Beach. "I didn't know the sharpies down there then," Presley recalls, but he nonetheless succeeded in convincing the manager of a low-priced hotel to quote a $4.50 per person nightly rate for his tour group. Armed with that figure, he went to hotel after hotel until he persuaded a highly rated hotel to register his group at the same price. Presley booked over five hundred people on that first tour for only $99 apiece, and barely cleared expenses.

Now in his late eighties, Presley remains active in the nationwide tour-bus company that grosses him $7 million annually. "I've never tried to make money," Presley insists. Indeed, he loves to play tour guide; at eighty-four, he personally led a caravan of fifteen tourist-filled buses to the Grand Ole Opry in Nashville. "No matter what your surroundings, in large communities or small," says Presley, "you can do well if you keep learning, keep your mind sharp and motivate yourself to move ahead." Not one of the successful people we interviewed opted for the status quo. "The most distinguished hallmark of American society," says Eric Sevareid, "is and always has been—change." That applies no less so to the over-sixty American.

THE SECOND C: CURIOSITY

A seventy-year-old man in the garment trade found himself the only noncollege graduate at a seminar attended almost exclusively by Harvard-trained professionals and academics. Each was asked why he was there, and when it was his turn, the septuagenarian shrugged and replied, "Because I want to die an educated man."

The hunger for knowledge does not abate with age. In fact, *the more we know, the more we know we don't know*—and the more we want to learn. Without exception, curiosity is a driving force in the lives of all people over sixty seeking to achieve success.

At seventy-seven, Amanda Hahn, who had dropped out of the ninth grade, spotted an article on an adult center offering a high school graduate equivalency degree. She rode the bus to school, took the five-hour test and passed with flying colors. She then discovered that with thirty credits she could be certified as a teacher's aid at Lincolnland College. Hahn's years at Lincolnland were the happiest of her life; she made many friends among the faculty and students, and her quest for learning inspired those around her to realize that the mind need not atrophy. Hahn graduated in 1980 with a bachelor's degree in education.

Francis Budinger's innate curiosity and desire to learn served him well in the insurance industry. As its president and driving force for decades, Budinger built Franklin Life, based in Springfield, Illinois, into one of the largest insurance companies in America. Along the way, he was honored as the first citizen of Springfield.

But along with his honors and achievements, Budinger also carried throughout his life the knowledge that he had never graduated from college. So, at the age of seventy-three, Budinger enrolled in Illinois's Sangamon State University to pursue his formal education. It was not uncommon to see him on campus, a dignified, white-haired man in a business suit deep in conversation with a group of his blue-jeaned classmates. Now in his eighties, Francis Budinger pursues his interests in music, photography and golf.

In Atlanta, Anne Eaton was devoting most of her time to volunteer work. She realized that she would have to learn more if she was going to really make a difference, so at sixty-nine she returned to school and earned a master's degree in sociology. Now she is working harder than ever as a co-founder of Life Enrichment Services, a nonprofit Atlanta group whose sole aim is to improve the overall quality of life of men and women in their seventies and above.

Eaton supervises the educational part of the service—setting up courses on subjects ranging from investment financing to languages to cake decoration. She works full-time without taking pay, and she says this is the most satisfying work she has ever done in her long working career as credit manager for a fashion chain, as a commercial artist or as director of social work in a nursing home.

Anne Eaton's thirst for learning has made her an authority

in her newly chosen field; in 1980, she traveled to Germany to address an international conference on aging.

THE THIRD C: COMMUNICATION

Connecting with others is another essential ingredient in our Success Over Sixty recipe. Each individual has something unique to offer, but no man is an island unto himself, as the great poet said. We benefit immeasurably from the cross-pollination of ideas and knowledge that we have accumulated through years of experience. The network we weave, in addition to serving as a source of information and support, doubles as a bank of opportunities. Jobs, business proposals, social and economic contacts of all kinds proliferate in an atmosphere of friendship, trust and mutual interest.

Jules Z. Willing's *The Lively Mind* is one of the best commentaries ever published on the need not only for continuing to learn but *sharing* what we learn throughout our lives. His book, completed a few days before he died in 1981 at the age of eighty-one, encourages respect for the uniqueness of one's own mind, and also urges the free exchange of what he calls "the mind's riches."

For two decades, Willing had been personnel director at Revlon, a company *Fortune* magazine called the most stressful corporate environment in the country. Upon his retirement in 1977, he devoted himself to his two lifelong interests, teaching and writing. He taught at the Duke Institute for Learning in Retirement in Durham, North Carolina, and at Shared Learning in Chapel Hill, North Carolina, where he lived.

"For me," explained Willing, "the acme of lively mindedness, of creativity, is the connection with others, the reaching out and touching, the sending of the message and the receiving of the response, the act of joining and evolving. It is this contact, the joy of engagement, that is self-enlarging and self-energizing, that evokes fresh vigor and constantly replenishes joy.''

Sidney Kaufman, a scientist with thirty-eight years' experience at the Shell Oil Company, also decided to use his experience in a teaching situation—to use his bank of knowledge to help others. The seventy-two-year-old geologist joined the faculty of Cornell University in 1974 as an acting professor of geology, teaching graduate students and directing the Consolidation for Continental Reflection Profiling, a group that studies the earth's deep crust.

His second career, Kaufman notes, has turned out even better than expected. ''There is a certain pleasure in working with bright, young graduate students. There's another reward in trying to help them,'' he adds. ''*You* feel better.''

THE FOURTH C: CONFIDENCE

Philip Begley could feel his confidence eroding during the last year before he retired. His fellow workers at the muffler company where he had been a regional sales director for twenty-three years were too deferential toward him; they pampered Begley and ignored his mistakes. However good his friends' intentions, Begley was left with a definite sense of inadequacy and isolation. It was not until his wife pointed out to him that he was suffering from a serious case of self-doubt that he took steps to shore up his self-image—and turn his life around in the process.

Once he was reminded of just who he really was and how much he was still capable of accomplishing, Begley teamed up with two recently retired friends and opened a small garage. They pledged their confidence in each other's abilities merely by investing their time and money in the venture, and were soon sharing in the profits of a booming business. Begley discovered one immutable truth: others will believe in you only if you believe in yourself.

THE FIFTH C: COMMITMENT

Guts, fortitude, perseverance—once you have reached your fifties there is no way to build a future for yourself without them. Dorothy Stattler knew years before retiring from a major paper products firm that she wanted to own her own gift shop, specializing in the arts and crafts of picture-perfect northwestern Connecticut. She spent a full six months scouting for the right location (she found it in a newly constructed shopping mall), then went to eleven banks before convincing one to put up the necessary starting capital—about $30,000. Four of the bankers who turned her down were honest enough (off the record, of course) to admit that her age—sixty-three —was a major factor in denying her the loan.

The store opened in early 1983, and two weeks later a storm ripped through the town, flooding her out. It would take another month for her to clean up and reopen. But almost as soon as she did, the shop began doing a land-office business. Was it worth it? "If it had been too easy," smiles Stattler, "I wouldn't be enjoying my success half as much."

Changing, building confidence, nurturing curiosity and communicating with others are important elements for Success Over Sixty, but they are meaningless unless you are willing to make the *commitment*. "What convinces," as Lyndon Johnson once said, "is conviction." Our purpose is to show, through the lives of successful men and women, that at any stage in your life you can make your star rise on the horizon. But nothing happens until you are motivated to make it on your own. Katharine Hepburn puts it: "Maybe the pendulum will swing back, but first somebody's got to push it." That somebody is you. Now that you have been introduced to the all-important Five Cs, if you want to stay in the mainstream after fifty, you'll want to know how each letter in the word "live" can provide the key to living life to the fullest.

L—*L*ook and analyze your present situation *now,* particularly if you are fifty or older. Decide what you want to do, how and where, and with whom you want to do it.

I— *I*nvest your time in investigating and weighing the various options open to you. *Success Over Sixty* provides a list of the latest resource material and organizations available geared specifically to you. One of your many significant advantages, for example, is that you have through seniority earned more vacation time, more freedom in your work schedule—precious time that can be utilized in finding and laying the groundwork for a second carrer.

V— *V*alidate your decision using the Success Over Sixty techniques described in Chapter 6 for matching your background, skills and desires to the right postretirement career. Sometimes the results are surprising—in part because, unlike most people in the job market who are young and looking for ways to compensate for lack of experience, experience is the over-fifties strong suit.

E—*E*xecute. Turn your ambitions for a successful second career into reality. For example, Success Over Sixty stresses that in getting the things you want, *who* you know can be as important as *what* you know. Don't make the mistake of letting pride or a misguided sense of decorum stand in the way of using whatever contacts you've made during your lifetime (social as well as professional), and remember that even the most casual, most tenuous acquaintance can often help you get a foot in the door. Success Over Sixty also provides step-by-step plans for getting that job, starting that business, finding that volunteer position in which you can do the most good—even foolproof ways to improve your body and your mind.

The Success Over Sixty program is drawn from human experience—the case histories of hundreds of people who, living by the Five Cs, shaped their own destinies. An assistant department manager for Sears, for instance, felt that, since he had spent the last twenty years in retailing, he would have to look for a job as a sales clerk once he retired. But once he had gone through rigorous self-analysis, he recalled that during his midtwenties he spent one of the most enjoyable periods of his Sears career in the store's nursery. Though never a gardener, the knowledge he accrued on that job concerning the business of running a nursery led him to start one with a friend —with an eye toward devoting himself full-time to the nursery business after retirement.

In another case a vice-president in the Bankers Trust International Credit Division felt he had reached the end of the line in banking—he was not likely to get any farther in terms of salary ($49,500) or position, and he was frankly tired of the same old thing after twenty-five years at Bankers. He realized that what he most enjoyed was traveling to the bank's various offices around the world to run seminars on corporate credit and meet with the bank's biggest customers. He learned that with a mere $10,000 credit line and an investment of only a few weeks, he could buy into a small travel agency in the New Jersey town where he lives. By the time he retired from the bank, this vice-president was well on the way to earning $50,000 a year in the travel business.

After nineteen years in the personnel department of a major magazine publisher, one sixty-year-old woman executive determined that when she retired she wanted to fulfill an original ambition to teach. She not only arranged her work and vacation schedule (she is senior enough to make these demands) so that in her spare time she could complete the required studies toward a teaching certificate, she also found a way to learn about her next job. At the publishing house she took on the task of personally visiting high schools and colleges to recruit young people for the company. Thus she got on-the-job training for her second career and made all the right contacts in the teaching world, while still meeting her current work obligations.

Stop and look around you. Look in the shopping malls, on the streets and in the office. Look at the driver alongside you as you wait for a stoplight, at the face in front of you in the checkout line. America is aging rapidly, and if you are not already a part of this trend, you will be.

When we get there we will all want—and deserve—more than a gold watch, a farewell banquet and a handshake. We all fear, particularly if we have worked many years for the same company, what will become of us. We do not want to join the walking dead.

There *is* another way, a path toward living a full, creative, useful and rewarding life past sixty. Success Over Sixty is not a sociological treatise, nor is it a manual for planning your pension. It is a blueprint for conquering the psychological and emotional obstacles that stand in the way of making the most of your talents; it is a practical guide for ensuring that your future will be at least as bright as your past. You are about to embark on your greatest adventure yet.

2 Retirement: The Myth and the Reality

A perpetual holiday is a good working definition of hell.
—George Bernard Shaw

Life is like riding a bicycle. You don't fall off until you stop pedaling.

—Claude Pepper

Once the American dream, retirement has now for millions become the American nightmare. "Finally! My turn to jump off the old treadmill, get out of the rat race and have a good time." Sound familiar? Millions of American workers have spoken these words (or similar ones) to themselves as they prepared to leave the workforce, collect their pensions and head for a life of leisure.

Some got what they bargained for. Most did not. Millions encountered financial difficulties because of inflation, or a lack of realistic financial planning, or a combination of the two. For these, the strain of making ends meet was multiplied by increased medical expense. Those men and women over sixty-five, as might be expected, are twice as likely to incur medical expenses than, say, someone forty or younger. And though Medicare has alleviated the pressure, on the average it pays for no more than 60 percent of the individual's health-care costs.

These problems aside, disengagement from society at sixty or sixty-five often proves psychologically devastating. That, in turn, invariably takes a profound physical toll. So wrenching is the experience of retirement that Dr. Thomas Holmes, professor of psychiatry at the University of Washington ranked it as the ninth (out of forty-three) most stressful event in one's life (behind the death of spouse, divorce, separation, a jail term, the death of a close family member, personal injury or illness, marriage and being fired).

Retirement shock is felt by the blue-collar worker, executive and professional alike. "Work supplies a lot of basic psychological needs that suddenly are cut off when a person retires," said Leland P. Bradford, who retired as director of the National Training Laboratories of Arlington, Virginia, in 1970. "As a worker, you have a sense of belonging to the producing part of society. Work helps to give you an identity. It is a source of human contact. It defines your goals and gives you a sense of accomplishment and affirmation."

These needs do not go away when you stop working, and failure to locate other ways of meeting those needs can produce emotional upheaval. Even someone as "prepared" as Bradford, a behavioral scientist, suffered severe retirement pangs which he described in his book, *Retirement: Coping with Emotional Upheavals*. "The first year was awful," Bradford wrote in an article that first appeared in the *Harvard Business Review*. "The organization moved on without me. No one called for advice. I found that golf did not fill a day. Life felt empty. I became uncertain of my identity. I knew who I had been, but I was not certain who I was."

This failure to find alternatives will often, as we have pointed out, result in a decline in health. "Those who retire to the rocking chair," says Dr. Erman Palmore, professor of medical sociology at Duke University's Center for the Study of Aging and Human Behavior, "tend to find that their body atrophies for lack of exercise and they become withdrawn and depressed."

Those who disengage fully from society survive an average of only six years past their retirement date, and compared to men and women the same age who have either stayed on the job or found other careers, suffer from significantly more heart attacks, strokes, cancers and psychological problems severe enough to seek psychiatric help.

Why has retirement in its traditional form been so destructive? Work, it appears, is good for us psychologically and physically. It helps to keep us alert and healthy. Work also defines what we are capable of doing and provides a structure for the way in which we will spend our day. Retirement of the total-withdrawal variety often removes the source of identity, self-worth, competence and time structure. Depression is frequently the result, followed by the predictable onset of major illness.

The American Medical Association has gone on record as recognizing that psychological problems resulting from the stagnation that too often results from retirement can actually trigger diseases, intensify them, and then serve to interrupt the healing process. Worry can cause high blood pressure, strokes, heart disease, ulcers and may even be at the root of some cancers. Boredom, stagnation and dissatisfaction can also spur or aggravate a wide range of problems, from asthma to migraines and kidney disease. As one gerontologist told us, "Most of my patients owe their physical problems to emotional and psychological ones. They've been told by their bosses, their younger coworkers, their neighbors and their children that the game of life is over. They feel worthless, shoved aside, and they get the big hint society has been giving them: go home and die. The ones who buy the old idea that retirement means dropping out often do that—they succumb to all these ailments and diseases."

No one comprehends the extent of the damage better than Maggie Kuhn, founder of the Gray Panthers. "Have you ever seen what 'senior citizens' do?'' asks Kuhn, who established her Philadelphia-based, nationwide organization after she was forced to retire as director of the Presbyterian Church's missionary program at age sixty-five. ''The best of them feel that they have worked most of their lives and tired themselves out, and all they want to do is rest, rest, rest. Resting is deadly and they soon die, especially if they are male.''

More and more people who saw retirement as some sort of panacea now realize they have been sold a bill of goods. A life full of golf carts and golden-age cruises may appeal to some, but increasingly we hear the voices of men and women who want more. Tennis was Allen Graham's consuming passion ever since his college days, and when he retired after thirty-five years as a supervisor with the conglomerate, TRW, he moved to Hilton Head, South Carolina, with his equally sports-minded wife with the intention of ''at least seeing how good a player I could be if I set my mind to it.'' The Grahams played four hours a day every day, and though they made new friends at Hilton Head, they realized after six months that they had made ''a serious mistake. I always told my friends that I worked to play and it occurs to me now that my work was as enjoyable to me as my tennis game. A steady diet of candy gets tiresome after a while,'' says Graham.

Though they would appear to have little in common, Allen Graham has a kindred spirit in Catherine Pullman. She spent more than thirty years with the same communications firm in New York, and when she retired in 1980 at the age of sixty-three she was a senior corporate secretary earning $40,000 a year. A widow, Catherine Pullman owned the condominium she and her husband had shared until his death in 1977. Since she would be collecting Social Security as well as a $30,000 yearly pension, Pullman looked forward to spending her retirement traveling, and going to museums, the theater and the ballet.

"Lonely. I'm lonely and I'm bored," says Pullman, who, after two solo trips to Europe, decided she missed the camaraderie of the workplace. When she realized what was lacking, she called up some of her old coworkers and got together with them for lunch. "That only made me feel worse," she recalls. "All they did was talk about the office—things I was no longer involved in or familiar with—and I just felt like a fifth wheel." Pullman dealt with these feelings by taking a third trip—a cruise to the Caribbean. On her return, she experienced severe back pains which her doctors diagnosed as stress-produced.

More and more Americans in their fifties are looking up from their work long enough to see that problems such as those experienced by Allen Graham and Catherine Pullman may lie ahead for them. Ideally, we should give ourselves as much time as possible to come to terms with reality and start planning for our retirement. But most of us do no constructive planning because we are so overwhelmed by fear and uncertainty. Lewis Oppenheim, now in his late fifties, has listened intently to his older brother's horror stories about retirement. "Not enough money is one complaint," says Oppenheim, whose brother was a district sales manager making $65,000 when he retired, "but it's not the main thing bugging my brother." The main thing, Oppenheim explains, is "the feeling that he is sort of invisible. His friends from work no longer call him, no one asks his advice or opinion, and gardening, chess and reading just aren't enough for him anymore. I sure as hell don't want to end up like that," says Oppenheim. "But my brother has been retired for four years, and he still doesn't know how to solve the problem."

Douglas Sanderson is also facing his retirement, which is imminent, with trepidation. Sanderson has worked for a major manufacturer of optical supplies since 1960, the last seven of those years as manager of his own department. He will depart with an excellent retirement package, including a lump-sum payment from his profit-sharing plan and a $36,000 pension. What Sanderson's corporation did not provide him with, however, was a sense of confidence about his future. "Oh, I'll be comfortable financially, all right," he allows, "but who the hell cares? I don't see myself sitting around on my duff all day long sipping Margaritas, but somebody tell me, what's the alternative?"

Work, and what is wrong with that? Achievement is measured by most of us by how we have fared at our jobs. Is it a great surprise, then, that we suffer from life-threatening depression when the trap door lever is pulled on us? Nevertheless, if your sense of self-worth, of womanhood or manhood are dependent on your work, that, insists Alex Comfort, "is a worthy conviction, so act on it."

At least 25 percent of those people retiring today will keep working, full-time or part-time, after they leave their present employers however. Keeping that in mind, you will take a long, hard look at your various postjob alternatives years before retirement day arrives. Should you stay in your own field, or embark on something entirely new? Making this judgment can be tough, and of course it must be coupled with financial planning that will enable you to maintain your standard of living through your sixties and beyond. Economic factors shift constantly with changes in the laws and regulations governing pensions, Social Security benefits, individual retirement accounts and Keogh distributions. The single most important decision you will make is what you will do with the rest of your life, your talents, your abilities.

Like millions of others, Robert Black found that the blissful world of retirement he had anticipated was empty without some regular work to give it meaning. A General Motors engineer, he retired on a $28,000 pension in 1979 but soon discovered that he hadn't prepared himself for the shock. "My wife didn't want me around the house," he recalls, "and there was nobody to talk to. If I had thought about retirement before, it was only in terms of the myths of what people are supposed to do when they retire." Even though he had lifelong hobbies—playing golf and painting figurines—he found both pursuits unfulfilling once he retired. Black endured what he calls "idle agony" for three years before returning to work as a vice-president for IGW Systems, an aerospace firm based in Indianapolis. Laws that forbid age discrimination permitted Black, who was then in his early sixties, to land his $65,000-a-year position with IGW within months of the time he started looking.

Sam Barker was not so fortunate. He, too, expected retirement to be all happy foursomes and lots of lounging by the pool. Without direction, without *purpose,* Barker began to founder, and like Robert Black, he began looking for a job in his old line of work. Unlike Black, he did not embrace the Five Cs. He was not interested in *changing* the nature of his employment. Black, on the other hand, eagerly embraced the notion of switching from the automobile to the aerospace industry. Nor was Barker *curious;* unwilling to learn anything new, he insisted on reentering the workforce at precisely the same place, doing the same job as he had done for thirty years.

Neither had Barker maintained the lines of *communication* with friends and coworkers that Black had, nor sought to communicate his thoughts, desires, aspirations to others in a way that might have landed him the position he wanted. Job interview after job interview proved fruitless, eroding his *confidence* to such an extreme that it undermined his *commitment*—his resolve to return to the sort of existence he found satisfying.

Barker became bitter, and that bitterness began to manifest itself in a series of ailments, none of them life-threatening, but collectively dispiriting nonetheless. In his mid-sixties, Barker has even given up those games that he once thought he would find fulfilling in his "golden years."

Of course he is wrong. There have been plenty of injustices perpetrated against him, to be sure, and in subsequent chapters we will explore ways to overcome such injustices. But our "golden years" tarnish only if we let them. Once you have decided that *doing* is what keeps you alive and happy, it is up to you to make the adjustments and display the requisite flexibility and adaptability.

It helps to lay the groundwork as early as possible. "I began planning early for things that I would want to do when I would have to retire," says Harry Essrig, now in his early seventies. Before he reached sixty, Essrig, then intracommunity coordinator for the Southern California Board of Rabbis, started editing and publishing a magazine of sermons for rabbis, *The American Rabbi*. By the time the board told him he had to retire, he had his lifeline to his profession—and a solid source of income—in place. Essrig's magazine not only pays the bills, he notes, it also "keeps me in touch with the life of the pulpit. I'm still in the swing of things, and I can work at my own pace."

The Five Cs are also an integral part of Violet Francis's postretirement life. When Francis, an accountant, left her job as a supervisor in the customer service department at Kaiser/ Permanente in northern California, she moved right into another, entirely different line of work that she had already prepared for. An avid fisherwoman, she was intrigued by the prospect of setting up a business that would supply bait to people who shared her passion for the sport. Violet and her husband, who also faced retirement, decided that the best way to obtain the answers they needed was to get in touch with the experts. "My husband and I analyzed the situation," she says. "We sent a questionnaire to nearly 500 worm farmers to get a sense of the business." Business was good, they discovered. Armed with the capital (her pension from Kaiser/Permanente, which she took in one fat lump sum) and the personal commitment to make it as a worm farmer, she boldly made her move. Her wriggling livestock was soon providing Violet Francis with an annual income of $80,000—more than twice her former salary.

If you have been far-sighted enough to lay the groundwork for a new life after sixty, you increase your options dramatically—even if you decide to try "traditional" retirement for a time. "Ideally," says Alex Comfort, "retirement isn't the occasion, for 'leisure' as packaged by the golden age promotions is Dead Sea fruit; you can read and play shuffleboard just so long." Top executives are not exempt; CEO's like John Kenneth Jamieson must discover this for themselves. Between 1969 and 1975, Jamieson truly had a tiger by the tail as chairman and chief executive officer of Exxon. For the last two years of his tenure, the world's largest oil company racked up the biggest profits of any American corporation up to that time: nearly $3 billion in 1974 alone. Jamieson, among the heads of the "Seven Sisters" of oil—Exxon, Texaco, Standard of California, British Petroleum, Royal Dutch/Shell, Gulf, and Mobil—was particularly well qualified. With a degree in engineering from M.I.T., he was equally comfortable in the executive suite and on a rig, and oversaw the entire $30 billion-a-year multinational from a football field-sized office dotted with Eskimo sculptures.

The size of his task did not keep Jamieson from more restful pastimes—fishing for salmon, gardening with his wife, Ethel, and working on his fourteen golf handicap. As he was then

46 SUCCESS OVER SIXTY

less than a year from mandatory retirement at sixty-five, he
had even purchased a home off the ninth fairway in Houston,
where he planned to put down roots for good.

After a month on the links, Jamieson knew he had had
enough. "I guess I always knew I'd never be able to retire in
the conventional sense," allows Jamieson. "That's why I
moved back to Houston. There were all sorts of things happening here." Jamieson took on the chairmanship of Crutcher
Resources, an oil and gas exploration firm. It has by no means
proven to be a cushy job; in 1982, profits for Crutcher nose-
dived. "As you can see from the grim expression on my
face," read an accompanying note when he sent us a copy of
Crutcher's 1983 annual report, "it has not been a good year."

Still, Jamieson was not so overwhelmed with the challenge
of turning Crutcher around that he couldn't take on another
assignment—a spot on the board of California's Raychem
Corporation—and continue his globe-trotting. "I have five
trips planned for the next year—to places like Alaska, British
Columbia and Norway," he told us. And then there's always
time to squeeze in some salmon fishing and, of course, golf.
"My nickname at the club," says the oil industry mover and
shaker, "is 'Jet Lag Jamieson.' "

Jamieson, who is earning significantly more now than he
did when he was running Exxon, blames the American workers' growing dependence on large corporations for the doubts
and fears that prevent many from striking out on their own in
search of new jobs, new careers, new challenges. "Most people at Exxon, for example, started there right out of school.
They never worked anyplace else, and so this becomes the
only world they know. They're afraid to look anywhere else.
There's just too much corporate hand-holding in this society,
but ultimately it's up to the individual to cut the umbilical
cord."

For retirees, continues Jamieson, that also means cutting

the cord that tethers them to a community of elderly peers. "The last thing I'd ever do," he bellows, "is move to one of those retirement communities." As he says in mock horror, "I don't want to be associated with those damn old people!"

The decision to go on working is one of the most important you will ever make. Art Beechum and Ned Krementz worked for the same company for twenty-five years, retiring within weeks of each other in 1979. Both men, then sixty-two, had risen to the same midlevel management position and retired on the same sized pension. That is where the similarities in their stories end, and there is no better way to highlight the differences than to briefly describe how each spends his day.

Beechum rises around 10:30 A.M., pours a cup of coffee and spends the next hour reading the morning paper. Edith, his wife of thirty years, has already been up for hours, and since she cannot bear having her husband underfoot, she makes sure her housework is done and she is headed for the supermarket by the time he gets up.

When he's finished with the paper, he begins watering the lawn, pulling up weeds, doing whatever small gardening chores he can find to take up what little remains of his morning. Around 1:00 P.M., Edith returns home with the groceries and Art helps her unload the car. She gets his lunch, and shortly before 3:00 P.M. they leave together for the shopping mall. There they split up; she heads for the dress department of Penney's, he goes off to pick up a new hammer at the hardware store. Home by 4:30, he goes off to the little workbench he has set up in the garage. But now that he has all the time in the world to work at it, Beechum's lifelong hobby, carpentry, is no longer that much fun. The shelves he has been working on for the past six months remain unfinished, and so, feeling guilty, he spends another hour hammering and sawing. Beer in hand and TV tray in lap, Beechum sits down in front of Dan Rather and begins to eat the dinner Edith has prepared. Around midnight, after a solid six hours in front of the tube, Art goes to bed. Before he does, he takes Maalox for his ulcer.

Ned Krementz is up by 7:00 A.M. and runs two miles before he starts out for the office at 8:30. Two years before he actually retired, Krementz tested the employment waters in his town and found that an old college chum was looking for an experienced manager to help him run his small chain of furniture stores. Krementz's new salary is marginally less than what he was making, but he finds the new and unfamiliar demands of the full-time job to be "stimulating—a real challenge." Change, curiosity, communication, confidence and commitment are all part of Krementz's life and make it possible for him to shape for himself a "stimulating" life after sixty.

Krementz often meets his wife, Ruth, a realtor, for lunch, and generally is home by 6:00 P.M. The Krementzes have made a point to invite his new coworkers over for dinner or for a weekend game of tennis. His hobby, bridge—infrequently played with friends from his *old* job—remains just that: a hobby. Hence he still finds it pleasurable.

For Ned and Ruth Krementz, nothing is more enjoyable than a quiet evening spent together at home—sending out for a pizza or Chinese food. Like Art Beechum, they'll catch the evening news and watch their favorite shows. But it is rare that they stay up even through Johnny Carson's 11:30 monologue. After all, they must be up at 7:00 o'clock to get that headstart on the morning. They have chosen to stay in the mainstream.

It is a hard lesson, but you have learned it: regardless of what the brochures say, idleness is not for you. The same thirst for accomplishment and purposeful activity that made you so effective in your chosen career for twenty, thirty, forty or more years calls you back to the land of the living. And those same characteristics—the love of a challenge, the desire to learn and to grow and to prosper intellectually and emotionally (as well as financially)—can help keep you healthy in spirit and body. You have always lived by the Five Cs, using them to benefit your employer, your family and your community. Now it is time to put the Five Cs to work for you.

3 *The Enlightened Corporations*

> *For a variety of reasons—not the least of which are plain business and economic need—corporations must take aggressive action on the older work issue.*
> —Blair Hyde
> Atlantic Richfield Co.

> *The* myths *about older people should be retired—not older people!*
> —Robert Ewing
> Bankers Life and Casualty

The enlightened corporations of the 1980s not only recognize that their senior employees are their most valuable employees, they have acted on that conviction with bold new policies and programs. This development is long overdue. Having spent almost fifty years in the corporate world, working at every level from stock boy to president and CEO, Albert Myers has evaluated firsthand the personnel policies of scores of companies, as well as his own. What he found was that though for decades most Americans in their fifties and above have wanted to go on working, the doors of business and industry have only recently begun to open to them. At last, corporations realize they have two choices: they can be among the first to tap the senior workers' vast reserves of experience, knowledge, skill and energy. Or they can be left behind.

One reason for this sudden awakening on the part of the business community is that the *average* age among the top *Fortune 500* executives is higher than it has ever been: sixty. These executives are their own proof of the importance of lifelong experience at the top. A survey of 1,200 chief executive officers of California-based corporations and major utilities disclosed that when confronted with labor shortages, more than 75 percent had recalled their own retirees for temporary or longer term jobs, while 82 percent have hired men and women who retired from other organizations.

Not only do older workers possess the know-how required for the job, but they are thought to be model employees in many other ways. The *Wall Street Journal* reported that 84 percent of personnel directors polled feel that this group is also more productive than their younger counterparts. In another study, a group of corporate personnel directors listed six other leading reasons why there is a shift in policies regarding the retaining and hiring of older workers:

- They have fewer absences
- They have fewer on-the-job accidents
- They are more satisfied with their jobs
- They have fewer psychiatric problems
- They use less alcohol and have far fewer drug problems

Now that the business world is awakening to the fact that it can no longer afford to turn its back on them, the number of workers aged sixty-five and older is expected to grow by 28 percent in the next few years. This will meet the needs of 75 percent of those people over sixty-five who indicated in a 1981 Harris poll that they wanted to continue working.

Nevertheless, among the 3 million businesses in America, corporate preretirement programs remain limited, and many still offer nothing more than a pension and that Solid Gold

Handshake. A 1979 survey of CEOs and personnel directors of the *Fortune 500* companies indicates that only 37 percent provided any preretirement program at all.

Fortunately, those companies that are in the vanguard of recognizing the enormous value of employees over sixty are among the largest in the nation, including IBM, McDonald's, Polaroid, Aerospace Corporation, and Mutual of Omaha. William Sanders, who as vice-president in charge of corporate personnel and employee relations at Sears has the welfare of 400,000 employees in mind, points out that the enlightened corporation is giving as much thought to the worker reaching retirement age as it is to recruiting new employees.

No longer willing to throw away the years of experience accumulated by the senior employee, some of the most prominent corporations in America are shaping programs involving part-time and gradual phased "retirement" work options, retraining for new jobs within the company, training for second careers outside the company, reassignments, outplacements and recalling of retirees.

The following Success Over Sixty Corporate Top Ten lists major companies that now offer the most comprehensive and forward-looking retirement policies. While there is no perfect program as yet, these ten, for very different reasons, come closest to the ideal:

MUTUAL OF OMAHA

The world's largest family health-insurance firm made a corporate commitment to maximize the productivity of its older employees thirty years ago when Dr. Charles Mayo, head of the Mayo Clinic and a member of Mutual's board, stated, "Age should be viewed as a biological and physiological development and not solely chronological." Mayo's statement prompted Mutual's chairman and CEO, V. J. Skutts, to formulate a policy renouncing the concept of "corporate senility," abolishing mandatory retirement, and any age restrictions in the hiring of new employees. Of Mutual's 248 general managers throughout the U.S. today, 11 percent are over sixty-five, with the average age being seventy-one. The oldest is eighty-eight.

Among its nationwide force of agents are hundreds of housewives who got into the insurance business as a second career. Esther Ann Leid, for example, joined Mutual at fifty-four. Now eighty, she attends insurance school to update herself on the latest policies. Adele Levy, ninety, is a repeated winner of the highest sales honors and a life member of the $1 million round table. Mattie Henrick, eighty-five, has served both as a sales agent and manager, and she continues to generate business.

Not only does Mutual have a commitment to its older employees, but it has made a nationwide effort to help dispel the myths about aging (see Chapter 4), by sponsoring the radio program called "The Best Years." Produced and hosted by Lowell Thomas until his death at eighty-nine and now hosted by Helen Hayes, eighty-four, it showcases the continued involvement and productivity of citizens over sixty. V. J. Skutts sums up the policy that has long made Mutual of Omaha a trailblazer in its handling of older employees: "So long as there are people who need your help, you have a career."

ATLANTIC RICHFIELD

As with Mutual of Omaha, change at Los Angeles-based Atlantic Richfield (ARCO) came from the top down. ARCO President William F. Kieschnick gave the keynote address to a national conference on "The Older Worker: Issues for the 1980s" in which he proposed a new order—a coalition of business, family, community, church and other institutions to develop resources and programs for the older employee.

As with the other companies listed in our Success Over Sixty Top Ten, ARCO, under the direction of personnel policy manager Blair Hyde, has abolished mandatory retirement. It also offers educational assistance plans, fitness programs geared to over-fifties and is not reluctant to rehiring retirees who want to reenter the workforce.

ARCO is most noteworthy, however, for the preretirement planning curriculum it developed with the nonprofit National Council on Aging, Inc. Any employee fifty years or older can avail himself or herself of ARCO's twenty-three-hour course. Before he emerges with a personal retirement plan tailored specifically to his needs, the employee is given expert advice on:

- *Life-style planning.* How to figure out the right balance between work and leisure. How to decide how and where to live.
- *Financial planning.* How to determine how much one can earn without cutting into Social Security benefits, and what your best investments are.
- *Being healthy and fit over fifty.* How to devise your ideal diet and exercise program.
- *Interpersonal relationships.* How to cope with marital strains resulting from retirement, being cut off from co-workers and friends.
- *Community service.* How to pinpoint the best volunteer opportunities.
- *New careers.* How to assess your aptitude for a second occupation, or the prospects for going into a business of your own.

Why make this program available to people years away from retirement? "As you grow older," says industrial psychologist Dick Buckles, "you should look into the future and anticipate problems—the sooner you start planning, the better your chances of not just surviving but of flourishing."

THE AEROSPACE CORPORATION

Another trendsetter in helping people to help themselves is California's Aerospace Corporation. It is a private, nonprofit research and development firm that employs approximately 4,200 people: 2,300 are members of the technical staff, mostly engineers and scientists; one in four has a doctorate. Aerospace's contract sales for 1983 were more than $273.7 million.

Dr. Eberhardt Retchin, president and chief operating officer, set the tone at Aerospace when he articulated the "corporate memory bank" theory—that the cumulative knowledge of experts working over a twenty-year period constituted one of Aerospace's major assets, an asset not to be squandered through forced retirement.

For those who do want to retire, Aerospace Director of Personnel Operations Robert Rubenstein has implemented an extensive preretirement workshop; the company also furnishes source material at its library on second careers, housing, financial planning, learning, nutrition, exercise and leisure.

Aerospace has been so skillful at preparing its staff for retirement that from a recent sample of seventy-six Aerospace retirees, two became school district administrators, twenty went into business for themselves, five became building contractors, two became horse breeders, two got engineering jobs, one became a licensed optometrist, another became a cattle rancher and yet another a lawyer.

By actively seeking out people who have been forced into retirement by other companies, Aerospace replenishes its own "memory bank." For example, Eric Selinger, an engineer hired at seventy, recently invented a rotary transformer for Aerospace. Now seventy-two, he is a key member of the company's guidance and control division, a handful of staffers directing the course of Aerospace's technical efforts. The Aerospace example proves one thing: when a corporation bets on the future of its older employees, everybody hits the jackpot.

McDONALD'S CORPORATION

We were surprised to find one of our most enlightened corporations in the youth-oriented fast-food business. Throughout its worldwide system of 7,000 restaurants, McDonald's hires older workers with flexible hours on a part-time basis.

Of course, teenagers and people in their early twenties still make up the vast majority of McDonald's employees. Increasingly, however, the company has come to realize that hiring older people is in McDonald's own self-interest. "There is maturity, a sense of responsibility and pride exemplified by regular attendance, consistent job performance and steadiness," explains McDonald's vice-president, Robert M. Beavers. "They are usually more stable and lend continuity and dependability to an often rapidly changing part-time workforce. They also comfort and reassure our young managers, many of whom are supervising others for the first time." In short, says Beavers, "they are a role model for our younger crew."

Consequently, McDonald's stresses in its job advertisements that age is not a factor in hiring; and it gave a grant to the National Council on Aging to fund the publication of *Job-*

Seeking Guide for Seniors, which the chain then distributed at its participating restaurants in the hopes of attracting older job applicants. McDonald's also works closely with ABLE, an organization that identifies job opportunities for people in this age group.

McDonald's enlightened policies also extend to its thousands of franchise owner-operators. Age is not a factor in determining who gets a franchise, nor is age considered when the original franchise agreement expires after twenty years and comes up for renegotiation. Each year, hundreds of franchise agreements are rewritten with operators in their sixties and seventies. No wonder. Ken Props, McDonald's director of franchising, is seventy-nine.

UNION CARBIDE

The nation's tenth largest employer has taken bold steps to make sure that the scientific, technical and managerial expertise of its retirees does not go to waste. Toward that end, William Morro, a top Union Carbide executive in his sixties, received the go-ahead from Company Chairman Warren Andersen in 1978 to establish the Carbide Retiree Service Corps.

Today the nonprofit corps' 4,500 members advise volunteer groups, government agencies and small businesses on a wide range of problems. One corps member, for example, traveled to Chile to help a local chemicals producer organize his marketing operation. In a joint venture with the U.S. Department of Health and Human Services, other Union Carbide retirees have helped design new lines of kitchen appliances and bathroom fixtures specifically for use by the handicapped. The disabled will also benefit from another corps research project: redesigning elevator doors so that they will not close too quickly or with too much force. The American Red Cross, the

International Executive Service Corps and the Small Business Administration are just a few of the agencies and organizations that now draw on the know-how of Union Carbide's retirees.

POLAROID

Under the direction of Joseph S. Perkins, Corporate Retirement Manager, the company that has become synonymous with innovation in the field of photography is also breaking new ground with its "rehearsal retirement" and "phased retirement" policies. If an employee is thinking of retiring from the company to pursue other interests but wants to test the waters first, he or she is given an unpaid leave of absence. At the end of the leave (the average duration is three months), an employee can either retire or return to his or her old job at Polaroid.

One of the first employees to take part in the company's rehearsal retirement program was Allen Metcalfe. "It left me free to make my own decision," he says, "without worrying about whether or not I would be able to go back to my old job." Metcalf, as it turned out, never came back. Now in his mid-sixties, he has parlayed his hobby of cutting and polishing semiprecious gems into a lucrative jewelry design business.

Under Polaroid's phased retirement plan, an individual may choose to taper off his or her work schedule, rather than retire outright. A gradual reduction may be made in the hours worked per day, the number of days worked per week, or the number of weeks per month. Employees continue to be compensated according to the amount of time put in on the job, and to retain their company benefits. Robert W. Woodward, sixty-seven, now works an average of four days a week in Polaroid's Cambridge, Massachusetts, laboratories. "I have seventy-six days off a year," he explains. "I was in Florida three weeks last spring. I took three weeks off in the summer. I'm going to Philadelphia to play grandpa for a long weekend. Then I'm off on the QE II for ten days next month, and I still have twenty days left." With such options available to them, it is little wonder that after turning sixty-five, more than 80 percent of Polaroid's employees go right on working for the company.

ASC AMERICA INC.

A leader in the field of training older employees is ASC America, Inc. of New York City, a subsidiary of the Ware III computer software company. Refuting the commonly held belief, particularly in high-tech fields, that anyone over fifty is resistant to change or even incapable of learning, ASC set out to hire restless retirees from other fields and teach them to be computer programmers.

"This was not organized as a social program," says Eric Knudson, ASC's chairman. "There was no altruistic purpose behind it. It was simply putting to good business use an economic resource that had largely been ignored in the computer industry. That the program redounds to the benefit of the employee's self-esteem and finances is a happy circumstance, but not the purpose of the program."

Today, the average age of ASC's programmers is sixty-three and a half. The oldest is eighty.

IBM

Thomas Watson, Jr., is considered a business visionary by most of his peers—an executive's executive. Watson, who at sixty-five stepped down in 1979 as chairman of IBM's executive committee, remains the company's most influential board member.

He has seen to it that IBM's 200,000 employees have the option of continuing in their jobs (there is no mandatory retirement age) or embarking on second careers within the corporation. Since 1970, more than 17,000 IBM employees have assumed new responsibilities. Assemblers have moved into office jobs, engineers have been trained as computer programmers, programmers have become sales representatives and systems engineers.

For those who do choose to leave the company, IBM's Retirement Assistance Program provides potential retirees *and their husbands or wives* $2,500 *each per year* in tuition. This stipend starts three years before the individual becomes eligible for retirement and extends two years beyond retirement, allowing the employee a total of five years to prepare for his new career trajectory.

Of the 1,200 IBM retirees who completed their courses of study five years ago, many are now active in real estate or in television, radio, electronic and automotive repair. One used half his IBM tuition money to finish college and the rest to attend a series of tennis clinics; he is now a pro at a San Diego country club. Another took voice lessons and is singing professionally, while a twenty-year IBM veteran studied small business practices and now runs his own picture-framing shop. A midlevel executive became a gemologist, and an information systems programmer began studying Chinese cooking three years before retiring so she could give lessons herself and start her own catering business.

BANKERS LIFE AND CASUALTY

This Chicago-headquartered insurance company with 5,000 home offices, and $1 billion in assets has never had a mandatory retirement policy. Nor does Bankers Life discriminate in hiring. For example, after a career with the Internal Revenue Service, George Morton went to work for Bankers Life and stayed twenty-five years. Hersheld Bold, who was hired by Bankers at age sixty-eight after forty-two years with the post office, remains a valued employee at eighty-five.

But Bankers Life's biggest single contribution to the lot of the senior worker is an intangible one. For most of the employees we spoke to, Bankers Life is simply an uplifting, inspiring place to work. "The management really wants to know what you're thinking," says one. "They don't patronize you." Management knows what it's doing. "Positive mental attitude has been one of the primary assets of the older people among our work group," says Robert Ewing, the firm's president. "Our experience shows it is bad business to exclude competent people from the workforce on the basis of age alone. The presence of older employees also enhances the general working climate," adds Ann Marie Buchmann, vice-president of human resources at Bankers Life. "We find that older persons, given the opportunity, respond to the challenge and offer creative suggestions," says Buchmann. "We also find that intergenerational exchange, friendships, and mature role models benefit young, middle-aged and older employees alike."

THE GRUMMAN CORPORATION

If any corporation approximates the perfect corporate policy toward older workers, it's Grumman of Bethpage, New York. "If discrimination because of age is to be avoided," says Grumman's director of personnel, Robert W. Bradshaw, "a clear policy opposing it must be part of the company's overall commitment to equal employment opportunity. Top management at Grumman fully endorses this policy and supports its implementation throughout the company."

The partial inventory of Grumman's programs and policies which follows can serve as a model for corporations seeking to make the most of this tremendous human resource.

Rehiring Retirees

Grumman conducts an effective rehiring program for retired employees who are interested in returning to work on a full-time or part-time basis. Such employees are returned to the payroll as "job shoppers" until they can fill the slot in the company that fits them specifically. No age limit or qualification is attached to this program. Generally, these workers are fifty-five and up. All are on Grumman pensions. Many are over seventy years of age. Retirees are recruited for this program in several ways. In many cases, a department will request an individual by name. The director of personnel also sends a letter periodically to all retirees asking if they are interested in coming back to work. Information on job opportunities for retired employees is conveyed to and through Grumman's very active retirees' club.

Work schedules for retirees who return to work are variable and flexible. A wide range of skills is represented in the retirees who return to work, including engineers, inspectors,

accountants, mechanics, security guards, buyers, editors and
executives. Apart from the appeal this program has for retirees interested in returning to work, it has many advantages
for the company. Returning retirees are immediately productive; they require no orientation or training period, no break-
in time. The experience of the retiree is again available to the
company at large and, in particular, to younger workers. The
presence in the workforce of experienced, enthusiastic and
productive older workers is a most effective antidote to prej-
udice or discrimination based on age.

Mid-Career Training Programs

The career education and development department at Grumman gives many courses that are designed to update the basic
engineering, management and mechanical skills of the worker
whose formal education ended many years in the past. These
courses are especially helpful to older workers who completed their formal education before the age of the computer.
They enable engineers and technicians alike to catch up and
keep up with the state of their art in a rapidly changing and
competitive environment. While no age limit or qualification
is attached to these courses, they are favorable to the middle-
aged and older worker.

Job Exchange Service

Grumman also participates in community programs to help
older workers find employment. In conjunction with the Department of Senior Citizens Affairs of New York's Nassau
County, the company is actively involved in the "Ability is
Ageless" Job Fair, conducted to provide free employment
services to individuals fifty-five or over.

Workforce Analysis by Age

Each year, Grumman conducts an analysis of the workforce by age. National workforce statistics and Department of Labor Employment and Earnings Charts are used for comparison purposes. The workforce analysis provides a tool for monitoring the distribution of the workforce by age. Such information is helpful in estimating employee needs for training, and for designing programs to prevent discrimination based on age.

Employee Attitude and Behavior Survey

This survey makes available the experience and perceptions of the employees themselves on such topics as discrimination, working conditions and opportunities for development. These perceptions are analyzed carefully by the personnel department and become the basis for new programs to foster the development of the workforce regardless of age.

Phased Retirement and Preretirement Planning

Grumman is now putting into motion a plan similar to Polaroid's, which would allow employees to move gradually into retirement by shifting from full-time to part-time employment. As with each of the other corporations in the Success Over Sixty Top Ten, Grumman also offers an extensive course aimed at preparing the individual for retirement. And Grumman goes one step farther by emphasizing that retirement is by no means compulsory so that, says Personnel Director Robert Bradshaw, "no employee will feel compelled to make a premature or uninformed decision to leave the workforce."

Older Women as a Resource

A study by the Denver Research Institute revealed that there were over 900,000 women with undergraduate mathematics and science degrees across the nation, and that 47 percent of these were unemployed. Recognizing the potential for recruiting educated, older women, Grumman has made a special effort to seek them out through two programs that cater specifically to older women: the Professional Awareness Workshop is for women who once were employed outside the home, have been absent from the workforce for a number of years, and now want guidance in redefining career goals. The Women's Responsibility Training Center provides an opportunity for on-the-job training in various Grumman departments. Grumman intends to make its policies regarding older employees stick. "Our policy of not discriminating because of age," says Bradshaw, "is inculcated in management training programs and is a criterion in all performance appraisals —particularly for managers and supervisors." This approach seems to be working. The average age of Grumman employees is now over forty-five, with more than 25 percent over fifty-five.

These are by no means all of the corporations acting to improve the lot of the older worker, but merely the ten we feel deserve to be singled out for special praise:

- *Mutual of Omaha* for developing a twofold corporate policy toward the individual employee and the public at large that recognizes the skill, value, experience and healthy longevity of the older American.
- *McDonald's* for realizing the value of over-sixties as part-time employees and as franchise owner-operators.

- *The Union Carbide Corporation* for demonstrating that managerial and scientific personnel who have retired can continue to make significant contributions to society through application of their professional expertise.
- *Polaroid* for encouraging their employees to determine their own retirement age through "Rehearsal Retirement" and "Phased Retirement" programs.
- *ASC American, Inc.*, for proving that retirees can be trained to be effective computer programmers and to enter high technology fields.
- *Atlantic Richfield* for developing one of the best preretirement programs in America.
- *Aerospace Corporation* for recognizing the "corporate memory" of its senior employees as the company's greatest asset.
- *IBM* for creating one of the most extensive training and retraining programs anywhere, and for paying tuition costs to launch retiring employees on the second career of their choice.
- *Bankers Life and Casualty* for encouraging an atmosphere of respect for the older worker that motivates many of them to succeed well into their eighties.
- *Grumman* for an overall policy that should be read by every corporate president and personnel manager in America, and for its unique program to train older women.

The policies being devised and vigorously pursued by the Success Over Sixty Top Ten will almost certainly be adopted by all U.S. corporations in the coming years. But for now, we cannot ignore the fact that prejudices and myths still prevail in many boardrooms. Albert Myers experienced them first-hand when he sold his chain of retail department stores to the Swiss conglomerate, Maas-Nordmann. Myers was told by Maas-Nordmann's president that Myers, then sixty-two, was "too old" to be running any large company. In fact, Maas-Nordmann's official policy is that no one over forty-five is to be hired as a president or CEO in the corporation.

This came as no great surprise to Myers, for although the "too old" myths exist in every industry, they are especially pernicious in the retailing and banking fields. One documented case involves a chain of fifty department stores whose policy was to employ only young males for its management training program. All women, and any men over forty, were excluded. In day-to-day operations, these young management trainees did essentially the same work as the rank-and-file, most of whom were women over fifty who had worked for the store an average of twenty years. Stymied in their efforts to be promoted and to obtain salary raises that would at least bring them up to the pay levels of the trainees, these longtime employees took legal action and won their right to equal treatment in the courts.

It should be noted, however, that major department stores like Macy's and Penney's do not have mandatory retirement *except* for their executives (we hope this will change) and have been industry leaders in hiring retirees on a part-time basis.

Banks have also been slow to open up opportunities for older employees. One bank president we interviewed staunchly defended his policy of forcing all employees into retirement at seventy. He also conceded that his hiring strategy was to recruit men under forty for executive training, with one or two young women for window-dressing purposes.

We pointed out to him that older women with experience and training might prove particularly adept at dealing with the problems of older depositors—particularly widows and other single women with sizeable accounts. At our suggestion, he sent a woman who had been forced into retirement after thirty years with the bank through their executive training program.

At sixty-eight, she is now a vice-president. As a direct result of her success, the bank has abolished its mandatory retirement policy, hired scores of men and women over sixty, and has managed to attract hundreds of older, more affluent customers to the bank.

Business shouldn't be required to go it alone. Government is going to have to pitch in to make sure that every citizen can achieve Success Over Sixty. The nation's largest employer—the federal government—now offers little to government workers in the way of preretirement planning, and a mandatory retirement age of sixty-seven remains in force.

The federal government could also give a shot in the arm to Americans through programs that now cost private industry millions. Federal tax credits for capital improvements have been used effectively to spur expansion and growth. So why shouldn't tax credits be given business and industry to find programs that encourage the development of *human* resources? Why not give an investment tax credit to companies that have the foresight to help employees make the most of their lives over sixty? With such tax relief, programs like those pursued by IBM, Union Carbide, Polaroid and the other Success Over Sixty Top Ten companies would almost certainly become the norm. Certainly, keeping this fastest growing segment of the population productive is in the long-range interest of the economy.

Higher education is already involved in the training and retraining of older employees. More and more companies are following IBM's lead and paying full tuition fees for those who want to learn new techniques or skills. *The New York Times Guide to Continuing Education,* by Frances Coombs Thompson, lists hundreds of colleges, universities and specialized schools that provide adult education opportunities. Most cooperate with the leading employers in their area to aid senior employees. Grumman, for instance, worked with Pratt

Institute to prepare older employees for work in the field of electrical power engineering, an area of high occupational demand. Grumman also joined with the State University of New York at Stony Brook to initiate a three-year study program for senior employees, leading to a degree of master of science in computer engineering and science. Both programs delivered formal graduate education in a rapidly advancing technology to engineers whose skills otherwise were becoming increasingly obsolescent.

A number of independent organizations are also helping corporations to forge new personnel policies for the 1980s and beyond. The American Association of Retired Persons' AIM (Action for Independent Maturity) Program, which conducts eight-hour preretirement planning seminars for people aged fifty to sixty-four still in the workforce, has been picked up by 1,600 companies, educational institutions and government agencies since 1971. Levi Strauss, Polaroid, and Northrop have each used AIM's program as the basis for their own expanded preretirement workshops.

The most effective corporate partner is the National Council on Aging (NCOA), the nonprofit, Washington-based consortium of major corporations (Bristol-Myers, the Container Corporation of America, Equitable Life, General Mills, General Electric and others) and unions, including the United Steel Workers and the American Federation of State, County and Municipal Employees. In addition to collaborating with Atlantic Richfield in formulating what is perhaps the most comprehensive preretirement planning course offered anywhere, NCOA has also been tapped by Travelers Insurance to form a retiree "job bank." Through the Travelers job bank, the company's retirees can register to fill temporary positions as they open up, as well as assume permanent jobs if they wish to work full-time. Appropriately, the job bank is run by two retirees in their seventies.

As America's workforce grows older, so too do its business leaders. That is a good thing. Now, as top corporate officers reach the age at which they have traditionally been expected to step aside, they typically feel their capacity for work is largely undiminished. And they become aware, in a very personal sense, of just how noxious the sixty-five-and-out rule really is.

In our free enterprise system, the private sector—not the state—invariably points the way toward progress; which is simply because in its search for profits, a corporation must find the better way. Herein lies the essential purpose behind corporate Success Over Sixty; beyond all humanitarian concerns—it's good business!

4 How Not to Be Your Own Worst Enemy

Youth is a quality, not a matter of circumstances.
—Frank Lloyd Wright

No matter how enlightened an organization's policies toward its older employees, or how comprehensive its plans and programs for retirees, only one person is ultimately responsible for your becoming a Success Over Sixty. That person is you. It is up to you to take a realistic look at yourself, to assess the opportunities that lie before you and to take the reasoned action—often the calculated risk—to ensure that your future will be a productive, fulfilling and rewarding one.

Before you can do that, however, you must appreciate the full extent to which society at large and you as an individual have been led to believe that the golden years should be a time of benign resignation. No group has suffered more from being stereotyped than this segment of the population, and the fact is that most older people feel subconsciously compelled to live up to society's lowered expectations of them. Maggie Kuhn of the Gray Panthers argues that her contemporaries have actually been "brain damaged" as a result of being so often shunted aside. "There are *so* many stereotypes," laments Kuhn. "The worst part of it is that older people believe these lies about age, and younger people are taught to expect them! Old people drool. They take laxatives all the time. Their sex organs are dried up. They are stuck in the past. Senility is judged an inevitable part of age. But old age," Kuhn argues, "is not chronology. It's self-image and mind."

By perpetuating these age-old myths, society programs us to feel that we will inevitably break down like a gas-guzzling clunker long before we've reached the end of the road. We have been brainwashed from infancy to believe age turns us all into old bags of bones. "We know," says psychologist Eda Le Shan, "that if someone is told enough times that he or she is stupid or crazy or whatever, it's only a matter of time before that person is convinced that it's true—and starts acting that way."

For Donald Payne, the subtle demoralization started at the architectural firm where he designs medical offices. "At work, I suddenly realized that I was the only person who remembered Dean Acheson or Bernard Baruch or Marlene Dietrich," he recalls. "Everybody around me was suddenly forty or younger. It was sort of funny at first—people kidded me about being the 'Old Man' or the 'Gray Fox.' But after a while, I stopped getting the really challenging, big-money assignments. When I went to my boss—he is thirty-eight, tops —and asked what was wrong, he said it was all for my benefit. He seemed amazed that 'at this stage' I was complaining about having my work load lessened."

From that point on Payne began to worry about the inevitable day when the axe would fall—when he would be "asked" to take early retirement and make room for those bright (and inexperienced) young talents everybody is always talking about. "That's when I started to think, 'What's the use?' "Payne's devotion to his job had been undermined. He began coming into the office late, missing deadlines, sloughing off in general. The sense of diminished self-worth and aimlessness crept into his personal life. "My wife and I had always had a wonderful sex life—somehow my work sort of charged me up. But when I started feeling worthless at the office, I just didn't care about sex anymore. My wife, Laura, kept asking what she was doing wrong, but I just stayed glued to the tube until 2:00 A.M. So one night, she turned the set off and she made me talk it out. We talked until 6:00 in the morning, but when I went to work three hours later with no sleep, everything seemed perfectly clear to me.''

When Donald Payne recognized what the ageist attitudes of his boss's and coworkers' prejudices were doing to him—and what he, in turn, was doing to himself—he began to plan for a second career. With two friends from other firms—a man and a woman both in their fifties—he laid the foundation for a small design firm of his own. As a result, Payne's life turned around dramatically, and Payne, not surprisingly, is back to wanting Laura.

We Challenge the Myth of Age as the Great Equalizer

At a time when major inroads are being made toward overcoming racial, religious, ethnic, economic and sexual prejudices, little effort is being made to eradicate this myth. When students were asked to look at a group of older men and women of varying heights, weights, races, classes and cultures, then asked to list the first thing they noticed about each individual, all of them came up with precisely the same answer: Not that the person was obese or skinny, male or female, black or white, dressed in a business suit or a loincloth. The first characteristic they noticed about each individual was his or her *age*.

And yet, by the sheer force of their breadth of experience, there is no more diverse group of people in the land. By the time one approaches sixty, he has inevitably seen his share of marital joys and troubles, personal tragedies, financial booms and busts, wars, political scandals, disasters, and so on—all grist for the making of a unique personality. This is "a more diverse, heterogeneous group than any other," says Dr. Robert N. Butler, director of the National Institute of Aging. "One may be at different 'ages' at one and the same time in terms of mental capacity, physical health, endurance, creativity and emotions."

We Challenge the Myth of Senility

Though certainly age-related, this nonspecific state is diagnosed in only about 1 percent of the over-sixty-fives—which is far lower than the number of people who suffer from severe mental problems at younger ages. Yet none of us are immune to this deplorable myth. Even before he racked up a number of impressive primary victories in the fall of 1980, Ronald Reagan, then sixty-nine, had to deal with the public's fear that he might become senile in office. The candidate dealt with the possibility head-on. He told the press that he was as alert as he approached his seventies as he was in his fifties, that he did not suffer memory loss or any other disability commonly linked (though often unfairly) to aging. To further reassure the electorate, he promised that if the White House physician ever determined that he had become senile, he would "walk away" from office.

That the issue of senility was even raised during the presidential campaign of 1980 appalls Dr. Butler. "I doubt that anyone in Germany ever asked that question of Adenauer, or of De Gaulle in France," says Dr. Butler. "It has to be an American cultural disease, part of the idea that senility is an inevitable concomitant of aging. I'm firmly convinced," he adds, "that senile dementia—and all of the change that occurs before its symptoms emerge clearly—has a lot to do with the negative images and fears about old age we develop as children."

Fortunately, those people with signs of mental disorientation are ṇo longer routinely dismissed as senile and incurable. Recent advances in the understanding of brain chemistry have resulted in a new arsenal of drugs to combat the disease. Through various forms of drug and psychiatric treatment, about one-quarter of all "dementia" cases are now reversible. "There has been a revolution in thinking about senility," asserts Dr. Peter Davis of Albert Einstein Medical College. "People no longer view it as hopeless. For the first time they're thinking, 'My God, we may be able to do something about the problem.' "

"Any blunting we do see in the absence of actual disease," writes leading gerontologist Dr. Alex Comfort in his excellent book *A Good Age*, "commonly results not from age but from put-downs, boredom and exasperation. Going out of your head, losing your memory or becoming 'senile' is statistically an unlikely misfortune. The word 'senile' itself is less a diagnosis than a term of abuse—you're senile if you make waves. That indicates only that your brain is still functioning and they haven't washed it for you."

Conclusion: intellect per se does not decline with age; on the contrary, older people usually have a wealth of knowledge that gives them a decided mental edge over their juniors.

We Challenge the Myth of Complacency

Never before in the history of this country have older people been more discontented—which has led octogenarian Florida Congressman Claude Pepper to become a kind of unofficial spokesman for the nation's 60 million senior citizens (America's largest political constituency) in his capacity as chairman of the powerful House Rules Committee. There he has battled endlessly against reductions in Social Security, Medicare cutbacks and ripoffs of the elderly. The Gray Panther's Kuhn, as well as dozens of other antiageist leaders, also make it clear that their contemporaries are far from complacent; more and more are mad as hell and they're not going to take it anymore.

One symptom of this unrest which has only surfaced in recent years is a sudden surge in crimes, ranging from assault to shoplifting, committed by people over sixty. During the 1970s, while the number of Americans fifty-five and over increased 22 percent, felony arrests of seniors for rape and theft each climbed a staggering 300 percent. The most prevalent crime, of course, is shoplifting, a diversion for some, for others a means to scrape by on a meager budget. But for most, say some experts, this is a way to lash out. "Overage criminals feel they are no longer bound to a system that has no place for them," suggests criminologist Gary Feinberg of Biscayne College in Miami, one of those cities with an even higher incidence of crime committed by the elderly. "They are adrift, and society has provided them with neither map nor itinerary nor friendly shore."

So severe is this crime wave that it has created a crisis for the criminal justice system, which is simply not geared to handle the problem. "There is really no room in the system for the sixty-seven-year-old woman caught stealing a can of tuna fish," says Donald Newman, dean of the School of Criminal Justice at the State University of New York at Albany. "A three-year sentence may be life for an elderly offender." As Donald Pappa, a municipal court judge in Asbury Park, New Jersey, says, "When these people come before me, I feel as if I'm standing in judgment over my own parents." While the immediate goal may be to channel those elderly accused of minor offenses into counseling programs instead of the courts, that is, of course, just a stopgap measure. Inevitably, society will have to come to grips with the alienation and rage of its older men and women.

We Challenge the Myth of Sexlessness

Doctor: "When did sex stop for you?" George Burns: "At 3 this morning." There is no clinical reason why sexual activity should cease or significantly decline in the sixth decade of life. In fact, the millions of people in this category who do not succumb to the stereotype lead active sex lives into their seventies, eighties—and beyond.

There are, to be sure, some changes associated with age in the sexual performance of males: orgasm becomes less frequent, occurring perhaps during every other act of intercourse instead of every time, and more direct stimulation is sometimes needed. But potency is largely unaffected, and frankly, many couples would not complain if it takes twice as long to reach orgasm.

Interestingly, statistics dating back to 1926 on the sexual activity of older people show that 4 percent of all males aged seventy to seventy-nine were indulging in sex every third day, and another 9 percent were having intercourse at least weekly. In 1959, Dr. A. L. Finkel found that 65 percent of men polled between the ages of fifty-six and sixty-nine were active regularly, and that nearly half those over eighty had intercourse roughly every five weeks.

Why, then, is there reluctance in the 1980s to admit to ourselves that everyone can and—if they wish—should be sexually active till the end? "Our adult children," explains Maggie Kuhn, "are perpetuating the myth that we can't have sex. They are embarrassed to think that their mother and daddy have, or had, sex activity. They have an immaculate conception of their own creation. Most children find it difficult, especially when they are in their own middle life, to allow thought of their mother and father or their surviving parent enjoying sex." Instead, they often brand their sexually active parents and grandparents as "dirty old" men and women. "They ought to be grateful and encouraging about a lively sexual attitude in parents," continues Kuhn, "but they are often judgmental and mad. They try to break up romance and feelings of affection. They are prudes, and some go so far as to bully their parents into sexual nothingness. A lot of people let their children do them in that way. But some older people leave home—are driven out, really—and start a new life for themselves away from their ashamed children."

We Challenge the Myth of Inflexibility

Given the opportunity, over-sixties have been found to be just as adaptable—to a new job, a new environment, a new challenge—as their younger counterparts. Old dogs *can* be taught new tricks. As Justice Oliver Wendell Holmes explained when he began studying Greek at the age of ninety-two: "When else would I have had the time to take it up?"

We Challenge the Myth of Unproductivity

This myth is particularly onerous, since it serves to justify a negative attitude toward employees that takes a dreadful economic and human toll. Despite the cruel practice of forcing people out of the workforce through mandatory retirement, an astounding 69 percent of men and women over traditional retirement age still manage to work on a full or part-time basis, and it is not insignificant that as we pointed out earlier, men over sixty run most of the *Fortune 500* companies. As for these companies' older workers, the results of a 1983 poll published in the *Wall Street Journal* showed that 84 percent of business personnel directors feel older workers are *at least* as valuable as younger ones. They also have an absenteeism record that is 20 percent better than average, and have far fewer injuries, since the number of industrial accidents decreases with caution and experience. But once the older employee has, in essence, perfected his job, he is all too often rewarded by being booted out.

We Challenge the Myth of Obstinacy

Older people have every right to be outspoken and they have learned that a dash of what Alex Comfort calls "bloody-mindedness" helps them to command the respect (if tinged with fear) that so often eludes older people. "Bloody-mindedness," Comfort explains, "subsumes feistiness, cussedness, orneryness, with overtones of heroic obstinacy. It is the ultimate resource of the senior person. Bloody-mindedness is an index of self-respect." Cranky and difficult? Refreshingly direct.

Finally, business is beginning to chop away at these stereotypes. In a statement before the House, Claude Pepper acknowledged that "older Americans—some as old as eighty—are being trained right now on the most sophisticated technological equipment to be computer programmers, retired engineers are being rehired to build jet aircraft and design robots; fast food chains, grocery and clothing stores, life insurance and oil companies are redirecting their corporate policies to encourage their veteran workers to stay on the job rather than retire. These are the signs that experience counts in American business." And that the age-old ageist myths are eroding. What matters most, of course, is that we over-sixties no longer believe them ourselves.

A NEW FORCE IN THE MARKETPLACE

There is no more effective way of getting the attention of the powers that be than by becoming a force in the marketplace.

Teenage models in tight jeans will almost certainly be splashed across magazine pages and flashed on television screens for years to come, but they are already beginning to give way to models with a more "mature" look. Long thought to possess little clout as consumers, people fifty-five and up are emerging as a major spending group, accounting for nearly half a *trillion* dollars in annual personal income and more than *one-quarter* of all consumer expenditures.

Whatever it is called—the gray market, the older market, the mature market—this segment of the population, through sheer force of numbers, has led American business to begin to revise its thinking about older people. According to *Nation's Business,* this consumer force is growing at a rate double that of the overall population. One in three U.S. households is headed by someone over fifty-five, and contrary to popular belief, only a small fraction—around 7 percent—live either with their children or in nursing homes.

Conversely, the youth market that business has been scrambling to satisfy is shrinking dramatically. From the 1950s through the 1970s, it was enough for corporations to zero in on the under-twenty-fives. But no longer. The number of men and women under the age of twenty-five will not only stop growing in the next few years, it will drop by some 12 million as the baby boomers careen headlong into middle age.

For those of us who have either reached that point or gone considerably beyond it, manufacturers have at last come to the belated realization that we are not poor and that we have the power to make the economy cater to us. "Historically," observed Washington, D.C., psychologist and marketing consultant Dr. Carole B. Allan, "the marketing community has turned its back on the older consumer for one basic reason— a belief that the age group has limited spending power." Add to this the belief that the group had limited consumer needs (with the exception of health-care products), less inclination to spend, and lacked distinctive marketing characteristics and only one conclusion seemed logical—marketing strategies targeted to the over-sixties would not justify the costs involved.

Item: Nearly 80 percent of all money in savings and loan institutions is controlled by people fifty-five and older (nearly two-thirds of whom are women).
Item: More than 30 percent of total personal income in the U.S. is earned by over-fifty-fives.
Item: Per capita expenditures for travel are highest in the fifty-five to sixty-four age group.
Item: Households headed by older Americans account for 30 percent of all expenditures on food and liquor, 40 percent of every dollar spent in beauty parlors, and fully one-quarter of all money spent on cosmetics.

"When one looks at the per capita expenditure figures," continues Dr. Allan, "it becomes clear that the 55-to-64-year-old household becomes the single most important consumer market in the country today. It is a time of life when, freed from the constraints and financial responsibility of child-raising, spending on self becomes the order of the day."

For the over-sixty-fives the pattern is "even more striking," according to Dr. Allan. "Indications are that an increasing number of persons 65 and older are joining the 'Me Generation'—spending money on themselves rather than saving for their children, as was once the case. The philosophy of the day has become if not now, when? Indeed," Allan continues, "persons 65 and older who fall within the prime income categories are among the most conspicuous spending groups in the country for a wide range of luxury goods and services." "Over-sixties," according to one banker who has set up a special financial service for older depositors, "offer the greatest profit potential there is." In fact, 29 percent of all

discretionary money in the consumer marketplace is controlled by the over-sixties—double that in households headed
by people in their late twenties and thirties, and thirty times
the money in pockets of under-twenty-fives.

If somewhat slow on the uptake, a number of major corporations have at last made a serious effort to target the gray
market. Hence Gerber Products, convinced there was as
much money to be made at the other end of the life cycle, has
abandoned its slogan—"Babies are our business, our only
business"—and launched a line of health-care products for
the over-sixties. Amtrak, Greyhound and Eastern Airlines are
among the many transportation companies trying to attract
the older traveler with package deals and bargain rates, while
McDonald's, Pepsi (a new Pepsi Generation?), General
Foods, Colgate Palmolive, Procter and Gamble and even
youth-conscious Levi Strauss are concocting new strategies
to capture what they correctly see as the growth market of
the 1980s and 1990s. And Wilson, Head, AMF and other
major manufacturers of sporting goods are taking square aim
at what they now see as their most lucrative market—men
and women with the cash to spend and time to play. Dr. Allan
points out that Elizabeth Arden, Estée Lauder and other cosmetic companies are pleased that in the 1980s they, too, have
jumped on the bandwagon. Helena Rubinstein's "Madame
Rubinstein" line for the mature woman has doubled its business every year since it was launched in 1977, and Arden's
"Millenium" cosmetics, put on the market in 1980, have enjoyed a similarly spectacular success.

Seeking a fresh source of big profits, companies, having so
long ignored the older consumer, now clamor for information
about the characteristics of this emerging market of affluent
Americans. What are they like? What do they want? For the
first time ever the over-sixties are being courted by industry;
misreading this group can be costly. For example, in 1980,

Heinz introduced a line of easily digestible, pablumlike "senior foods," presumably to be "gummed" by toothless consumers. The line was a complete flop. What business is learning is that there is no homogeneous consumer profile for this group, no way to pigeonhole older people. We do not, as we have been led to believe, become more alike as we get older; we become increasingly diverse. The challenge to the business community is not merely to crack the code that will ensure success with this segment of the population, but to be innovative in accommodating the myriad needs and desires of the over-sixties.

DEFYING THE MYTHS

All the evidence points in the same direction. "Older people who see themselves as doing useful and interesting things fare better in every way than ones who merely take it easy," says B. F. Skinner, eighty-one, the famed Harvard psychologist. Dr. Charles B. Huggins, who reached eighty-two in 1983, concurs: "It's commonly held that old age is a shipwreck but that need not be so. You can be young at ninety or old and washed up at thirty-five. The important thing is whether you use your bean. If you don't use it, you lose it." Dr. Huggins should know. At the age of sixty-four he was awarded the Nobel Prize for physiology and medicine for his research in the field of cancer. In his eighth decade he continues to exercise his "bean" every day in his laboratory at the University of Chicago, where he is professor emeritus of surgery. "Why should I retire as long as I love my work and can still do it well?" he asks, sounding more than just a bit incredulous at the suggestion. Huggins is not alone among older overachievers. Consider the brief, decade-by-decade roster of over-sixties in their prime.

After reaching ninety-six in 1983, Broadway producer George Abbott (*Pal Joey, On Your Toes*) remained a force in the American theater and got married, to boot. Pathfinding psychiatrist Karl Menninger continued to unravel the complexities of the human mind as he approached his hundredth birthday in 1984. Marc Chagall and Georgia O'Keeffe, artistic giants of the twentieth century, were still painting when they celebrated their ninety-fourth birthdays in 1983. Comparative youngster George Burns achieved his greatest fame in his eighties, kicking off his ninth decade with an Oscar as best supporting actor in *The Sunshine Boys*. At eighty-seven, he wrote his best-selling *How to Live to Be 100* and recorded his second Country-Western album. Sculptors Henry Moore and Louise Nevelson have continued to produce masterpieces well into their eighties, as have composers Aaron Copland and Virgil Thomson. Meantime, James Cagney emerged from a twenty-year retirement in 1981 to star in the film *Ragtime* at the age of eighty-one. Also octogenarians, actresses Helen Hayes, Lillian Gish, Eva Le Gallienne and the irrepressible Ruth Gordon (who won her first Oscar for *Rosemary's Baby* at the age of seventy-four) are busier than ever with stage, film and television projects. Norman Vincent Peale keeps preaching in his eighties, pianist Vladimir Horowitz, eighty in 1984, continues to dazzle audiences around the world.

At eighty, ex-Coca Cola executive Walter Mack started up the King Cola Corporation to compete with his old employer, and seven years later he was still calling the shots. William Paley was eighty-one when he finally stepped down as head of CBS, the giant communications conglomerate he founded, only to buy up a controlling interest in Whitney Communications and take on the responsibility of pulling that company out of the red. Benjamin Spock remained active in politics and pediatrics as he entered his eighties. Isaac Bashevis

Singer won the Nobel Prize for literature at seventy-five, and was at the peak of his literary powers when he turned eighty. (Bob) Hope springs eternal. Hope was honored on his eightieth birthday in 1983 with a star-studded nationally televised party at Radio City Music Hall; later that year he took his Christmas show to U.S. servicemen in Beirut.

When one begins to consider the number of major figures who are still going strong in their seventies, the field becomes crowded indeed. Ronald Reagan, who turned seventy just a few weeks after he was sworn in as the oldest elected president in history, is a year older than House Speaker Tip O'Neill. In his mid-seventies, Philip Johnson remains the country's leading architect. Harry Helmsley and William Levitt, both in their mid-seventies, are arguably the country's two most active names in real estate. In his seventies, Jacques Cousteau still explores the world's seas. Katharine Hepburn continues, in her mid-seventies, to place high in polls rating the world's most-admired women. Laurence Olivier, meanwhile, entered the second half of his seventh decade with a much-acclaimed TV production of *King Lear*.

As for those celebrated movers and shakers sixty and above, just consider that one-third of the United States House of Representatives, more than half the Senate, most of the President's cabinet and the vast majority of America's business leaders fit into this category.

HOW YOU, TOO, CAN BE A DEFIANT ONE

First and foremost, you must determine the specific ways in which you may be thwarting yourself by trying to be what you have always been told someone your age *should* be. Once you recognize the extent to which you may have fallen into this trap—though you may be one of the few who haven't—there is a way out. As an important step toward self-discovery, complete the following statements:

1. Compared to five years ago, I like myself
   —more
   —less
   —about the same.
2. Compared to my younger colleagues, I am
   —more
   —less
   —equally
   productive.
3. Because of my age,
   —more
   —less
   —the same
   should be demanded of me.
4. These days, I find that I'm
   —more
   —less
   forgetful than I was five years ago.
5. At my age, sex is
   —very
   —moderately
   —less
   important than it once was.

Now, answer *true* or *false*:

6. There are no new worlds left for me to conquer.
7. Things are changing so fast, I am too old to adapt.
8. I leave ambitious plans to younger men and women.
9. I think of myself basically as a survivor.
10. I'm not the person I used to be.

11. I'm sleeping far more than I used to.
12. I read far less than I once did.
13. I'm concerned that when I die, I won't be leaving my children a large enough estate.
14. I am less concerned about things going on around me than I used to be.
15. I'm too mature to let things rile me.

If you answered *less* to any of the first five questions, and have answered in the affirmative to even one of the true-false statements you are probably undermining yourself. This can be the first nail in your psychological coffin.

Before you have succumbed to all the stereotypes and declared yourself obsolete, take the following steps:

(A) Walk into the bathroom, and take a long, hard look in the mirror. Since the way we feel about our appearance has a tremendous amount to do with our self-esteem, a thorough inventory in this department is essential. Sure, we now have to contend with gray or thinning hair, crow's feet (let's call them laugh lines), the whole bit. But many of us will find that age may have actually *improved* our looks. In men, those crags, creases and silver temples add that touch of distinction. How many times have we heard women complain that men grow handsomer as they grow older? It is less often said, but the same thing frequently goes for women.

Of course, no one is entirely satisfied with his or her appearance. If there is something about your reflection that displeases you, change it. Set out today to lose those extra pounds and tighten those sagging muscles. If your baldness bothers you, buy that toupee (but be choosy; make it a good one) or get that hair transplant. Too much gray? Color your hair—that goes for men as well as women. And if you are really vexed by bags under your eyes or a badly sagging chin, don't be afraid to consider cosmetic surgery. The better (not necessarily younger) you look, the more confident you'll be —and that is half the battle.

(B) By way of exploding the myth that you've lost your memory, your marbles or both, sit down with a blank piece of paper and write down the ten events you lived through that shaped our times, and recall just where you were and what you were doing when they occurred. The Depression, World War II, the Korean War, the dawn of the nuclear age, and so on. Living in the past? Not really. These earth-shaking occurrences are an inexorable part of you. Because you have lived through such complex times, you have a wealth of personal knowledge and experience that cannot be matched by youth. You're right when you assume many of them don't want to hear about it; there is a disturbing inclination on the part of today's young to discount much of what has gone before. "That was before my time" is used to excuse even the most astonishing gaps in a young person's knowledge. But this list should serve as a personal reminder that you, as much if not more than they, have a right to be here.

(C) So you're supposed to be unproductive. On another piece of paper roughly calculate how much money you have earned in your lifetime. If you are, say sixty, that figure may fall somewhere between $500,000 and $1.5 million. Then figuring in the rate of inflation over the past thirty-five years, multiply that sum by four. If you have been a housewife all that time, just pay yourself $35,000 for each of those years, because that is what your job is worth today. Putting a dollar value on one's worth is as American as the chili dog. Even if you haven't managed to keep much of it, take pride in your proven capacity to work—and to bring in the bucks.

You'll note that a disproportionate part of your income was earned *after* you hit fifty-five—the period when you shouldered far more responsibility than younger men and women

on the job. Contrary to the myth, you have not sloughed off
with age. Your fat paycheck is proof positive of that.

In subsequent chapters, we will tell you how to make your
specific capabilities and achievements work for you in the
coming years. But first, you must be sure that you have rid
yourself of the burden of the age-old old-age myths. "It's the
steady drip of misinformation that prepares people to be vic-
timized at sixty-five and the rest of us to help victimize them
until we get there ourselves," says Alex Comfort. The ultimate question remains: why condemn one-fifth of the population on the basis of lies, when that's where the rest of us
eventually wind up?

LIMITED RISK: TAKE IT!

You have now taken that first step toward unburdening yourself of the heavy psychological baggage of the ageist myths.
The second step toward Success Over Sixty is more personal:
it is to conquer your fear of the future. It is a known fact that
most people approaching retirement postpone personal deci-
sion-making and planning till the last possible moment. Often
this reluctance stems from the understandable fear that once
we begin thinking about our postretirement lives, we somehow jeopardize the job we are in. So delay becomes denial.
"What are you planning to do when your company retires
you?" we asked scores of working men and women. The
standard answer: "Oh, there are *plenty* of things I can do."
Translation: "I'm too damn scared to even think about it,
much less plan for it."

According to Gail Sheehy's best-selling book *Pathfinders,*
"If retirement is not planned, if no new goals are set or hori-

zons sighted, the *Playboy* lifestyle many people envision soon becomes monotonous, leaving them with a beer in one hand on the poop deck, bobbing like a cork in the bay. But when retirement is used as a channel to possibilities never attempted when there was no time, then there is every reason for refreshment.''

Risk? Of course, there is always risk involved in starting out again, in trying something new. But there is far more risk in letting events overtake you. And if you are to get a handle on your postretirement plans, why not make it sooner rather than later?

No one is more of an expert on the subject of limited risk than Albert Myers. When he stepped down as president of Myers Brothers, Al went ahead with plans he had begun formulating years before to develop a chain of travel agencies. After organizing sixteen offices, he resigned from that enterprise (though he remains on retainer as a consultant to the agencies) to start an exporting firm called Pan Pacific Coal. He then went on to organize the Myers Sport Balloon Company, which manufactured hot air balloons, become a marketing partner in a new credit card company, to market a new Swedish invention that attaches buttons to fabrics using ultrasonic waves and obtain the patents on a fitness testing machine.

Of course, the risks taken by Myers did not all work out. As he says, "You don't roll sevens every time," and on the Pan Pacific deal, no "seven" came up. After flying to Japan and negotiating contracts with Mitsui, Mitsubishi, Sumitomo and other major corporations there, the oil glut that began in 1979 sent coal prices plummeting. The Japanese no longer needed to import coal from the U.S., so Pan Pacific suffered tremendous losses.

Such an experience can be emotionally and financially wrenching, but it can be more than offset by life's successes as long as you try to hedge your bets. Once again, when we speak of risks we are not suggesting that you jeopardize your security. In Myers' case, the hot air balloon and travel business continued to flourish; while the Combi-Tex button machine shows signs of actually replacing the needle and thread. Myers took the kind of *limited risk* that can reap tremendous rewards without ever imperiling his finances. He was not afraid to begin thinking about future projects before the current ones were finished.

It took him longer than Myers, but George Becker also took a limited risk and won. A Notre Dame graduate, Becker served as a navy fighter pilot in the Pacific during World War II, and as soon as the war was over signed on with American Airlines as a pilot. For the next thirty-five years, Captain Becker, like nearly all of his colleagues, devoted himself almost entirely to his job, with an occasional skiing or fishing trip to unwind. Becker never gave any thought to retirement, even though American Airlines, like all major air carriers, has a compulsory retirement age of sixty. Instead of planning a second career Becker merely waited until American booted him out, then, not surprisingly, he began to founder.

Fortunately, he was able to maintain a connection with the world of work through the Gray Eagles, an organization of his fellow retired pilots. An association of about 9,000 pilots, the Eagles are working to persuade both the airlines and the FAA to reconsider the compulsory retirement rules now governing the industry. Beyond that, they serve as a network to help men like Becker, who find themselves grounded in their prime, to become airborne again—on the wings of another career. After rising to the presidency of the Gray Eagles, Becker finally found his calling. In the summer of 1983, his mechanized farm in Durango, Colorado, started cultivating its first crop. The lesson he learned was a bittersweet one. "A guy can log 1 million miles in the air flying through everything from typhoons to pea-soup fog," says Becker, "and still not face up to the fact that he's going to have to take charge of his own life. Because I was unprepared, I lost three years of my life trying to find which direction to go on my own." At least by sixty-three George Becker managed to set himself on a course for personal fulfillment.

Government jobs are often the most difficult to leave. One who chose to take the risk was Clarence Klassen. For thirty-five years, Klassen was Illinois's chief sanitary engineer. When the state established its own Environmental Protection Agency, Klassen was chosen to head it. He resigned over a disagreement with the state administration, and in his late sixties gambled on his ability to make it as an environmental consultant. He succeeded spectacularly, and now approaching eighty, his income as an internationally recognized consultant to corporations and utilities is *five times* what it was when he worked for the state government.

Always looking ahead, Klassen is now formulating plans to spend his eighties making documentary films for commercial travel agencies and shipping lines. He has also taken up painting, with an eye on art as a career for his nineties. Meantime, Klassen maintains his interests in music and photography and is on the technical committee of the Indianapolis Speedway, which supervises the running of the Indy 500. His philosophy: "There are no breaks in life. As the Boy Scout motto says, 'Be prepared'—to take advantage of opportunities when they come along."

For millions of men and women who have mortgaged their independence for the stability that comes with working for a large corporation, making it on one's own may often seem an unattainable dream. Lulled into a false sense of security, the corporate employee is often ill-prepared for life outside the company womb. The shock is that much greater if, in his fifties or sixties, he is fired or forced into unwanted early retirement. The resulting sense of betrayal does little to bolster confidence; having been abandoned by his employer after years of faithful service, he is not about to ante up what little self-esteem he has left on a wager that he can make something of his future.

GLOOM AT THE TOP

Such feelings extend right to the office of the chairman. Virtually all of the retired chief executive officers we interviewed admitted that the prospect of stepping down was an unsettling one. The pension may be 100 percent of the salary, but even for a CEO it isn't easy to face retirement. No more aides to do the legwork, no company limo waiting at the airport, no more secretaries to take calls, no more lavish office suite with its fine paintings and amply stocked liquor cabinet in the corner. But more important than the loss of perks is the loss of power, the knowledge that all eyes are on you when you enter a meeting, that your every word is being heeded. "As you come up through the ranks, you keep shaking your head," recalls one retired CEO. "You say to yourself, 'Don't these old geezers know they've gotta step aside? Do they think they're gonna last forever?' Of course, when it comes to you it's a different matter, particularly if you've worked your way to Number One. I mean, that's the brass ring, isn't it? Then it hits you: you've been at this job for thirty years, maybe longer, with your sights on one thing. But even if you're lucky enough to make it there by your late fifties, you've only got a few years to go before *you* have to leave. And boy, do they come fast! So you really don't think about what you're going to do when the time comes for you to retire, and you wind up grumbling just like those old geezers you marveled at twenty years ago."

What surprised this particular CEO, too, was the attitude of his successor. "He told me to stay away from the division managers and my friends in the company. I was pretty angry at the time but I think, in retrospect, he was probably right. It was a time for the changing of the guard. A new commander had taken over, and the troops had to get accustomed to the new chief."

Actually, most executives insist that they have the right to continue personal friendships that have been forged at their companies over the years, and many corporations encourage retirees to maintain their ties by serving on company boards and committees, consulting and keeping an office—however modest—at headquarters. But even then, a retired CEO must be careful not to tread on the territory of his successor.

WHAT TO DO IF YOU'VE "TOPPED OUT"

If those at the top of the heap have difficulties fending for themselves outside the familiar framework of their companies, at least they have the satisfaction of knowing they have bested their peers at the game of corporate success. But what of the other 99 percent who never realize their goals within a company? "There comes a time around forty-five—maybe fifty, tops—that you realize the path to the Number One spot is blocked," the sixty-one-year-old vice-president (we'll call him Jack) of one of the biggest communications companies told us. "That's when you know you've been topped out. You're not going anywhere, no matter how much harder you work, how much better you get, or what miracles you perform for the company."

Jack, a tennis-trim, immaculately dressed man with dark eyes, coal black hair and a perpetual Palm Beach tan, knows he is the very best in his incredibly demanding business: he has kept his department functioning smoothly (and profitably) for all of the ten years he's been in charge. But he also knows that he is unlikely to fulfill his ambitions to be part of the company's ruling triumvirate. "Bitter? Damn right I'm bitter. You play by the rules, always expecting to be rewarded for your efforts, and if you're lucky, for a long time you are rewarded. If you're outstanding in one spot, they may just decide that's where you'll serve them best. The top spot usually goes to someone with a knack for political maneuvering. It really has very little to do with who has contributed the most to a company, or who could do the best job of running it." So what are Jack's plans? "To stay right where I am and do my job until I retire," he says. "But my real life now is spent on my boat, and improving my tennis game."

It is a critical moment when an executive realizes he has been passed over. If his rage does not result in a bleeding ulcer or worse, the executive may continue through the motions, doing his job but not enjoying it—an attitude that invariably spills over into other areas of his life. Or he may become destructive, directing his venom at his coworkers, doing his best to undermine the plans and programs of others. If he cannot be captain, he figures, why not scuttle the ship?

There is yet another way in which the frustration of being passed over may manifest itself. In an effort to prove to everyone—especially himself—that he is indispensable, the executive may plunge deeper than ever into his work, taking on more clients and projects and working unimaginably long hours. Having defined himself almost solely on the basis of his work, he now puts even more eggs into that one basket. A formula for disaster, and one that Timothy Friedrich followed to its inevitable conclusion.

After thirty-two years with a leading Madison Avenue advertising agency, Friedrich had risen to the key post of vice-president for creative affairs. He was collecting a salary of

$60,000 plus bonuses (a hefty sum in the early 1960s) when the firm's founder and chairman died, setting off a scramble for control. When the dust settled, workaholic Tim, always too enmeshed in his job to pay much attention to office politics, and two other vice-presidents were called in by the new chairman and summarily canned—the first of five top-level firings. The new chief wanted to start fresh, with his own "team" behind him. At age fifty-three, Friedrich was adrift.

To try to help him recover from the blow, Friedrich's wife, Katherine, reminded him of his long-cherished dream of writing. Wasn't this the perfect time to polish his outline and send his sample chapters along to a publisher? And what about that offer from his friend at Time, Inc.? Couldn't Tim offer some expert advice on putting together a promotional campaign for that new magazine they were launching?

Friedrich brushed aside both of his wife's proposals as too risky. Instead, he devoted the next eighteen months to one thing: a desperate search for a position with another ad agency. By the time he found a job, his hair had gone from reddish-brown to white, he had lost weight, his marriage was shaken to its foundations, and his confidence had been dangerously eroded. Finally, he did find a job and he gave all to it. But again, a boardroom scuffle resulted in his being axed.

Now would he dust off that book proposal, Katherine pleaded? Nope. Tim had been on that one company track virtually all his adult life. He had to get back on it, he argued, rather than waste time chasing a dream. One long year later Tim, now fifty-nine, was miraculously welcomed back into the fold by his original employer. Now that his team was firmly entrenched and the economy was booming, the man who had fired him without warning thought Tim was just the man to handle the agency's flood of accounts. True to form, Tim labored fifteen-hour days, took on a workload that was twice that of his fellow executives, and kept it up until he retired at age sixty-five in 1982. Seven months after his farewell party, Tim Friedrich suffered a stroke in the living room of his Central Park West co-op. Like thousands of other passed-over employees, he overcompensated to prove himself in the corporate environment at the expense of his health —and a dream. The book outline still sits in the bottom of a desk drawer, untouched since the day he put it there in 1955.

Robert A. M. Coppenrath, president of Agfa-Gevaert says, "European executives are better suited to handle retirement because they are trained early in life to be multidimensional," and he is right. The single biggest mistake we make is to allow ourselves to be defined by any one thing. If we fail to diversify, we pay the price of unhappiness.

Look at the following statements and assign a percentage to each as you would most like it to apply to you, the total not to exceed 100 percent.

1. ____ I have met or exceeded all my career goals.
2. ____ I am sexually attractive.
3. ____ I am a good spouse and parent.
4. ____ I work to keep myself in good shape physically.
5. ____ I live the best part of my life outside the office.
6. ____ I am expanding my horizons, growing as an individual.
7. ____ I have no regrets about not taking other career paths.
8. ____ I am active in community affairs.
9. ____ I am a spiritual person.
10. ____ I am envied by my fellow workers.

If you assign more than 35 percent to any one statement, you may be defining yourself too narrowly—and that can be dangerous. If your figures for statements 1, 7 and 10 add up to 50 percent or more, you have invested too much of your sense of self in your occupation.

DON'T RETIRE, RETREAD

For many people it is not difficult to pinpoint that one moment when they realized that they had become someone they did not like; they looked in the mirror and were not happy with the image that stared back at them. For one wholesale merchandise sales representative, it occurred while he was giving a pep talk to a group of junior salesmen. "It was the same routine I'd been giving for twenty-seven years," he told us, "but all of a sudden it seemed as if somebody else's voice was coming out of my mouth. I interrupted the speech, excused myself, called my wife and told her I was quitting."

Soon he got together with another member of the restless fifties and bought a fast-food franchise. While his partner, who had retired two years earlier from his job as a warehouse foreman, ran the business, the merchandiser started negotiating with his superiors for the best early retirement package possible. Within eighteen months, he joined his partner in running their now-profitable hamburger outlet. "We split up the time," says the retired sales rep, "so that he runs things for three months while I sail, and then I run the business for three months while he tools around the country in his RV. We have the best of both worlds—work and play—and nobody can retire us."

As for the risk; "I could have lost the $40,000 I put up for my half of the franchise, but I still owned my house and had ten years to go at the company before compulsory retirement. If things hadn't worked out, I'd have chalked it up to experience, stuck with the job I had a little while longer to build up another nest egg, and tried something else. Look, nothing in life is certain, is it?"

Kaylan Pickford knew that better than anyone. When her

first marriage ended in divorce in 1961, she got custody of her two daughters. One month after her second marriage, to a Washington, D.C., hotel owner, he discovered he had cancer, and four years later he died.

Grief-stricken, alone in her fifties, Pickford wondered what she would do with the rest of her life. A strikingly attractive woman with white hair and dazzling blue eyes, she decided, after weighing her options, to take the plunge and try her luck with modeling—a daring move, considering the fact that back then, in 1975, "mature" models were not very much in demand, being pretty much confined to the denture and arthritis pain-formula aspirin ads. "Advertisers were never interested in anyone over twenty-five," she remembers. "I used to go weeks without a job. Then I'd work for one hour and come home at night and cry." It was as if older men and women did not drive automobiles, drink, smoke cigarettes or use cosmetics and hair products (even dyes to hide gray hair featured models in their late twenties).

But Pickford would soon help change all that. By the time she came to our attention in 1980, she had already made a few television commercials and done print ads for every product from DeBeers diamonds and Bufferin to Piper-Heidsieck champagne, though she was still earning under $10,000 a year. Then she was featured in *People* magazine, which led to small movie roles and any number of other modeling opportunities. She is no longer making $10,000. "She is an inspiration," raved Eileen Ford about the star model, proud of her white hair, crow's feet and 34–25–36 measurements. "She has a smashing figure and marvelous skin. She is positive proof that being past thirty, forty or fifty doesn't mean your life and body are finished."

Pickford is quick to point out that she owes her success and her current happiness to an inborn willingness to take a chance. "The greatest strength is the strength it takes to explore your fears." Was it worth the risk? Replies Pickford: "I risk—therefore I have."

Pickford has a kindred spirit in Julia Montgomery Walsh, who immediately after graduating from Kent State University in 1945 joined the Foreign Service in Munich, where she was assigned. She met and fell in love with army Lieutenant Colonel John Montgomery. They were married in 1948, and Julia quit her job to raise their four sons. Julia was thirty-four when their father was killed on maneuvers.

She had not held a job for nearly eleven years, but she did collect $20,000 from her husband's life insurance. Julia carefully analyzed the stock market and decided to invest the entire $20,000 in four companies—Texas Instruments, Hewlett-Packard, Aerojet General and Reynolds Metals. With a 20–20 hindsight, we can clearly see that each was a high technology pioneer and a blue chip investment; in the mid-fifties, however, all but Reynolds were considered highly speculative. Less than eighteen months after placing the order with her broker, Julia had quadrupled her original bankroll—more than enough to purchase a large home for her family in Washington, D.C.

Buoyed by her initial success at playing the market, Julia enrolled in Harvard Business School in 1962, where she met a guest instructor, George M. Ferris, Jr., who was so impressed with her that he invited her to join his Wall Street securities firm. At fifty, she was named vice-chairman of the firm, no mean feat in the male-dominated world of high finance. Meantime, she had married banker John G. Montgomery and added eight children (his seven by a previous marriage, plus one of their own) to her original brood of four.

Realizing that it would be years—if ever—before she would run Ferris and Company, Julia struck out on her own in her late fifties, launching her own investment firm with three of her sons. "It was a very big gamble," she concedes. "The market back then was soft. But it was then or never." And once again, by zeroing in on the right high technology companies, as well as gold, oil and communications stocks, she triumphed. By mid-1983, when she sold Julia Walsh and Sons to the Boston firm of Tucker, Anthony & R. L. Day, Inc., for an undisclosed sum, Julia, now a bona fide Success Over Sixty, held seats on both the New York and American Stock Exchanges. Her firm employed thirty-five brokers handling more than 4,000 accounts.

A crisis or series of crises like the ones experienced by Kaylan Pickford and Julia Walsh can propel us to achievements that, in calmer moments, we might have thought impossible. The Chinese symbol for crisis is, in fact, the same symbol as the one for opportunity. Seizing the moment to turn a setback into a gain is one of life's great challenges.

Of course, this does not mean that one should court disaster just for the thrill of plucking victory from the jaws of defeat. If we wait for a crisis to bring change in our lives, we put ourselves at the mercy of unnecessary pressures. Still, using Success Over Sixty principles, at any point in the game, we may emerge as champions of our own destiny.

"I had reached my level of incompetence," allows tax attorney Tom Thornton, borrowing a phrase from *The Peter Principle*. "I'd been made an associate partner in the firm, and instead of handling the specific types of shelters I'd become a specialist at—oil and gas exploration credits, income property, that sort of thing—overnight I was overseeing twenty-five Ivy League lawyers involved in every sort of Big League corporate case. I'd gone from being so expert at my limited area that it bored me, to being in way over my head."

Ruddy-faced, pipe-smoking Thornton looked remarkably like the silver-framed photograph of his father that dominates his Park Avenue office. Thomas Thornton, Sr., had been one of the nation's leading corporate attorneys in the late thirties and forties. Dad had been a mover-and-shaker who instilled in his only son the desire to excell in the world of law—specifically business law. He also left no doubt in Tom's mind that he thought winning was everything, not only in the courtroom and in the boardroom, but in the mahogany-paneled inner sanctum of the firm itself. Dad wanted his son to be nothing less than senior partner—*the* senior partner—at one of the leading firms. Now that he seemed within a few years of finally achieving that goal, Tom, at the age of fifty-six, wondered if that was, after all, what he really wanted out of life.

Tom will never forget the look on the faces of the twenty-five other partners in the firm as he announced that he had just delivered his letter of resignation to the founding partner. "There was an audible sigh," he recalls. "It wasn't that they were that sorry to see me go—after all, it opened up a spot on the ladder—but they were genuinely confused because I was shaking their confidence in the dream. I had it made, as far as they were concerned. They wanted to be in my shoes so bad they could taste it, and here I was, saying I didn't want to play anymore. For at least a few seconds, maybe a few of them wondered if they wanted to play this game, either."

Thornton reached his decision to leave the firm with the support of his wife of thirty years. "Joan always felt I was far too cautious," says Tom. "Now I was about to take the only real risk of my life." On the strength of the knowledge of income real estate he had acquired over the years, he started his own real estate investment firm, building subdivisions and condominium complexes in the Northeast. Tight money nearly dealt Tom, along with the entire housing industry, a death blow, but he hung in long enough to reap enormous profits with the turnaround of the early 1980s. Tom is now earning perhaps three times what he would have had he made senior partner.

Looking back, he sees it as a move he had to make. "They would have found me out eventually," says Thornton. "I knew in my heart I wasn't cut out for the top spot at that firm, or any other huge law firm for that matter. I just didn't want to wait until a crisis came along a few years down the road." By reassessing his dream and reshaping it accordingly, Tom succeeded in an area that was no less challenging than the one he started in and was even more lucrative. Though he did not wield the power that would have been his at the firm, he found personal satisfaction as captain of a smaller ship.

Should you take the leap, expect a period of uncertainty—like Kaylan Pickford's $10,000 income from modeling during her first year out, Julia Walsh's "big gamble" on a soft market, or Tom Thornton's near-bankruptcy as a result of the sagging economy. This goes hand-in-hand with the thoroughly human feelings of uncertainty that accompany leaving a structured job for a comparatively structureless existence. So hunker down and weather the storm; it is, we have learned from scores of career-changers, apt to last anywhere from a few months to a year or so. And remember, particularly if you are starting your own business, once it's underway *nobody* will be able to tell you when to retire.

Time and again in our research we encountered men and women for whom the continued willingness to take limited risks seemed almost an end in itself—a constant source of excitement, a way to stay alive, really alive. Wilton Jaffee started taking such risks early in his fifty-year career with H. Freeman, one of the country's largest clothing manufacturers. Recognizing the commercial possibilities for skiing in Aspen, Colorado, he put his career in the clothing business on hold after World War II and went to Aspen to map out ski runs for a future resort. He then returned to H. Freeman, but took another leave to run a ski school at Aspen; later, he purchased a ranch nearby while still in the employ of H. Freeman.

When it came time for him to retire as one of the company's top executives in the mid-1960s, Jaffee had enlisted the aid of his son Wilton Jr. in running the Colorado spread, which had by then grown to 375 acres. On a ski trip to Peru, Jaffee stumbled across "high-altitude" potatoes—potatoes grown at an altitude of 8,000 feet—which, because of the low moisture content, are firmer, crisper and bigger than the closer-to-sea-level variety. Jaffee began raising his own high-altitude crop in 1982, and the following year, Wilton's organic seed potatoes hit the market. Jaffee's newest venture: high-altitude garlic. Over the next decade, Jaffee plans to make substantial investments in what he is convinced will be a booming industry in high-altitude crops.

Not that his commitment to profit-making schemes has lured Jaffee from the slopes for long; at eighty-one he is a paid ski instructor at the Highlands resort in Aspen. And in 1983, he won the downhill slalom in the over-seventy class, competing against men ten years his junior. "My future looks great," Jaffee told us, "and when I stop risking, dreaming and learning, you'll know it—'cause I'll be dead."

Harold Koplar feels the same way. Having already established his own motel chain, Lodge of the Four Seasons, purchased his own television station, and engineered a major land development deal in the Ozarks, Koplar kicked off his sixty-fifth year by announcing the formation of a new commuter airline. "The trick," says Koplar, "is to plan meticulously, to research every angle before going ahead. Provided I've done the spadework, I'm never afraid to take a calculated risk."

But no matter how much homework we've done, most of us are still reluctant to do so as a result of a fear that stems from three primary sources: (1) Obligation. You tell yourself that your family, the corporation, the community all need you so much that there is no choice but for you to sacrifice your desires in order to preserve the status quo. (2) Fear of Failure. This is the most obvious hurdle, though it can take several forms. We may fear financial loss, but we may also fear the unknown, loss of love, loss of friends, loss of comfortable routine. (3) Fear of Success. This fear is a little more subtle, perhaps, but just as real. "What if I *do* make it? Will I change? Will the people around me change? Won't I lose the security of the life I've become so accustomed to? Won't I have to try even harder to *keep* what I've won?

Every single person we interviewed was gripped by one or all of these fears at one time or another. But none of them regretted taking a calculated risk, whether they succeeded or not. Now is the time to decide whether you should take the plunge. It takes real courage to start things rolling, but it is infinitely easier if you ask yourself a few basic questions and *answer them honestly!*

1. Is it time for a change?
2. Where do I want to be in five years? Ten?
3. Is it necessary for me to take a risk in order to reach my goals in life?
4. If I make a change in my life, what will I gain?
5. If I make a change in my life, what will I lose?
6. Does my experience qualify me to succeed in whatever I am planning?
7. Have I researched and carefully planned out what I am about to do?
8. What are my alternatives?
9. How does my risk-taking affect those closest to me?
10. Will I have more control over my life if I change?
11. Whom can I expect help from in making a change—Family? Friends? Business contacts?

12. Do I have the confidence in myself to accomplish my goals?

These are only very preliminary questions—teasers, if you will—to get you thinking seriously about your general feelings regarding change. You may want to come back to them periodically to see if your answers have remained the same. As we look at the various opportunities opening to older Americans, we shed many of our initial doubts.

William Hersey had made a lifetime practice of reassessing his status and, at the appropriate time, boldly moving on. Hersey was managing a Mobil gas station (the pay was $29 for a sixty hour week) when he married Fairlee Towsley in 1935. He became a service station supervisor the following year and went on to the Mobil personnel department three months later, but a reshuffling of Mobil's organization resulted in Hersey's first setback: demotion to statistical marketing clerk. Following a stint in the army during World War II, Hersey returned to Mobil, worked his way up to vice-president in charge of job evaluation and salary administration and then, on his fortieth birthday in 1950, resigned. He had been with Mobil eighteen years. "I could see no further opportunities," Hersey explains, "in the area of my principle interest: me."

From 1950 to 1953, he worked on the training staff of Eastern Gas and Fuel Associates, a Boston-based utility that owned coal mines, a railroad, stores and gas companies. Hersey's primary duties were to conduct seminars for new managers. It was during this period that he began investing in the stock market, and in 1954 Hersey joined the sales force of Investors Diversified Services. That same year he was about to give a talk on mutual funds to a small Rotary Club in Sharon, Massachusetts. The program chairman mentioned offhand that the previous speaker, a local politician, had memorized everyone's name and challenged Hersey to do the same. "Somehow," said Hersey, after being introduced to everyone, "I named every man and his business and got a standing ovation. I knew a good thing when I saw it and started to talk to a club a week to advertise my business."

Hersey was running out of places to deliver his investment spiel when, with $6,000, he launched "Hersey's Short Course for Short Memories." It was not an idea whose time had come. Within a year Hersey was thinking of quitting. But in 1961, after an editor had read a newspaper article about the course, Prentice-Hall approached Hersey and asked him to write a book. The book was published in 1963, on Hersey's fifty-third birthday, and has since sold 250,000 copies.

Hersey retired from Investors Diversified Services on his sixtieth birthday, after convincing the federal Civil Service Commission to use his memory course for its employees. Since then, he has taught the course to thousands of people around the world. At seventy, he taught himself Spanish to open up the Latin American market to his teaching methods. Among the clients of Hersey's National Memory Training Institute: IBM, Time, Inc., General Electric, Pepsico, Xerox, Century 21 Real Estate, Raytheon, Scovill Manufacturing, Boston University, Northeastern University, Cornell University, New York State University and the states of Kansas and Maryland. He has conducted over eight hundred seminars for the U.S. government. "When I was twenty-one," concedes Hersey, "I expected to live to be fifty. Now I plan to accomplish as much between seventy-one and eighty-five as I did between twenty-one and thirty-five. If I live to be one hundred, I want to die young."

Overcoming the ageist myths is a great stride in the right direction, but there often remains a nagging hesitation about the future that may have more to do with a lifelong reluctance to risk than the fact that you've reached a certain age. The concept of limited risk is essential if you are to make the adjustments in your life called for by Success Over Sixty. Such risk may involve orchestrating a smooth segue from one career to another, a continuation of a familiar line of work but for a different employer, an abrupt shift to a completely new field of endeavor or, in the case of hundreds of thousands of women, embarking on a fresh career outside the home now that the kids are grown.

Why indulge in risky business? "There's more here than just survival," says Yale University psychologist Daniel J. Levinson. "If you try for the change you may fail miserably. On the other hand, if you don't try for change, you'll be dead in a few years because you'll be stagnant." You can get nowhere without some investment, be it an investment of money, effort, pride or all three. You will act prudently, you will weigh all the alternatives and draw on your experience, but you *will* act. You may not always win in the short run, but you will only have gambled what you could afford to lose. And you will try again. Because you have cast aside the ageist myths and overcome your own resistance to risk-taking, you will eventually walk away a winner.

5 Stimulating the Creativity within You

You're never too old to become young.
—Mae West

"Me, creative? Oh, I've structured budgets, come up with some pretty clever marketing plans, and managed people effectively for years. But I know I don't have it in me to be creative." Most people, regardless of age, have convinced themselves they cannot come up with new ideas, fresh approaches to turn their lives around. Routine jobs certainly reinforce this feeling, but even those of us in the most challenging fields grow accustomed to acting on the instructions of others, to doing what we are told. And the longer we refrain from thinking creatively, the deeper the rut and the harder it gets to climb out.

According to Bud Grossman, founder of the Minnesota-based, $650 million-a-year Gelco Corporation, automation is making things worse. "The new office technology is a step backward," he asserts. "The worker gets bored as hell with what he is doing. It may have been hard work, but a person used to sit down and type a letter and identify with it. Now we put it into a damn machine, change a few words and produce 1,000 different letters. We have succeeded in dehumanizing him." Grossman has launched an aggressive program to tap the creativity of his managers. "Even if a guy risks and flops," says Grossman, "he learns a lot. He also gains a certain confidence from the company because it backs him up. We have to be damn sure that we don't make anybody so scared that he will be afraid to float a suggestion or try something. Ideas are really all we have.''

George Bernard Shaw wrote in *Back to Methuselah,* "You see things and you say 'Why?' but I dream things that never were, and I say 'Why not?' '' This eloquent statement applies to everyone—we all have the capacity to dream, and to create.

"It is commonly held that there is such a thing as 'the creative spark,' '' writes Douglas R. Hofstadter in *Scientific American,* "that when a brilliant mind comes up with a new idea or work of art there has been . . . a 'quantum' leap from ordinary mortals. People such as Mozart are held to be somehow divinely inspired, to have magical insights. But I contend that the 'creative spark' is not the exclusive property of a few rare individuals, but rather part of the everyday mental activity of everyone, even the most ordinary people.''

Only in the last few years have scientists attempted to find a rational explanation for the creative process. What they have discovered thus far is that the human mind follows the line of least resistance, and it is most likely to be creative when at rest. As Hofstadter puts it, "The bottom line is that invention is much more like falling off a log than like sawing one in two. Einstein didn't go around racking his brain, muttering to himself, 'How can I come up with a great idea?' As Mozart used to say, things should 'flow like oil.' And Mozart ought to know.''

A case in point is the nineteenth-century German chemist, Frederich Kekule, who had been struggling for endless hours to figure out the structure of the benzene molecule. Finally, in a state of complete exhaustion he sank into a chair and stared into the fire. It was then that a vision came to him of a snake biting its own tail, which made him realize that the core of the benzene molecule was a ring of carbon atoms. Kekule could not explain how this vision came to him, but he did concede that the revelation came, not when he was trying hard to find the answer, but after his mind had slid into a sort of reverie.

If there is any common denominator among the hundreds of Successes Over Sixty we have interviewed, it is a knack for innovative thinking, and few have displayed that knack more brilliantly than George Demestral. One day, after a long hike, Demestral, then in his sixties, pulled a number of burrs out of the coats of his hunting dogs and began absent-mindedly sticking them together and then pulling them apart. In this easy, daydreaming state, it occurred to him that if he could simulate these qualities in a fabric, they might make a cheap, effective fastener. He took his idea to Du Pont, where they put 100 loops per square inch on one piece of nylon and made a straight ridged line on another piece for the loops to fasten onto. The result was a thistlelike adhesive surface. Velcro, as it was christened, is now used in hundreds of products from purses and billfolds to coats, shirts and even shoes. Demestral, now in his eighties, collects millions of dollars in royalties for this idea alone.

Similarly, Bertha Jackman, a ninety-year-old great-grandmother, who has long taught volunteer classes in crocheting and sewing, turned a washrag into a puppet for small children. She dubbed it the "Scrub Puppy" and went on to make a small fortune marketing the clever item across the country through major department stores like Macy's and Marshall Field. Her newest venture—"floral" arrangements made from seashells that she sells through florists as "Poke-Up Plants."

The creative mind is often kindled by association, as in the case of Dr. Leonard Morehouse, professor of kinesiology at

UCLA. In his sixties, Morehouse invented the heart-rate controlled bicycle, wrote the best-selling book *Total Fitness,* and was selected by the National Research Council as senior scientist to help deal with metabolic problems of astronauts in space.

His successful collaborations date back to his student days at Springfield College in Massachusetts where Morehouse earned the nickname "Hammer" for assisting his physiology professor in a study for Stanley Tools, in which they worked at reshaping tool handles. During his postdoctoral studies in industrial physiology at the Harvard Fatigue Laboratory and the Harvard Graduate School of Business Administration, he studied the effect of shoe soles on foot function, which led to the invention with Nathan Hack of the ripple sole. Working with engineers at Douglas Aircraft, Morehouse began work on the first ejection seats to help pilots withstand the forces of gravity during space flights. He then designed tractor seats for John Deere, and at seventy designed an office chair solely by computer. He also invented a power-building hand-grip exercise, and was awarded a patent for invention of a system for regulating exercise according to heart rate.

Before interviewing Dr. Morehouse, Al Myers went to UCLA to go through the physical-fitness testing program Morehouse had developed there. While taking tests on about ten different machines, it occurred to Al that while we have long had fitness equipment (weights, bicycles, trampolines, rowing machines) in our homes and in gyms, no one had come up with an office machine to test such things as our pulse count, blood pressure, breath record, hand-grip strength, weight—a single testing device that would fit in an executive's desk drawer. As a result of this cross-pollination of ideas and expertise, Morehouse and Myers will build a "Fitest" machine for home and office consumption.

"If I am born again," said nature photographer Ansel Adams, another example of creative genius into one's eighties, "I want a Leica in my crib and my name to be Eisenstaedt." Alfred Eisenstaedt got his first assignment in 1929, photographing Thomas Mann receiving the Nobel Prize for literature. In the fifty-five years since then, Eisenstaedt has become a major force in the world of photography, famous not only for his portraits of the great (Winston Churchill, Harry Truman, G. B. Shaw, John F. Kennedy) and the glamorous (Marlene Dietrich, Marilyn Monroe, Sophia Loren), but also for capturing moments of great emotion such as his memorable photograph of a sailor kissing a nurse in Times Square on VE Day.

Celebrating his eighty-sixth birthday in 1984, Eisenstaedt keeps a schedule that would daunt a man half his age, publishing books, lecturing, crisscrossing the country and the world on assignment.

Eisenstaedt, who neither smokes nor drinks, has lived alone in a New York apartment since his wife Kathy died in 1971. He is always up at 5:15 A.M. ("I don't want to be rushed") and does thirty pushups before heading out to his first appointment by 9:00 A.M. at the latest. When he had his first major health problem in seventy years—a mild heart attack in 1981—Eisenstaedt was outraged. *"Imagine,"* he said, utterly mystified that this could happen to him, "I eat only the right foods, don't smoke and don't drink—and *I* get a heart attack!" Of course, he recovered quickly and completely, in plenty of time to attend a special showing of his work at the Smithsonian.

Eisenstaedt is the perfect example of an individual remaining creative because he remains curious, or even a bit naive.

It is that sense of wonder that propels us forward, at any age, toward new discoveries, new achievements. "I cannot see something," he says, "without asking myself, How? Why? And then I make it my business to find out." A precise definition of what makes a good photographer is another matter. At a Chicago exhibition of Eisenstaedt's work, the photographer overheard a visitor saying to his young son, "I'm going to buy you the same types of cameras and lenses and you'll take pictures just as good as this." Laughing, Eisenstaedt held up his hands. "I have two hands just like Rubinstein and Van Cliburn," he told the man, "but I can't play the piano. It's all," he said, tapping his head, "up here."

While Eisenstaedt continued doing what he has done so brilliantly for the past fifty-five years, Helen Santmyer waited all that time for her 1,300 page book, *And the Ladies of the Club,* to be published by a major New York house and to be chosen as the main selection of the Book of the Month Club for September 1984. Santmyer gained instant fame at the age of eighty-eight.

Anyone with imagination has the power to think creatively. Our Success Over Sixty creativity quiz will test what hidden talents for innovative thinking you may already possess—and will also help you spot your weaknesses:

TRUE OR FALSE:
1. I spend too much time daydreaming when I should be working.
2. Prime time television bores me. I only watch the news.
3. There is no substitute for hard work.
4. There is no such thing as a new idea.
5. I don't have time to read.
6. I never write a letter when I can pick up the phone.

7. No news is good news.
8. Nobody really wants to hear what I think.
9. Curiosity killed the cat.
10. If I haven't set the world on fire by forty, I never will.

If you answered "True" to any of the above, you are probably sabotaging your creative impulses. (1) Daydreaming? *Don't* apologize for letting your mind wander. That is when the fresh idea, the new angle is most likely to strike. (2) TV bores you? Renowned psychologist B. F. Skinner attributes much of his mental agility in his seventies to "relaxing" the brain with regular doses of prime time pap and even soaps. The mind cannot be working full steam without fatigue; you need to let your brain go blank sometimes. (3) Oh, yes, there is a substitute for hard work—inspiration, and as we have noted, that usually comes when we're not sweating it out. (4) So you think there is no such thing as a new idea. . . . What is significant here is the defeatist tone of the statement; you're less likely to open your mind to something new if you've convinced yourself that it is an impossibility. (5) Make time to read. (6) You may prefer the phone, but letter writing is an effective way of clarifying your thoughts and an opportunity to think creatively.

(7) The "no news is good news" philosophy implies a resistance to change, to new ideas. You're not about to be very creative if you want your world to remain as is. (8) "Nobody wants to hear what I think" is one of those self-defeating (and self-pitying) statements that undermine our will to succeed. We are often too afraid to look stupid, afraid to be wrong. But a bad idea is usually quickly forgotten; a good one can lift you far above the crowd. At any age, it's vitally important to risk a bad idea in the hopes of coming up with a good one. (9) Curiosity killed the cat? "What if . . ." are part and parcel of the creative person's working vocabulary. A lack of curios-

ity kills creativity! (10) The "if-you-haven't-set-the-world-on-fire-by-now-you-never-will" blues: another bit of defeatism that tamps down our creative fires—fires that burn as we keep them stoked.

Among the mentally alert and physically healthy, recent studies have shown that intelligence does not inevitably decline. "In some areas," says Dr. Harry R. Moody of New York's Brookdale Center, "as in tests measuring insight into problem situations, in creative understanding and metaphoric processing, older people show actual statistical *gains*." But the negative self-image can send an elderly person into a spiral of depression. "So much of the feeling of the depression," says Dr. Moody, "can be traced to the feeling of 'I can't grow' or 'I can't be creative.' "

Seventy-four-year-old Elizabeth Layton lives in the same Kansas farm town where she was born and where her father was publisher of the weekly newspaper. At the age of sixty-eight, following the death of her son, Elizabeth enrolled in an art class. Her first drawings were angry outpourings over the loss of a loved one and against a male-dominated, youth-obsessed culture. But soon Elizabeth Layton's drawings of herself and the world around her became less downhearted, reflecting her love for her family and a sense of humor about herself.

Elizabeth feels it would be immodest of her to display her work on the walls of the home she shares with her husband, Glenn. Nor will she sell her drawings. But she is admired as an artist nonetheless. In 1980, she was awarded first prize from among 600 entries in a juried exhibition at the Nelson Gallery of Art in Kansas City, and that same year she was named one of three "Governor's artists." By 1983, her work was included in one exhibition sponsored by the National Endowment for the Arts, and another at New York's trendy Soho 20 Gallery. "I am tempted to call Layton a genius," proclaimed Kay Larson, *New York* magazine's art critic. "These simple self-portraits are distinguished by a complex, sophisticated wit." The *Washington Times'* Jane Addams Allen concurred, "She is the Van Gogh of contour drawings. . . . With her colored pencils she shows us her inner world; her patient lines quiver with emotion."

The object of all this idolatry will have none of it. "I'll tell you," laughs Elizabeth Layton, "everybody is a genius. What I can do, everybody can do."

Not that everybody can expect to be another Grandma Moses. If you couldn't paint at twenty, you're just as likely not to be able to paint at sixty-five. But, argues Dr. Rose Dobroff, executive director of the Brookdale Center on Ageing at New York's Hunter College, "Creativity can mean having the opportunity to attend to parts of ourselves that we never had the time or the energy or the chance to develop earlier in life. There is the opportunity to be honest in a way we've never been able to be before. There is a deep and different sense about human beings and situations, one that just isn't possible when one is younger."

Psychiatrist Robert N. Butler has discovered that older people begin to undergo a spontaneous resurgence of early memories—something he calls the "life-review process." The generation of these memories, dismissed for years as senile flights into the past, is actually "a natural, healthy way of coming to terms with ourselves," explains the Brookdale Center's Dr. Moody. "It's a life-affirming process that can integrate one's experience, a process that can be used for learning, for creation."

Marc Kaminsky started the Arts for Elders project of New York City's Teachers and Writers Collaborative in 1979. "The life-review process is the cutting edge where gerontology and the humanities meet," says Kaminsky. Older people's reminiscences can be shaped into journals, poetry, novels and plays. They can create works of power that have personal meaning for them and great resonance in society. Six books, dozens of plays, works of poetry, sculpture and painting have come out of the Arts and Elders project. At eighty-one, after surviving the Russian Revolution, two world wars and a career in the fur business, Norman Hofferman discovered the pleasures of writing through his involvement with the project. "I see the beauty in things," he muses. "I stand back and speak the truth the way I see it. My instincts are very strong. I feel more creative than ever before."

Why don't you sit down with a blank piece of paper and analyze what your experiences have taught you and how you can use those experiences to create a rewarding life after sixty. Start with interests and talents you might have begun developing as far back as childhood—ambitions you may have abandoned decades ago. One retired oil company executive, a one-time collegiate swimmer who gave up the sport to join Mobil, finally came close to realizing his lifelong dream in his midsixties by setting up a series of swimming and lifeguard clinics. A similar case is the California insurance salesman who never had the time to pursue his passion for woodworking as a youth. So at sixty-two, he opened his own antique refinishing shop in San Francisco.

FOILING THE BANDITS: MAKE THE TIME TO BE CREATIVE

One eighty-year-old Swiss gentleman who decided to take inventory of his life, calculated that he had spent twenty-six years in bed, six years eating, twenty-one years working, six years being angry, five years waiting, two hundred and twenty-eight days shaving, showering and brushing his teeth, twenty-six days scolding his children, eighteen days tying his necktie and shoelaces, eighteen days blowing his nose, eighteen days lighting his pipe, and only forty-six hours laughing. He recorded not a single second for thinking. And though it might sound like hyperbole, we're all in danger of being consumed by the kind of mindless routine that this man's inventory suggests. If you are not fully employed, or engaged in part-time work, then like the rest of us you will probably fill up those "free" hours with household chores, errands and the like. But don't be afraid to take the time to daydream.

Time, of course, is not enough. What is required for creativity at any age is an open mind, an appreciation of those around you and of your environment. We were flying across the country not long ago with a plump, affable salesman in his late fifties. Right after takeoff, he ordered a double martini and announced to us that he was fortifying himself for the boring six-hour flight. After another martini, he rang for a pillow and blanket. Our route took us over some of the most spectacular scenery in the world, including the Rockies and the Grand Canyon. The earphones offered excellent music for every conceivable taste, the movie was *Tootsie,* and our fellow passengers were charming. The salesman had six hours to watch the film (which he told us he had not seen), read, write, listen to music, whatever. Instead, he got bombed and fell asleep.

Even the involved, energetic and industrious individual may be cheating himself out of "creative time." Not long ago, certainly not much earlier than the early seventies, someone coined the term "workaholic" to describe those of us who consider ourselves driven. Since then, the word has been much overused—probably because we all love to see ourselves as diligent and selfless. Science writer K. C. Cole insists that she does not consider herself a workaholic: "I recently read a book about workaholics and laughed at their poor, misguided life-styles until I realized I was laughing at myself. True, I do not spend eighteen hours a day at an office, but without fail I am at my typewriter from 10:00 A.M. to 6:00 P.M. Any interruption of my schedule is an unwarranted 'waste of time.' " For Cole, not even weekends are exempt: "My husband and I often measure weekends well spent by museums visited and errands accomplished." Once she was aware of how packed her schedule was, Cole started making the effort to free up more time for reading, and "just plain relaxing."

Nobody wants to see life slip by in wasted moments, but when it comes to making every minute count in terms of work, there are limits. At one hotel in Washington, the operator placing wakeup calls to guests greets them with "Have a successful day." There are exercise classes in New York where women bend and stretch while watching the news, and more than one executive we know has a television in his bathroom so that he won't miss anything while showering and shaving. There are even those who feel strongly that sleep is a waste of time.

But what we are so quick to call "wasted" time is often the most fruitful of all. How often has the proverbial lightbulb flashed on while you were taking a drive? How many times have you been tempted to shout "Eureka" because a solution to a problem suddenly dawned on you in the shower or the tub? Time spent in transit—driving or riding to and from work, heading for the store—these are moments when you might regroup mentally, collect your thoughts.

For whatever reasons, it is particularly difficult for women to come to grips with the fact that one doesn't always have to be on the move to be productive. "Women especially seem to have a hard time accepting the legitimacy of time spent doing anything that doesn't directly relate to a paycheck or a clean child or a cooked meal," observes K. C. Cole. She is right; her husband may come home exhausted from the office, plop in his favorite chair and unwind with a beer. But a woman—whether she is a homemaker or has a job of her own outside the home to go to—tends to regard moments spent on herself as "wasted." If you are female and over fifty, you've most likely been cheating yourself in this manner for most of your adult life. Now is the time to stop. Be sure to allow sufficient time for yourself to do absolutely nothing—or at least as close to nothing as is humanly possible, such as watching those sitcoms. You will discover what the scientists and artists already know: the idle brain is fertile ground.

ZEN AND THE MBA

Can creativity be taught? "All people have the same amount of creativity at birth," says Stanford business professor, Michael L. Ray, "but they have different capacities to tap that creativity." Toward that end, May and Rochelle Myers, a San Francisco painter and a violinist, began teaching second-year students at the Stanford Graduate School of Business how to "unlock" their potential.

The Stanford "Creativity in Business" course is, well, very California. In a darkened classroom, for example, twenty-five students sit on the floor in a semicircle, backs straight, legs crossed, chanting in unison as soothing Hindu music plays in the background. Or they sit on the floor and draw circles on paper, then create designs inside the circles using brightly colored pens. These drawings, called "mandalas," are a 3,000-year-old Indian art form meant to relax and free the mind by breaking down inhibitions. Freewheeling corporate "retreats" or bull sessions are designed with the same pur-

pose in mind. At the Hewlett-Packard Corporation, for example, executives meet annually at a seaside resort to
consider company problems and participate in no holds-
barred discussions in small groups. "When you take people
with business skills and teach them to be creative, you enable
them to deal with new types of business problems," explains
David L. Bradford, a professor of organizational behavior at
Stanford. "Creative business people tend to look at business
problems more broadly. They have a different mind-set."

To be all we can be in our fifties and after, it is crucial to
adopt that "mind-set." Everybody's brain is capable, as Dr.
Ray points out, of generating new ideas. But, like a computer,
it's got to be turned on first. Here are a few practical suggestions for slipping on the switch.

1. *Think Positively!* There is nothing that will cramp your
life more than a negative attitude ("It's too late," or "Life
has passed me by"). Think of it—a person of sixty in good
health will probably live at least twenty more years—25 percent of his life is still ahead. The fantastic maturity and experience each of us has had by the time we are sixty qualifies us
to succeed in a number of areas. A positive person looks
forward to the future. He or she imagines, improvises, plans,
dreams and follows through and is a happier, *more capable*
person for doing so.

2. *Brainstorm.* Take the brakes off your mind. One way to
start: fill out our *Creative Living Chart* (p. 123). Under each
category, write down something specific to improve your life,
your family, your work situation (if you are still engaged in
your first career or already into a second), your inventory of
skills and your community. This can be even more successful
if you get together with several people whom you respect and
trade ideas. Have each one write down his or her ideas on a

CREATIVE LIVING CHART

Ideas to Improve My Life	Ideas to Help My Family	Ideas to Improve My Career (first or second)	Ideas to Learn New Skills	Ideas to Contribute to My Community
1. Improvise a time management plan	1. Plan a new experience together	1. Suggest an idea that your life experience has taught you to make your job more interesting (more travel, for example, or customer contact)	1. Go to the library and research a subject that interests you, but that you know little about	1. Volunteer for community service
2. Consult a doctor to plan your best exercise program	2. Plan a family reunion	2. Spend an evening with the person you most respect in your field discussing ideas for improving your division of your company	2. Enroll in an adult education course	2. Contribute to a religious program
3.	3.	3.	3.	3. Join a civic club
4.	4.	4.	4.	4.
5.	5.	5.	5.	5.
6.	6.	6.	6.	6.
7.	7.	7.	7.	7.
8.	8.	8.	8.	8.
9.	9.	9.	9.	9.

subject that is of common interest. You will be amazed at the number of really good ideas that come from the session. Remember! Einstein, Fuller, Newton, Churchill, Monet, the Wright Brothers—all utilized other people's concepts and ideas to help them create.

3. *Dream.* The most effective way of giving birth to an idea. Some of our most creative moments occur during the middle of the night, so keep a pad by the side of the bed to record your thoughts. Take the time to daydream and see how much leaps from your subconscious to your conscious mind.

4. *Prospect for Ideas.* To search for a better way is part and parcel of progress. Within each individual mind is the mechanism to create ideas but it takes a little background, a little research. Head for the library and look up everything there is to know on the subject. Ask the experts. If at all possible, go into the field for a firsthand look.

5. *Get to Know Creative People.* They can take your life in new directions. It may be a full-blown collaboration, a team effort or just some friendly advice. No one has a corner on this particular market.

6. *Don't Be Overwhelmed.* Nobody we talked with came close to inventing the wheel. They were ordinary people who started with a small idea, usually at home, or while waiting for a bus or walking in the countryside. Witness Chicago baker Charles Lubin's better coffeecake—Sara Lee; or Burt Baskin, who started making Baskin-Robbins ice cream in his Westwood, California, kitchen. Spectacular ideas often have humble beginnings.

7. ***Follow Through.*** Putting an idea to work makes all the difference. It is one thing to incubate and germinate an idea, but another to have the courage and determination to see it through to reality. If we don't fully intend to act on our ideas, then we might just as well nod off with a bellyful of martinis as the world glides by.

6 Making the Most of What You Already Know: Matching Experience with a New Career

Experience is not what happens to a man. It is what a man does with what happens to him.

—Aldous Huxley

Having faced down the myths and our own anxieties, we now see ourselves as we really are—not the reflection in the fun-house mirror society has held up to us. We are ready to carefully map out our new lives after sixty, whether that time is years away or has already arrived. For most, the solution will probably lie in an adroit spinoff from the business we are in to one that will make maximum use of the talents and skills we have cultivated in the past.

But wait. Perhaps you are not sure if you want a second career; maybe you should stick it out for a few more years in the job you now have. Ask yourself if the job you're in is unsatisfying, a bore? If there is any chance for a promotion or a satisfactory lateral move within the company in the near future? If you are given enough responsibility? Enough independence? Enough *money?*

There are a number of factors that may militate against your making the switch. Your present employer may offer a superior life insurance and health plan (free membership in a cardiovascular fitness center *and* a comprehensive dental plan), a big expense account, eligibility for stock options, generous vacation time, bonuses, an impressive title. But very often, particularly for a senior employee, such fringe benefits are "golden handcuffs" that bind you to a job which at bottom you no longer find rewarding.

If you're still not sure whether you want to switch careers or stay where you are, think back to the Five Cs. Are you *c*hanging, growing in your current job? Is your natural *c*uriosity being tested, challenged? Are you growing in terms of self-*c*onfidence? Are you encouraged to *c*ommunicate your opinions, ideas and feelings to coworkers and superiors alike? Are you as *c*ommitted to your work as you were, say, five years ago? If the answer to one or more of these questions is "no," the Five Cs are pointing you in the direction of a major career move.

If the notion that you can't learn as much or more elsewhere is preventing you from action, consider this: a survey conducted by an executive search firm discovered that in 1981 executives making $30,000 to $45,000 received annual pay increases averaging 16 percent when they moved. Those earning $46,000 to $60,000 received 18 percent more, and those making $61,000 to $85,000 got a 21 percent boost. Meanwhile, executives earning $86,000 to $110,000 got 26 percent raises, and over $110,000, the average was a whopping 33 percent salary increase. So switching can be—and usually is— profitable. And in the majority of cases, executives also traded up in terms of profit sharing, insurance plans and other benefits.

Let's say, after weighing all of the above, you come to the conclusion that, for now at least, you just want to stay put. Should that be the case, let's take a look at the best plan for hanging in there in your present position.

First, it's important to realize that the law is usually on your side. According to federal law, employers of twenty or more workers cannot fire or refuse to hire individuals age forty to sixty-five simply because of their age, unless the job—say, modeling dresses for juniors—requires someone in a specific age range. Companies are also prohibited by landmark federal legislation of the late 1970s from favoring younger workers in pay, fringe benefits or promotions. And the same rules that apply to business apply to unions. If at sixty-six you meet all of the requirements, physical and otherwise, for being a stevedore, you cannot be barred from joining the appropriate union just because of your age. Help wanted ads cannot state age preferences anymore than they can say "Boy Wanted" or "Girl Wanted," and employment agencies are forbidden by law to refer a job applicant to an opening because of his or her age.

Specifically, no piece of legislation is more important to you than the 1978 Age Discrimination Act. This law, rigorously enforced by the Labor Department's Wage and Hour Division in Washington, D.C. (the zip is 20210 should you need to write or file a complaint), raises the legal mandatory retirement age for most people in the United States from Bismarck's old sixty-five-year benchmark to the equally arbitrary but more realistic age of seventy. Policy-making executives and tenured college professors are the only people still subject to the sixty-five-and-out rule, though what precisely defines a "policy-making" situation is still being thrashed out in the courts.

Two major concerns were voiced prior to the passage of the legislation. The first was that employees nearing retirement tend to slough off, biding their time until they can collect their pension. The second was that younger workers "kept down" because their superiors refuse to be put out to pasture might be tempted to move on to other firms with greater opportunity for advancement.

Hogwash! As we pointed out earlier, older workers have

repeatedly shown themselves to be *more* reliable than younger ones in studies done in both the public and private sectors. A study conducted by the publishing house, Prentice-Hall, concluded that "for many companies, keeping workers on the job until age 70 would pose very few problems." Another finding is that while the mandatory age for retirement is rising, the number of employees opting for early retirement is also rising. So, in fact, more rungs on the corporate ladder are opening up to young employees because the men and women who occupied them choose to hop off.

"No matter what your views on an individual," says financial columnist and author Sylvia Porter, "traditional discrimination on the basis of age alone is finally being eliminated from the law. Our society's attitude toward over-60s has been and is far more barbaric than the barbarians ever dreamed of. I hail the step, although it is only one minor move forward. It has been so long in coming."

STARTING OVER

But maybe instead of toughing it out, you want to try something different. Certain careers ease naturally into postretirement occupations—military careerists move into the arms industry as contract administrators and technical advisors, journalists write books, ballet stars and opera singers teach, athletes coach. But the joys of dramatically shifting gears, applying our talents and experience in altogether new and unfamiliar ways can be extremely rewarding and are by no means confined to the few.

Carl G. Sontheimer grew up in Paris and earned degrees in physics and engineering from M.I.T. before going to work for R.C.A. in the 1930s. In 1946, he set up his own consulting firm, and after it went public in 1958, he left to start up another firm that designed and manufactured microwave components. He sold the second company and retired in 1969 at age fifty-five "to a life of leisure and fun," he joked. One year later, however, Sontheimer was "ready to climb walls, but I didn't know how."

Sontheimer's thoughts turned to his childhood, which he had spent whipping up soufflés and pastries in France. "I knew French and had technical skills enough to evaluate appliances," he recalls. So he boarded the first available flight to Paris in search of "something to import." He came across a line of stainless steel cookware but, more important, a machine used to prepare food in the better restaurants. The manufacturer of the machine wanted to sell one model for home use, and in 1971 Sontheimer brought three of the curious-looking devices back home to Connecticut. Two years later, that number jumped to 1,000 and by 1974 Sontheimer, by then sixty-one, was importing and selling 10,000 of the machines in the U.S. Today, Sontheimer sells more than a quarter million of his Cuisinart food processors a year. "There's a great similarity to my other career," he observes. "I'm responsible for recipe development as I once was for engineering development."

John Burke joined the Brooklyn Fire Department in 1957 after a stint in the army and two clerical jobs. Over the next twenty-two years, he rose to the rank of lieutenant before retiring in 1979 to become a nurse at St. Vincent's Hospital in New York.

The shift was not quite as dramatic as it sounds; Burke had been preparing for his new profession even while he was in residence at his Brooklyn firehouse. "There was a nurses' training program at Hunter College," says Burke. "It gave men who were thinking of retiring the chance to get into nursing, and it was also meant to help give male nurses a better image." The two jobs meshed nicely. "There was a lot of emergency first aid,'' explains Burke. ''Also, it was the idea of saving a life.''

For more than a half-century, Stanley Marcus ran Neiman-Marcus, the Dallas-based department store chain that has become synonymous with high style and quality. In 1975, when the merchant prince of Dallas was seventy, he turned over the keys of his retail kingdom to son Richard. Hardly ready to rest on his laurels, Marcus set up his own marketing firm—an enterprise that soon kept him trotting around the globe four months a year on behalf of his clients. Marcus also started his own minipublishing house—*really* mini. His Somesuch Books prints Lilliputian volumes (one-half inch to under three inches high) of fiction for collectors of miniatures. And while adding to his private museum of pre-Columbian, African, Oriental and modern art, Marcus has enjoyed considerable success publishing books of a different sort—namely, his autobiographical *Minding the Store* and *Quest for the Best*.

''A little bingo, dinner with friends and lots of doing nothing'' is the way Ruth Bennett described her existence at age seventy-eight. That was before she unintentionally stole the show at a roast honoring her son Alex, a disc jockey on San Francisco's hard-rock station, KMEL, 106.1 FM. The next day, a station executive asked her if she would be interested in hosting her own rock 'n' roll show. At first she laughed the offer off, but a few days later she changed her mind. Since then Ruth, the widow of a violinist, has delighted her radio fans every Sunday night by spinning hit singles from The Police, Culture Club, Men at Work, and other top groups of the eighties. She also does the occasional interview; rock stars' mothers are favorite subjects. Is this any way for an octogenarian to act? ''When I was young we did the jitterbug and the Charleston,'' she shrugs, ''and our music was loud, too.''

California native Marion Cunningham did not read her first cookbook until she married lawyer Robert Cunningham, in 1942. "I had continual failures," she says of those first forays in the kitchen. "I could never get things to come out on time. If it didn't work I was very determined and I would continue to do it. But I had a few good dishes and people would encourage me."

Still, she never took a cooking lesson until she was forty-five, when on a lark she flew to Oregon to enroll in a class conducted by James Beard. They became fast friends, and when the publisher Alfred A. Knopf was looking for someone to update Knopf's *Fannie Farmer Cookbook,* Beard recommended Cunningham. At fifty-seven, after spending her entire adult life as a housewife and mother, Marion Cunningham achieved "overnight" celebrity as a cookbook author.

After retiring as an air force colonel in 1968, Robert Donahue went into the mortgage banking business and over the next decade expanded his firm's service portfolio from $11 million to $275 million. At the age of sixty, he combined what he learned in the air force with the financial management and administrative skills he honed as a top executive of a major mortgage banking concern to become director of the Division of Aeronautics for the state of Illinois.

William B. Macomber joined the government in 1951, serving first with the CIA and then with the State Department. John F. Kennedy appointed Macomber U.S. ambassador to Jordan in 1961, and after three years he returned to Washington. In 1973, he was named ambassador to Turkey by Richard Nixon, a post he held until Jimmy Carter took office in 1977. When Carter did not reappoint him to the post, Macomber suddenly found himself unemployed. He was fifty-six. "I knew I wanted a continued form of public service, but in the private sector," says Macomber.

Now Macomber heads the Metropolitan Museum of Art in New York City. He has been surprised to learn that he has been able to draw on administrative skills he honed as a career diplomat. "When I was in the State Department I tried to modernize the administration," he recalls. "Here, I'm worrying about personnel, budgets, public relations. The work isn't that different, but the setting is so different."

In 1986, Macomber reaches the Met's mandatory retirement age of sixty-five, but he is already contemplating his next career switch. "I learned from my idyll that I'll never retire," he admits. "At my age, most people have their heads down. But to go into something entirely different is so refreshing and invigorating. I feel like a whole new dimension of life has come to me."

Marvin and Claire Brigham have made much the same discovery in Placerville, a California hamlet nestled in the Sierra Nevada foothills that was known as Hangtown during the gold rush days. After Marvin "retired" as public works director for Marin County in 1962, he and Claire spent two years abroad. He worked as a consultant on various civil engineering projects, while she taught English to American high school students overseas. But in 1964 they spotted a newspaper ad that changed their lives. The ad merely read "Apples! Apples! Apples!" Still, it was enough to get the Brighams to hop into their car and drive up to the thirty-acre farm that was for sale near Placerville. A small house on a knoll overlooked the twelve-acre orchard of red and Golden Delicious apples, and Angora sheep grazed nearby.

Marvin Brigham decided to cash in his retirement account to pay the $44,000 asking price for the farm. Right after closing the deal, he took a short-term assignment which involved developing port facilities near Saigon. Meanwhile, Claire stayed on the farm and set out to learn how to run it. Six months later, Marvin was in Addis Ababa on another assignment. His wife turned the spread over to a sharecropping family and joined him. Soon she was teaching English to Ethiopians. When the sharecroppers left a year later, the Brighams turned their apple orchard over to a local grower who agreed to pay a fixed rate per box for their apples.

In 1974, the peripatetic Brighams returned to the farm, this time for good. Although they maintained their business arrangement with the grower, they took charge of the orchards which, in their absence, had only been turning a profit of $3,000 per year. They bought a tractor, enlarged the house and improved the irrigation system. Over the next seven years, the Brighams' apple production jumped more than tenfold—from 25 to 300 tons a year—making them one of the top ten growers in the region.

The farm is tough work—pruning, thinning, spraying and picking are all tremendously difficult jobs; and the return on capital is under 5 percent. "But it's the life-style we wanted," explains Marvin. "It's something we can do to keep busy and productive." Claire is more to the point: "If you just sit still and let life go by, you die."

CBS founder William S. Paley hasn't sat still since stepping down in 1982 at age eighty-one as chairman of the $4 billion communications empire that he had built over a half-century.

Even before he stepped down (Paley remains a CBS director, chairman of the executive committee and a consultant to the company), the broadcasting titan was determined to devote himself to a new position as partner in the Whitcom Investment Company. Paley's particular interest: the Paris-based *International Herald Tribune,* one-third owned by Whitcom.

Paley isn't the only illustrious CBS alumnus forging a new postretirement for himself in the 1980s. When in 1981 he retired at sixty-five as CBS anchor, Walter Cronkite was indisputably the most influential man in television news, pulling in a $1 million-plus annual salary from the network. But Cronkite soon grew restless because he wasn't, as one of his colleagues told us, "getting enough to do." Of course, by anyone else's standards, Cronkite wasn't exactly idle. His science series, *Walter Cronkite's Universe,* ran for three summers, and he also anchored a number of specials.

"On one hand, I want to do so many things," Cronkite says. "On the other hand, I want to play more tennis and do more sailing. Now I understand why people don't want to leave Sing Sing. It's easy to exist in a cocoon." But Cronkite intends to keep fighting for air time, to make good the promise he made to viewers during his farewell appearance on the CBS "Evening News": "Old anchormen don't fade away. They just keep coming back for more."

Stuart Mace keeps coming back for more—but never more of the same. At sixty-four, he has smoothly shifted professional gears more than a dozen times. During World War II, Mace taught mountain climbing to soldiers and trained sled dogs for Allied ski troops. After the war, with very little money, Mace built a small guest lodge and restaurant in Aspen, Colorado, and his World War II experience came in handy. This time Mace raised Alaskan sled dogs to take his guests on cross-country excursions.

Along with his wife, Isabel, Mace developed a mail order business to market their homemade jellies and jams nationwide; they also built an arts and crafts gallery adjacent to their lodge. The success of the lodge's restaurant led the Maces to build another, even larger restaurant in Aspen. As if this weren't enough, Mace took out a real estate license. By 1983 when he was in his mid-sixties, most of Mace's energies were spent on behalf of Aspen's Malachite Small Farm School. But in his spare time, Mace produced with Bill Moyers a TV documentary called *Living Free in the Rockies*. Moyers couldn't have found a more knowledgeable collaborator on that particular subject than Stuart Mace.

Perhaps the most striking example of someone taking his on-the-job experience in new directions is Ronald Reagan. Reagan saw an outlet for the powers of persuasion he developed as an actor, union leader and General Electric spokesman when at fifty-six he made his first bid for elective office, running successfully for governor of California in 1966. And, well, everyone knows the rest.

CASHIERED OUT? CASH IN!

The military, like many of our large corporations, rushes its careerists into early retirement. And we mean *early*. Many officers retire after twenty years of service, and that can make them all of forty. The skills and talents they developed in the armed forces also qualify them for important civilian positions, but it gives them the upper hand if military personnel research their alternatives *prior* to leaving the service.

Ed Hopkins, a seventy-year-old ex-brigadier general, has been equally successful as the chief operating officer of a global corporation. He graduated from college in 1932 and worked for the General Motors Acceptance Corporation until the outbreak of World War II, when he enlisted in the air force. He spent the next twenty-five years in the service and retired as a brigadier general and comptroller of the Strategic Air Command.

He left SAC and went to work for the International Executive Service Corps, a worldwide placement service for older executives, as vice-president in charge of finance. In 1982, Hopkins left the I.E.S.C. and currently is interested in the improvement of communications systems in underdeveloped countries. He is also developing a program to train citizens of South American countries in practical nursing skills, particularly where there are no medical facilities. Ed Hopkins achieved Success Over Sixty because he managed to apply abilities refined in the military to his life as a civilian.

Hudson Reid, a captain in the navy, retired at the age of fifty. He then went back to college at George Washington University to get an MBA degree. In the navy, Reid was an airplane accident investigator and a flight teacher, so UCLA hired him to teach a course in "Failure Mode Analysis." But when the school got a closer look at his record, they appointed him associate professor of aviation.

After five years at UCLA, Reid had a brush with cancer and he was forced to shift gears. When his health crisis hit him, he decided to leave the pressures of the academic world and to undertake a third career using the skills he had acquired in the navy. He went to Pensacola, Florida, and opened "Uncle Andy's Locomotive Works, Inc.," a first-class machine shop. He also started a cabinet-making shop in his home. Now he fixes and maintains items for all the neighborhood on a volunteer basis. He is also an excellent photographer, an ardent cyclist, a sailor and an amateur astronomer. In addition, he teaches basic surface navigation and celestial navigation at the U.S. Naval Yacht Club. As Reid's case proves, the training provided by the military is not only applicable to civilian life, it is often varied and extensive enough to see one through several careers.

SKILLS OVER SIXTY:
FIND OUT WHAT YOU'RE GOOD AT

"My husband is fifty and earns $44,000 as an assistant circulation director for a magazine. He has been with the company twelve years, so when we bought a larger house in Westchester three years ago we felt that, although the monthly mortgage payments and taxes were high, our income would always be growing to meet the demand. Our son is a sophomore in college, and we have two girls in high school. When my husband got his $2,000 bonus last year, it went for a down payment on a new Pontiac Firebird he'd been eyeing.

"This week Dick came home with the news that because circulation had been slipping, his boss was fired and everyone else in that department was told there would not only be no bonus this year, but that salaries and expenses were frozen. Dick thinks the axe could fall anytime. What should we do?"

Answer: Get to know yourself, your goals and aspirations better.

Of course, the threat of losing one's job always comes as a blow, particularly if it comes at a time when your obligations are great, or when you are at last feeling secure enough to spend freely (if not beyond your means).

And you probably haven't pounded the pavement in search of a job in years.

So perhaps you're in a crisis situation, but like any crisis, you can probably turn it to your advantage. Take what may be a once-in-a-lifetime opportunity to see if you've been doing what you really want to do with your life. And perhaps for the first time in a very long time, think *hard* about yourself. As diplomat-turned-museum director William Macomber pointed out, a second career can be energizing, exciting, ultimately more rewarding than your first—if you let it.

At this point, it would be very useful for you to sit down and make a list of the ten things that were most important to you when you were twenty-five. Then make another list— this time of the ten things you considered most important ten years ago.

Finally, compare the two lists, taking the best to make the most important list of all, a list of the things that are most important to you right now.

Now it's time to take stock of what we are equipped to do at this very moment. In order to do this, write a profile of yourself, a synopsis of your life and career—your qualifications, achievements, goals. Are you satisfied with what you have become? If so, how can you keep doing what you're doing? If not, how can you change your career and life direction?

To really know yourself, you must come to grips with why you no longer have the job you had, assuming the change was not voluntary. If you were a middle- or upper-middle-management executive, you may have lost your job because your company merged with another, which meant heads had to roll. In most cases, however, you were probably just retired by your company. Either way, a fast and thorough inventory of your skills is in order.

Take five pieces of paper and on each describe an achievement of which you are proud. If, for example, you are a manager who saved his company a bundle by shrewd belt-tightening measures in his department, then put that down, detailing in a few sentences what knowledge and skill that entailed. Or if you are a salesman who broke certain sales records, write down what it took to do that.

Now record those achievements on our version of Richard N. Bolles' "Fabulous Five" Transferable Skills chart (see pp. 142–47). Then go down the list and color in those skills which apply to each particular achievement. The purpose of this coloring? To see just how much our chosen career involves. So often we think of ourselves in terms of all-too narrow definitions. A telephone operator, for instance, may not realize that his work involves more than fifty skills until he is forced to sit down and check them off. Ultimately, you will use this inventory of skills to determine just which jobs leading to Success Over Sixty you are qualified for. However, it still remains for you to decide, with the help of the following chapters, exactly what it is you *want* to do.

ZEROING IN

The next step is to zero in on the kind of people you want to work with. John L. Holland provides a tool for accomplishing this in his superb *Making Vocational Choices: A Theory of Careers*. Richard Bolles suggests a "Party Exercise" based on Holland's work, which you will find on pages 148–49 here. This exercise gives you an aerial view of a room where someone is throwing a party. Naturally, people with like interests have all migrated to the same corner of the room. You arrive . . .

The Party Exercise will also help you define whether or not you are a leader, follower or an independent. Though by no means foolproof, this gauge of your career type tends to cast people who fall into the "E," "S" and "I" categories as leaders, while "R's" and "C's" tend to be followers. "A's" can swing either way. Again, there's plenty of margin for error here. All of us tend to see ourselves as leaders, but with some real soul-searching you can honestly determine whether you really like making waves, or whether you would rather not even rock the boat.

Another important question is where, geographically speaking, do you want to pursue your second career? Consider such variables as climate, terrain and recreational opportunities in making your decision. The perfect job is anything but perfect if you don't like where it takes you.

Maybe the best, most direct and least complicated way of deciding what it is you really want to do—particularly if you are one of those over-fifties of the opinion that you've already "done it all"—is to sit back and imagine what *working situation* you most want to be in. If, for example, this conjures up images of yourself in the great outdoors, the Bureau of Labor Statistics (you can write the bureau in Washington for even more extensive lists) offers the following partial list of occupations that may be just right for you:

athletic coaches
automobile service occupations: auto, bus, truck, mechanics; gas station attendants, others
beekeepers
boat-ride operators

(Continued on page 150)

List Your "Fabulous Five" Transferable Skills Here

YOUR "FABULOUS FIVE" TRANSFERABLE SKILLS

Example: The Budget-Cutting Feat

func·tion (fungk'shən) *n.* one of a group of related actions, contributing to a larger action. *(Webster's)*

1	2	3	4	5	*Name of Skill*	*Example of a situation where that skill is used*
					A. Using My Hands	
					1. assembling	as with kits, etc.
					2. constructing	as with carpentry, etc.
					3. or building	
					4. operating tools	as with drills, mixers, etc.
					5. or machinery	as with sewing machines, etc.
					6. or equipment	as with trucks, stationwagons, etc.
					7. showing manual or finger dexterity	as with throwing, sewing, etc.
					8. handling with precision and/or speed	as with an assembly line, etc.
					9. fixing or repairing	as with autos or mending, etc.
					10. other	

Adapted from the *Three Boxes of Life and How to Get Out of Them* by Richard N. Bolles, copyright 1978 by Richard N. Bolles. Used by special permission.

1	2	3	4	5	Name of Skill	Example of a situation where that skill is used
					B. Using My Body	
					11. muscular coordination	as in skiing, gymnastics, etc.
					12. being physically active	as in exercising, hiking, etc.
					13. doing outdoor activities	as in camping, etc.
					14. other	
					C. Using Words	
✦					15. reading	as with books; with understanding
✦					16. copying	as with manuscripts; skillfully
✦					17. writing or communicating	as with letters; interestingly
					18. talking or speaking	as on the telephone; interestingly
					19. teaching, training	as in front of groups; with animation
					20. editing	as in improving a child's sentences in an essay, etc.
					21. memory for words	as in remembering people's names, book titles, etc.
					22. other	
					D. Using My Senses (Eyes, Ears, Nose, Taste or Touch)	
					23. observing, surveying	as in watching something with the eyes, etc.
					24. examining or inspecting	as in looking at a child's bumps, etc.
					25. diagnosing, determining	as in deciding if food is cooked yet
					26. showing attention to detail	as in shop, in sewing, etc.
					27. other	
					E. Using Numbers	
					28. taking inventory	as in the pantry, shop, etc.
					29. counting	as in a classroom, bureau drawers
					30. calculating, computing	as in a checkbook, arithmetic

1	2	3	4	5	Name of Skill	Example of a situation where that skill is used
					(continued)	
✔					31. keeping financial records, bookkeeping	as with a budget, etc.
✔					32. managing money	as in a checking account, bank, store, etc.
✔					33. developing a budget	as for a family, etc.
✔					34. number memory	as with telephone numbers, etc.
✔					35. rapid manipulation of numbers	as with doing arithmetic in the head
					36. other	
					F. Using Intuition	
✔					37. showing foresight	as in planning ahead, predicting consequences, etc.
✔					38. quickly sizing up a person or situation accurately	as in everything, rather than just one or two details about them, etc.
					39. having insight	as to why people act the way they do, etc.
✔					40. acting on gut reactions	as in making decisions, deciding to trust someone, etc.
✔					41. ability to visualize third-dimension	as in drawings, models, blueprints, memory for faces, etc.
					42. other	
					G. Using Analytical Thinking or Logic	
					43. researching, information gathering	as in finding out where a particular street is in a strange city
✔					44. analyzing, dissecting	as with the ingredients in a recipe, material, etc.
✔					45. organizing, classifying	as with laundry, etc.
✔					46. problem-solving	as with figuring out how to get to a place, etc.
✔					47. separating important from unimportant	as with complaints, or cleaning the attic, etc.
✔					48. diagnosing	as in cause and effect relations, tracing problems to their sources

1	2	3	4	5	Name of Skill	Example of a situation where that skill is used
					(continued)	
					49. systematizing, putting things in order	as in laying out tools or utensils in the order you will be using them
					50. comparing, perceiving similarities	as with different brands in the supermarket, etc.
					51. testing, screening	as with cooking, deciding what to wear, etc.
					52. reviewing, evaluating	as in looking at something you made, to see how you could have made it better, faster, etc.
					53. other	
					H. Using Originality or Creativity	
					54. imaginative, imagining	as in figuring out new ways to do things, or making up stories, etc.
					55. inventing, creating	as with processes, products, figures, words, etc.
					56. designing, developing	as with new recipes, new gadgets
					57. improvising, experiments	as in camping, when you've left some of the equipment home, etc.
					58. adapting, improving	as with something that doesn't work quite right, etc.
					59. other	
					I. Using Helpfulness	
					60. helping, being of service	as when someone is in need, etc.
					61. showing sensitivity to others' feelings	as in a heated discussion, argument
					62. listening	
					63. developing rapport	as with someone who is initially a stranger, etc.
					64. conveying warmth, caring	as with someone who is upset, ill
					65. understanding	as when someone tells how they feel, etc.
					66. drawing out people	as when someone is reluctant to talk, share
					67. offering support	as when someone is facing a difficulty alone, etc.

1	2	3	4	5	Name of Skill	Example of a situation where that skill is used
					(continued)	
					68. demonstrating empathy	as in weeping with those who weep
					69. representing others' wishes accurately	as when one parent tells the other what a child of theirs wants, etc.
					70. motivating	as in getting people past hangups, and into action, etc.
✊					71. sharing credit, appreciation	as when working in teams, etc.
					72. raising others' self-esteem	as when you make someone feel better, less guilty, etc.
					73. healing, curing	as with physical, emotional and spiritual ailments, etc.
					74. counseling, guiding	as when someone doesn't know what to do, etc.
					75. other	
					J. Using Artistic Abilities	
					76. composing music	
					77. playing (a) musical instrument(s), singing	
					78. fashioning or shaping things, materials	as in handicrafts, sculpturing, etc.
					79. dealing creatively with symbols or images	as in stained glass, jewelry, etc.
					80. dealing creatively with spaces, shapes or faces	as in photography, art, architectural design, etc.
					81. dealing creatively with colors	as in painting, decorating, making clothes, etc.
					82. conveying feelings and thoughts through body, face and/or voice tone	as in acting, public speaking, teaching, dancing, etc.
					83. conveying feelings and thoughts through drawing, paintings, etc.	as in art, etc.

1	2	3	4	5	Name of Skill	Example of a situation where that skill is used
					(continued)	
					84. using words on a very high level	as in poetry, playwriting, novels
					85. other	
					K. Using Leadership, Being Up Front	
					86. beginning new tasks, ideas, projects	as in starting a group, initiating a clothing drive, etc.
					87. taking first move in relationships	as with stranger on bus, plane, train, etc.
					88. organizing	as with a Scout troop, a team, a game at a picnic, etc.
					89. leading, directing others	as with a field trip, cheerleading
					90. promoting change	as in a family, community, organization, etc.
✗					91. making decisions	as in places where decisions affect others, etc.
					92. taking risks	as in sticking up for someone in a fight, etc.
					93. getting up before a group, performing	as in demonstrating a product, lecturing, making people laugh, entertaining, public speaking
					94. selling, promoting, negotiating, persuading	as with a product, idea, materials, in a garage sale, argument, recruiting, changing someone's mind
					95. other	
					L. Using Follow-Through	
✗					96. using what others have developed	as in working with a kit, etc.
✗					97. following through on plans, instructions	as in picking up children on schedule
✗					98. attending to details	as with embroidering a design on a shirt, etc.
✗					99. classifying, recording, filing, retrieving	as with data, materials, letters, ideas, information, etc.
					100. other	

THE PARTY

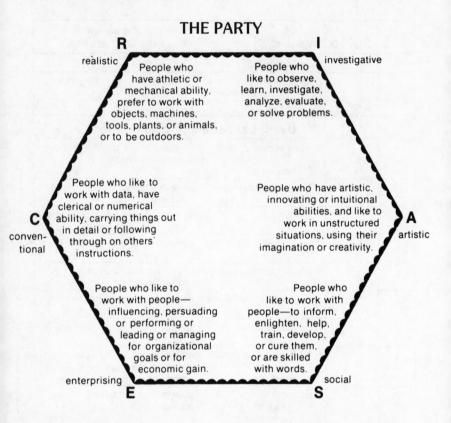

R realistic
People who have athletic or mechanical ability, prefer to work with objects, machines, tools, plants, or animals, or to be outdoors.

I investigative
People who like to observe, learn, investigate, analyze, evaluate, or solve problems.

C conventional
People who like to work with data, have clerical or numerical ability, carrying things out in detail or following through on others' instructions.

A artistic
People who have artistic, innovating or intuitional abilities, and like to work in unstructured situations, using their imagination or creativity.

E enterprising
People who like to work with people—influencing, persuading or performing or leading or managing for organizational goals or for economic gain.

S social
People who like to work with people—to inform, enlighten, help, train, develop, or cure them, or are skilled with words.

1. Which corner of the room would you instinctively be drawn to, as the group of people you would most *enjoy* being with for the longest time? (Leave aside any question of shyness, or whether you would have to talk with them.) Write the *letter* for that corner here:

2. After fifteen minutes, everyone in the corner you have chosen leaves for another party crosstown. Of the groups *that still remain* now, which corner or group would you be drawn to the most, as the people you would most enjoy being with for the longest time? Write the letter for that corner here:

3. After fifteen minutes, this group too leaves for another party. Of the corners and groups which remain now, which one would you most enjoy being with for the longest time? Write the letter for that corner here:

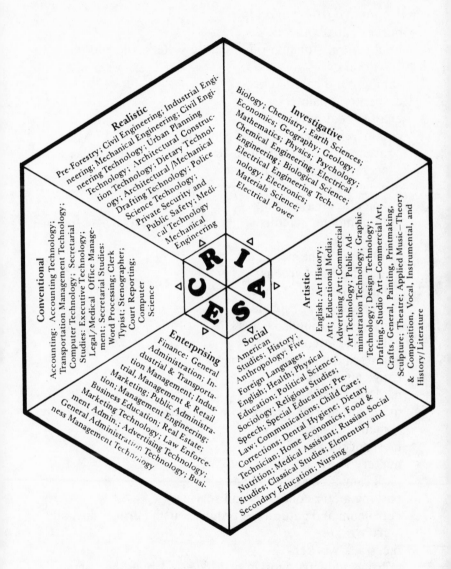

Adapted with permission from Richard N. Bolles's *Three Boxes of Life* and John L. Holland's *Model of Types and Environments,* Copyright 1975 by John L. Holland, Ph.D. Reproduced by permission of Consulting Psychologists Press, Inc.

(Continued from page 141)
border patrol officers
bricklayers, stonemasons, marble setters, tile and terrazzo
   workers
campground caretakers
carpenters, painters
charter-boat operators
commercial fishermen (and women)
conservation workers: foresters, forestry aides, range managers, soil conservationists
driving occupations: bus, truck, taxi
engineers: civil, mining
environmental scientists: geologists, geophysicists, ocean-
   ographers
farm equipment mechanics
fish and game wardens
fishing and hunting guides
fur farmers and trappers
gardeners, grounds keepers
golf-range attendants
guards and watchmen (women)
landscape architects
mail carriers
merchant marine occupations: officers, seamen, longshore-
   men
messengers
nursery workers
park rangers and caretakers
parking meter collectors and servicers
petroleum and natural gas production and processing industry workers
racetrack workers
railroad industry workers: bridge and building, signal department
recreation workers
ski resort workers

surveyors
telephone craft occupation: linemen (women), cable spli-
    cers, phone servicemen (women)
tour and sightseeing guides
tree surgeons
tree trimmers
vendors
well drillers
wildlife refuge workers
wrecking and salvaging workers
zoological workers

If you're housebound, here is a sampler of the occupations
you may consider:

accountant
babysitting clearinghouse operator
bookkeeper
clipping service employee
collection agent
commercial artist
custom needleworker
fashion designer
free-lance typist
income tax preparer
telephone solicitor
translator

And here are possibilities for those who wish to be self-
employed:

agent for writers, artists or artisans
airport chauffeur
answering service operator
antiques dealer
auctioneer

babysitter
caterer
Christmas tree farmer
clipping service operator
cooking instructor
dog walker
elderly visiting service
exercise instructor
fashion designer
firewood dealer
flea market or art show organizer
free-lance typist
garage sale organizer
home baker
housesitter
income-tax preparer salesperson
interior decorator
jewelry designer or repairer
mail order salesperson
odd-jobs person
party planner
personal shopper
photographer
private child-care center worker
private tutor
private tour guide
specialized gift service operator

Remember, these are only partial lists of jobs you may want to consider to stay active and alert after retirement.

IF YOU ARE A HOMEMAKER OVER SIXTY

The children are grown, and you and your husband have tasted retirement and found it lacking. Or you are widowed or divorced, and the challenge of forging a career for yourself outside the home suddenly appeals to you. Consider the case of Sally Ashley: "In 1975, when I tackled the job market," writes Ashley in her book *Connecting,* "I realized that the contribution I, an ex-housewife, could make was not what the corporate world had been holding its breath to receive. . . . It was clear: no one would hire me because I was 'just a housewife.' "

Ashley soon found out that not only was she eminently qualified for a number of positions, but that she did not have to start at the bottom—her first job was research manager and now she heads her own executive recruitment firm. What she did have to do was shake the feelings of inferiority she had long harbored vis à vis her husband and the Real World. "The world of work," says Ashley, "was a magic place where people spoke a language I did not understand, did things I was not able to do, earned money for accomplishing totally alien and mysterious tasks about which I knew nothing. I knew nothing about the Office except that David (like my father and grandfather before him) went there every morning and returned every night, and every couple of weeks brought home a bag of money from it. It terrified me to enter that world. I believed myself to be inept, incompetent and useless in such a place inhabited by Important Men with Briefcases. No wonder women like me were paid low wages. What a miracle to be paid at all!"

And yet more and more of the Important Men with Briefcases know in their hearts that their wives are capable of surviving, even flourishing, in the "magic" world of work. As a career homemaker, you have performed a job day in and day out for which you would have been paid somewhere in the neighborhood of $35,000 a year had you been working for strangers.

Bearing in mind that you were co-chairperson of Myers,

Inc. or Andersen, Inc. or whatever your surname is, Inc. for however many years, use Richard Bolles' Party Exercise and his transferable skills chart to make an inventory of your capabilities. Then turn to our "Sources Over Sixty" appendix for lists of businesses, organizations, books and other source materials to find the occupation that can be matched with your particular aspirations and qualifications. But remember, if you are serious about landing that job, then you will have to go after it with the same tenacity you applied to getting your kids to school or paying the bills on time.

SELLING YOURSELF

Nothing serves to clarify objectives, delineate marketability and bolster self-esteem more than a well-crafted resumé. The following sample offered by Sally Ashley could, with a few modifications, be used by every career homemaker in America:

Experience

I recently completed twenty years of experience as a suburban housewife and mother of two children. *General Management* responsibilities included development and implementation of short and long-range strategies and programs, including:

Budgeting. I was accountable for the allocation and disbursement of an annual budget averaging $25,000.

Purchasing. Planned expenditures ranged from low-ticket items to heavy capital equipment and services: sound systems, major appliances, musical instruments, automobiles, carpets, furniture, medical, dental and orthodontic services, club memberships, recreational devices, travel arrangements (tours and vacations), clothes and food.

Analyzing needs and supervising the use of all material and services:

Scheduling. Set priorities, met deadlines, often directed and accomplished several important tasks at once.

Recruiting, Interviewing, Evaluating, Selecting and Assigning Personnel. Persons hired and supervised included domestic workers, gardeners, painters, roofers, plumbers, handymen, electricians, carpenters, decorators, babysitters.

Persuading and Motivating. Formulated marketing strategies and sold the idea of personal development and goals definition in the form of participation in music lessons, swimming, tennis, soccer and ballet lessons, cultural events, the proper and regular use of libraries and the reading of books, visits to museums, galleries and the movies.

Acculturating, Teaching. For the two people whose development and well-being were under my care, I stood ready to respond to stated needs on a twenty-four-hour basis.

Selection, Design, Preparation and Provision of the Following Services. All meals, transportation, clothing (including scheduling and supervision in order to provide clothes on a regular basis), medical service and education.

Since you have probably been on the job far longer than twenty years—perhaps twice as long—you will most likely have more to put down on your resumé. This was only intended as a bare-bones example of the qualifications you have simply by virtue of the fact that you have run a household. What, then, does this experience qualify you for once you are over fifty and want to enter (or reenter) the job market? Here is just a small sample of the areas particularly well-suited to homemakers:

Arts and Crafts. A natural for many homemakers. She generally develops skills in such areas as needlepoint, crocheting (as did Bertha Jackman, designer of the "Scrub Puppy"), ceramics, quilting, painting, and so on.

Budgeting. A skill in which many women are most proficient, and with a refresher course at your local college, bookkeeping, auditing, computer programming and financial planning are but a step away.

Computer Programming. ACS America, Inc., of New York offers training programs in software for people up to eighty years of age (the average age is sixty-four). A college degree is not required; basically, anyone who can learn to type can learn the fundamentals of programming.

Decorating. We know a number of housewives who became interested in interior design after years spent decorating their own homes. One of Los Angeles's outstanding interior decorators started her career in her home, studied at the library, and then took an extension course in design from UCLA.

Designing. The graphic arts are wide open. Esther Kline graduated from Chicago Art School in the early 1940s, and after many years of raising a family, took a refresher course and is now a free-lance graphic artist.

Fashions. Most older women have been responsible for developing the fashion image of their families. They are the major buyers of fashions, and in many cases design and make their own clothes. Clothing and department stores, boutiques and fashion manufacturers themselves offer a wide range of employment possibilities for the determined and imaginative woman over sixty.

Food. Most homemakers today are experts at food buying, selling, processing and cooking. This qualifies them with solid background for gourmet cooking, working in gourmet product stores and restaurants, as demonstrators in the food and cookware sections of department stores, and so on.

Innkeeping. Many of the skills used in running a home apply to the hotel-motel field.

Modeling. Kaylan Pickford was the first, but in every community, attractive older women are now modeling clothing for department stores, charitable events, and so on. How old is too old for this line of work? Clara Fraser, eighty-four, recently modeled in a fashion show in Manhattan Beach, California.

Nursing. Many housewives have developed nursing and first-aid skills to handle whatever medical emergencies strike their families. Most colleges and junior colleges offer two-year nursing programs—an excellent field for older women.

Politics. Millions of housewives throughout America have had experience in grassroots politics. This is a fertile field for a woman who has been able to manage the "politics" of family life, as well as to become active in club politics, P.T.A. and civic affairs.

Professional Community Service. This area is a natural for many women who have done volunteer work over the years and have the skills and knowledge to help run a nonprofit organization. Lily Halpern was in charge of public relations for numerous Denver community projects over the years. Now she is the director of development at the Rocky Mountain Child Development Center (We will discuss Lily Halpern more extensively in our chapter on volunteerism).

Real Estate. More and more older women are studying for and obtaining their real estate licenses. As career homemakers, they are not only experts at rating property and its value, they also know their neighborhoods and the people who inhabit them inside out. Women are also drawn to real estate because it offers flexible hours and a considerable degree of autonomy. Not surprisingly, some of the top realtors in America are women who entered the field later in life.

Sales Jobs. The selling of insurance is a particularly lucrative field for women; Mutual of Omaha and other life insurance companies count among their most successful agents women who got into the insurance business only after raising families of their own. Again, their firsthand familiarity with the family—in this case the family's financial needs—gives these women the background to become insurance experts. Door-to-door sales jobs such as those offered by Avon and Fuller Brush also offer excellent opportunities.

Service Businesses. Women have been arranging for the services of housemaids, carpet cleaners, fumigators, window washers, telephone-answering services, plumbers, electricians, babysitters and other professionals to meet the daily requirements of maintaining a household. These homemakers know from firsthand experience what the consumer wants, and smart businessmen are hiring them either to sell these services to their fellow career homemakers or to perform these services themselves.

Travel. Women generally have been the travel planners of their families, and the world of travel can produce an exciting, satisfying life in later years. There are numerous husband-and-wife teams in the travel agency business.

Youth Organizations. Y.M.C.A., Y.W.C.A., Catholic Youth organizations, Boy Scouts, Girl Scouts, Boys Clubs—all need mature leadership, and many women who have had experience simply through raising their families are perfectly suited to these areas.

Everything in the job-getting game applies equally to housewives and $100,000-a-year executives, whether they be male or female. What we cannot stress enough is that *you must think positively* about your achievements in the home. Over and over again, we encountered women who refused to acknowledge that they had done anything since they gave up that job back in 1950 to marry their college sweetheart. Remember, a woman who has raised a family has probably had to be, among other things, a manager, a budgeter and bookkeeper, a self-taught expert on child care, a nutritionist, a recreation director, an active participant in community affairs, a savvy purchaser of necessities and luxury items, a decorator, a fashion consultant, a travel planner, a chauffeur, a teacher, a skilled craftswoman (not everybody can sew hems and mend draperies), a cook (don't forget Marion Cunningham) and a counselor to her husband and children on education, grooming, sex, morality, religion—and life in general.

NETWORKING

Many homemakers—and, for that matter, many seasoned executives who find themselves back in the job market—are reluctant to make the most of personal contacts. One woman we interviewed, for example, wanted desperately to get back into retail sales after twenty-one years devoted to raising her two sons, but bridled at the suggestion that she talk to her best friend, now the chief buyer for a major department store, about a job. "Connie's so busy," Rita told us, "I just wouldn't feel right about adding to her troubles. Anyway, this is something I should be able to do myself." So Rita is busy submitting her resumé to other stores in the hope that someone will hire her.

Rita's unwillingness to ask a favor of a well-placed friend is shared by Jim Street. At 12:30 P.M., Street was sitting at his usual table sipping his usual drink—a gin gibson, straight up. A ramrod-straight man of fifty-seven, Jim had been out of work for a year, since he and three other top executives were fired from the advertising agency they had been employed by for a collective seventy years—all victims of a new boss's "housecleaning." All four—two men and two women—were over fifty, and earning more than $50,000. Jim made no bones about his financial predicament and the emotional toll it was taking. He had submitted his resumé to more than one hundred firms across the country and had been interviewed by nineteen prospective employers. But what he had not done was contact any of his former friends and colleagues—well-connected neighbors, club members or golf buddies—directly. He felt it was "inappropriate" to capitalize on friendships and social relationships, though after he downed his second gibson, the real reason surfaced: "These guys know what I've done for them over the years, so why should I go crawling? They should come to *me*."

As if on cue, a man who had left Jim's old firm and taken on a bigger job with an agency down the street came up and slapped Jim on the back. We watched in utter amazement as Jim assured his old buddy that things were never better, that at long last he was enjoying the "life of Riley" and that he was thrilled to be out from under the old pressures and deadlines.

Unfortunately, both Rita and Jim are very misguided. It is a fact that more than 80 percent of all job placements in today's market result from personal contacts. If you know somebody with the authority to give you the job you want, don't be afraid to speak up. It may never occur to an acquaintance that you need his or her help *until you ask*.

Don't make the mistake of letting pride or a misguided sense of decorum stand in the way of your using every contact you've made during your lifetime (social as well as professional), and remember that even the most casual acquaintance can help you get a foot in the door. After all, they wouldn't do it if they didn't need you as much as you need them. If the first nineteen friends you approach turn out to be of the fair-weather variety, it will be worth it when the twentieth says, "I'm so glad you called. It just happens that we're looking for someone with your skills and experience." As for anyone who might be offended by your request for help or advice, that's their problem. After all, this is no game we're talking about—it's your future.

THE INTERVIEW: DO'S AND DON'TS
FOR THE OLDER APPLICANT

You are a fifty-eight-year-old who, after twenty-nine years
with Arthur Andersen, has retired. With the help of Success
Over Sixty you have rekindled the passion for nature and
conservation that led to a brief but low-paying job as a forest
ranger in your early twenties. Now you are up for a position
with the American Forestry Association that would make use
of both your knowledge of forestry and your talents for management and budget control. Or . . .

You are a sixty-year-old homemaker, and at long last you
have a chance to put that master's degree in art history to
work on the staff of your local fine arts museum. Or . . .

You are fifty-six and you have been squeezed out of your
middle management position because your company was gobbled up by a larger one. Now a tennis buddy of yours has
pulled strings and you have a shot at a public relations job
that would pay $10,000 more than your old job. Or . . .

You are sixty-five, bored senseless with the notion of retiring after a lifetime of work and looking for some part-time
clerical work just to keep the juices flowing . . .

Once you've gotten to this point, no matter what your background or your prospects, you all face the Interview. There
are certain pitfalls to be avoided by the older applicant at all
costs:

• It's usually a mistake to try to look younger by effecting
casual dress; why wear leisure suits and open collars when
you are of an age perfectly suited to a classier look? Neither
is it advisable to wear anything out of *Gentleman's Quarterly*
or *Harper's Bazaar;* the idea here is to look not like a fashion
plate, but like a conscientious professional with some meas-

ure of style. As a rule of thumb, men should wear a dark suit, a blue or white cotton shirt with button-down collar, solid or striped tie, black shoes, dark socks, and no flashy jewelry. In an interview situation, a woman cannot go wrong with a tailored dark suit, stockings, pumps in navy or black, a conservative blouse and, as with the men, as little jewelry as possible. No oversized rings, no more than one ring per hand, no dangling earrings, nothing clunky or trendy. Silly? Not at all. In all probability you have not had to go out looking for a job in quite a while, so you should be reminded that now, more than ever, image is important. It is essential that what sticks in the interviewer's mind about your appearance is not what you wore, but only that you looked great.

• Don't downplay the significance of this as "just a second job to make ends meet." Here is where your mastery of the third C, communicating, comes into play. You may want to appear calm, but the interviewer wants to know whether you really want this job. So start off with a firm handshake and be enthusiastic. It is up to the interviewer to break the ice, but you play an essential role in establishing rapport by responding positively to his or her overtures. In answering questions, be assertive and concise.

• Do not hesitate to ask for details about the position, the salary, the job requirements and responsibilities, the possibilities for personal and professional growth. Show that you've done your homework, that you know the basics about the prospective employer and his operation. Otherwise you wouldn't be there. You and the interviewer are, after all, in this business of exploring career and personal goals, work values and aspirations together.

• Don't, on the other hand, be so eager that it appears that you are desperate for the job. Strike a balance that communicates to the interviewer that you are serious about wanting to fill the job under discussion, but that the employer isn't the only pebble on the beach. If you hear something you don't like, ask for more information to see if this potential obstacle can be overcome. If you like what you hear, do be enthusiastic in your response.

• Don't apologize for your age, or for any physical limitations or disabilities. Again, federal law prohibits discrimination on the basis of age. You are also protected by federal statute if you do have a disability, and it has no bearing on your ability to perform the job in question.

• Try not to underrate yourself either during the interview or in your resumé. You wouldn't have gotten this far if they weren't interested in your qualifications, so you don't want to disappoint them now. Aim for the most you reasonably think you can get in the way of salary and benefits, and remember that a 15 percent to 35 percent increase over your previous pay is the norm.

Once an interview is underway, that intangible thing called chemistry takes over. Your qualifications are all right down there on your resumé, so how you answer the questions posed by the interviewer and how he perceives you as a person are the deciding factors.

Since you may have chosen to leave your employer after many years of service, or have perhaps decided to look for work after years of conventional retirement, you will have to grapple with some questions not faced by younger applicants. Be up-front in answering these queries. If you are being pushed into early retirement in your late fifties, stress that you have a lot to offer. If you are reentering the workforce after trying to build your life around a golf game, don't say you're seeking gainful employment simply because you are bored. Emphasize your continuing desire to expand your horizons and conquer new frontiers in the twenty or more active years remaining to you. In the past, as we said earlier, much of what you did was for others. Now you want to pursue the career which most excites you—so be positive! Barring the possibility that you are up against the boss's brother-in-law, in every instance you will win the interview game.

Launching a second career is a big challenge, but you are up to it—an estimated 9 million Americans do it every year. First, you must decide for yourself after weighing the pluses and minuses, whether you are committed to making the switch. Then you must find the area that most interests you. Next you must decide where and with whom you want to do it. Then comes the important process of making an inventory of your skills and tracking down the specific occupation to which they can best be matched. Networking—at long last cashing in on the contacts you have made over the years—gives you a tremendous edge. Even if your contacts are limited, the experience you have accumulated constitutes a major advantage over younger applicants. With what you have already learned from *Success Over Sixty*—and what you are about to—you will be able to avoid the obstacles that have stood in the way of countless applicants before you. You know who you are, what you can do, what you want to do and—most important—how to get what you want.

7 If You Want to Be Your Own Boss (at Last)

It is no achievement to walk a tightrope laid flat on the floor. Where there is no risk, there can be no pride in achievement—and, consequently, no happiness.

—Ray Kroc

Many people who have been under the wing of a large corporation have it in them to run the whole show themselves, but they never realize it. They have never had the courage—or the encouragement—that would have enabled them to strike out on their own. Of course, owning and running a business is not for everyone; though hundreds of thousands of older Americans find great satisfaction in answering only to themselves.

One reason most of us never consider taking this step is that, as corporate employees, we have become so specialized and involved in our specific assignment that we don't, as they say, see "the big picture." We overlook our basic abilities and talents that could be channeled into building a business of our own. We encountered scores of men and women who started thriving businesses after they turned sixty: a department store executive who used his managerial expertise to start his own employment agency; a sixty-year-old lathe operator who after thirty years with a steel mill summoned the courage to set up his own shop, making custom fixtures for stores in the Chicago area; and an executive who had been with a major hotel chain, who now manages his own inn in New England.

A national sales manager for Olin Industries, David Marvel collected art and antiques during his travels around the country. When it came time for Marvel to retire from Olin at the age of sixty-five, he and his wife Marcia opened their own fine arts gallery in Lewes, Delaware.

Then there's the Georgia housewife who tended beehives as a hobby and decided to market her own brand of honey. She now ships over $1 million worth of honey throughout the South each year. And Louis Goldblatt, founder of the Chicago department store that bears his name, who retired at sixty-nine and set up an artificial-flower-marketing business at seventy. Today, at ninety-two, he is running a $35 million-per-year enterprise. But perhaps the best example of septuagenarian ingenuity is the late Colonel Harlan Sanders, who started Kentucky Fried Chicken with his mother's recipes when he was seventy-two.

Statistics show that three out of every five businesses started in 1983 were opened by women, many of whom are mothers with grown children. In her fifties, Judy Reis used her talents as a cook to open her own restaurant, the Café Provençal, now considered one of the finest restaurants in the Chicago area. Judy Samuelson was in her late fifties when she and a friend pooled their savings and opened a fitness center. And Jean Flaxenberg started the French Creek Sheep and Wool Company in her garage with one used sewing machine and an initial investment of $2,000. Today, her company sells millions of dollars worth of sheepskin coats to major outlets throughout the country.

Such success stories—and there are plenty of them—are inspiring. But unfortunately, they must be tempered with hard facts. According to the Small Business Administration, 40 percent of all new businesses fail during their first year, and only one in nine lasts seven years. With the proper research and planning, however, your chances for success will be infinitely better.

ANATOMY OF A FAILURE

Jane R. is a divorcee who spent more than twenty-five years as a secretary-bookkeeper at an oil company in the Southwest. While on vacation she shopped at a women's specialty store and was so impressed with it that she inquired about the possibility of purchasing a "franchise" in her own community. The owner of the store had never sold a franchise to anyone before and was not in the franchising business. Nevertheless, she agreed to sell Jane a "franchise" for $12,500. For her fee, Jane got the use of the store's name and little else; the management and merchandising assistance she had been promised proved to be minimal.

Jane had a friend with some selling experience, so in her enthusiasm for her new venture, Jane offered her a partnership in return for a small investment. The friend knew nothing about managing a business, however. Within six months, Jane ended up buying out her "partner"—and losing a friend.

In selecting a location Jane did not do her homework and wound up paying A+ prices to lease a grade C location. She was also ignorant of the rule of thumb that your rent should never be more than 10 percent of your total operating expenses. She paid too much for furniture and fixtures, and initially, she drew out too much in salary both for herself and her partner. Because she did not set up a buying plan, Jane bought too much inventory and her record-keeping was inadequate. Also, because of her abysmal location, Jane's advertising costs were twice what they should have been.

Most important, Jane was badly underfinanced from the

day she opened. Realistically, she had no idea how much starting capital was necessary for a women's specialty store in her area. Accordingly, she was forced to borrow over $50,000 at 15 percent interest. She had to put up her home as collateral. In less than a year, Jane was headed for bankruptcy.

We are not recounting Jane's story to discourage you from becoming an entrepreneur—only to point out the pitfalls for anyone starting up a business of his or her own. Actually, you are probably in a better position than most to take this step because you have had time to accumulate some or all of the capital necessary to finance such a venture. Over the years, you have also established banking relations and a credit line. In addition, you probably have the broad base of friends, advisors, contacts and potential investors—not to mention potential customers—that can vastly improve your chances for success.

To avoid making the mistakes that ended Jane's small-business career before it ever really started, all you really have to do is refer once again to the Five Cs. Are you willing to make the *changes* in your life that will be necessary to meet the demands and pressures of setting up and running your own business? Do you have the requisite *curiosity* to research all the various aspects of the business thoroughly? Are you willing to establish and maintain lines of *communication* with experts in the field who can advise you, as well as with employees, suppliers, customers and others necessary to keep you in business? Do you have the *confidence* to make a go of your own enterprise—confidence justified by your own experience, familiarity with the business and homework? Finally, are you *committed* to your new role as independent businessperson? Are you willing to work long hours with no guarantee of a paycheck for a while? At the end of this chapter we have included a checklist to help you set up your business, much like the kind a cockpit crew must go over before the pilot can be given the go-ahead to take off.

EDUCATION FOR ENTREPRENEURS

Being *your own boss* means you've got to educate yourself. But don't worry, you've got plenty of time: fifty-five to sixty-five-year-olds starting their own businesses have an average of twenty-five to thirty productive years ahead of them. The Small Business Administration funds university business development centers at colleges throughout the country. These centers are designed for the specific purpose of educating aspiring entrepreneurs. Inventors, engineers and scientists seeking to make it on their own may also seek assistance from the National Science Foundation, which is sponsoring courses at Carnegie University, the University of Oregon, M.I.T. and other schools. In recent years, a number of colleges have also added academic chairs in free enterprise. We have listed these under "Sources Over Sixty for Entrepreneurs" at the back of this book.

PROFESSIONAL SERVICES

Be sure to arrange for the necessary professional guidance. It is possible to set up a business on a do-it-yourself basis. But if you want to reduce the risk—and protect your starting capital—it is essential that you hire an experienced attorney who can help you determine the correct legal form for your business (do you want to go into a partnership or incorporate, for instance), draw up all necessary contracts and secure whatever licensing may be required from the city, county or state. You should also hire an accountant or professional bookkeeper who is familiar with small-business record-keeping systems and tax laws. With the help of computers, many accountants now provide a wide range of services at relatively low cost, from monthly statements to long-term projections.

The right banker is essential, too, so shop around. You'll be counting on him or her for loans, checking accounts, billing and credit services.

The fourth professional you will want to turn to is an insurance broker who is willing to put together a package tailored to your business. You'll be needing fire, security and theft insurance, general liability, and probably medical-surgical insurance. Many small businesses have been saved by business interruption insurance, which covers any losses you may incur because you've had to close down due to illness or some other calamity. What you should look for is an agent who won't overload you with unnecessary coverage, and who takes a personal interest in your account.

RESEARCH YOUR MARKET AND BUSINESS

It is vital that you know your market. Who will be buying your product or service? Is the market growing or declining? How strong is the competition? Is there room for another business of this type in your area? To find the answers, talk to the local Chamber of Commerce, bankers, manufacturers, landlords, other businesses in the neighborhood —and your potential customers.

BUYING AN ESTABLISHED BUSINESS VS. STARTING FROM SCRATCH

If you buy an established business there are fewer variables. Your market and your competition are in place. You can check the profit and loss statement for the last few years and make a reasonable diagnosis of how healthy the business is, whether volume is expanding or shrinking, if there is long-term potential for growth. Among other advantages: there is an established clientele; the furniture, fixtures, equipment and stock are in place. The employees are already trained (you will be able to draw on their expertise) and you can judge by the customer traffic if the location is worth the price of the lease.

Given these advantages, it is not surprising that we encountered so many people in their sixties and seventies who chose to buy into businesses: the retired department store buyer who bought into a men's clothing store in Florida, the retired college football coach who bought into a fitness center in New York City, the high school art teacher who became a partner in a sculpture gallery, and the textiles executive who parlayed a lifelong interest in clocks into a part-ownership in two watch and jewelry stores.

For many older people, however, starting from scratch has more allure. There are, in fact, many sound reasons for not buying an established business. You can, for example, start fresh in determining the right location. In addition, you're not stuck with old inventory, you can hire and train employees as you desire, and you can avoid inheriting the mistakes of the previous owner. In short, you can have everything your way.

PICK A NAME—BUT NOT JUST ANY NAME

Your company name is a valuable asset, representing you on stationery, business cards and in advertisements. Check the Yellow Pages so that you do not wind up choosing a name that is already being used by a similar business in your community. If you want your company and/or product name to be protected by a trademark, simply have your attorney fill out the necessary application for you. His fee for this should be no more than $100, and it's well worth the investment. A trademark can only enhance the value of your business.

THE LEGAL FORM OF YOUR BUSINESS

We recommend that you consult an attorney before deciding whether to form a proprietorship, a partnership or a corporation. Of course, you may be confident that you can do this without the assistance of a lawyer, in which case we suggest that you read *How to Form Your Own Corporation Without a Lawyer for Under $50,* published by Enterprise Publishing, 725 Market Street, Wilmington, Delaware 19801.

There are advantages and disadvantages to each of the three forms of business:

A *proprietorship* is an enterprise owned by you, the individual. It is the simplest form of a business, giving you total control of its destiny. On the other hand, most attorneys warn that the owner is personally liable for all legal claims made against the business. Therefore, not only are the assets of the business vulnerable, but the owner's personal assets are vulnerable as well. Another drawback is that when you die, so does your proprietorship.

A *partnership* tends to be less risky. If you are over fifty-five you probably do not want to gamble all your life's savings on a new venture, so you and one or more partners share the risk by each putting up a portion of the starting capital. A partner may also bring to the business experience you lack. For example, you may be a whiz at financing and organizing the business while your partner's areas of expertise may be marketing and promotion. And since you are dividing up management and responsibility, neither of you has to spend his whole life minding the store.

When a partnership clicks, there is probably no better, more personally satisfying business arrangement. For example, we encountered two executives with a major food chain who decided to take early retirement, each collecting his pension in one lump sum. Each invested $50,000 and together they opened a gourmet food store in a resort area. The partnership worked splendidly: one was an expert office manager, one was a first-rate salesman, and both knew the food business inside out. Their gourmet shop is so successful that they now plan to open several more.

Unfortunately, business marriages—like the other kind—can turn sour. More often than not, clashes over how the business should be run, how profits should be split, and so on eventually arise. If left unresolved, such conflicts can sink a business.

Generally speaking, your best bet is to set up a *corporation*. This is, in essence, a legal entity that exists without reference to the particular individuals who share its ownership and direct its activities. The corporation itself can make contracts, pay its own taxes and absorb liabilities (actually, the legal liability of the corporation's owners and stockholders extends only to the amount of their individual investment). The corporation does not terminate with the death of its owner, ownership is in fact easily transferable, and management control can still be concentrated in the hands of the corporate officers.

Many small businesses incorporate under what is known as an "S Chapter corporation." Basically this allows the owner the protection of limited liability; in the event of disaster, the corporation goes bankrupt—you don't. You also escape any heavy corporate tax burden—in an S Chapter corporation with ten or fewer stockholders, the I.R.S. permits each stockholder to report his share of corporate income on his *personal* return. Setting up an S Chapter corporation is simple and inexpensive. Your lawyer can do the paperwork for about $100.

SET GOALS

Establish your objectives. You've now made the decision, studied up on what it takes to be an entrepreneur, talked to professional advisors and researched your market. You've even picked a name. Now you need a plan. And if you were part of management at a large company, you did plenty of planning. You formulated two-year plans, five-year plans. It's no different with a corporation of your own.

Set goals for intervals of one month, three months, six months, one year and five years. For example, think about where you expect the business to be after one year in terms of projected volume, rate of growth, expansion, increased profits, and so on. By way of monitoring your progress, you are looking for one of two things: proof that you are doing well, or signs that the business is in jeopardy. If it becomes clear that it isn't going to succeed, it is obviously preferable to get out as soon as possible and cut your losses. Sylvia Porter provides the following guidelines for keeping track of a small business, and she suggests that you write down on a table like this the criteria necessary for your business to succeed:

Time	Criteria for Questionable Survival	Criteria for Likely Success
First Month	Little foot traffic: few calls or letters; if they come in, they don't buy; if they buy once, they don't buy twice.	Active foot traffic; people calling, writing, and coming back with friends. Sales volume picks up every day.
Third Month	Promotional campaign brings some sales, but little repeat business. Revenues cover only one-third of operating expenses. No referral business.	Building some referral and repeat business. Revenues cover operating expenses during the best weeks.
Sixth Month	Revenues increasing slightly, but by year-end capital will have been used to cover operating deficits.	Revenues are covering expenses. Biggest season ahead.
First Year	Revenues barely covering expenses during peak months of biggest selling season. No cushion to fall back on. No more capital available to cover operating deficits. No revenue for pay increases. Promotional campaigns bring "one sale" customers; no repeat business.	Revenues covering expenses. Rebuilding capital. Revenues sufficient for pay increases and slight expansion. Some left over for me.

As you begin your first year, then, you have established the criteria by which you can judge your success or failure as you go along.

FINANCING A SMALL BUSINESS

The main reason most small businesses fail is a lack of adequate financing at the outset. That doesn't mean, however, that you should sink every penny you've got into the business. Even if you have managed to accumulate a sizeable nest egg, only invest that amount you can afford to lose on a new venture. If necessary, take on a partner to minimize your risk. And never pay major starting costs in cash. Like a young consumer, a new entrepreneur must establish a credit line. That means you must borrow. Go straight to the Small Business Administration for any one of the many types of financial assistance they make available to entrepreneurs: direct loans, participating loans, guaranteed loans and lease guarantee loans—at interest rates lower than those offered by banks.

Whether your financing comes from the S.B.A. or a bank, you won't get a cent unless you make a clear and convincing case for your enterprise. Bring a personal resumé, a personal financial statement, a detailed profit and loss statement (if you are acquiring an established business) and/or a projected sales forecast in units and dollars, as well as proof of adequate insurance. You will also have to be prepared to offer a thorough description of the nature and purpose of the business itself. If you have already printed up a few brochures and product information booklets, this could make the task significantly easier.

A word of caution: do not underestimate your start-up and operating costs. Even before you open your doors and frame that first dollar, you will have to pay for legal fees, permits, licenses, sales tax deposits, insurance, furniture and fixtures, office equipment, remodeling and redecorating, signs, stationery, advertising, and public relations.

Once again, undercapitalization has caused the immediate

downfall of many businesses. But it can be avoided by taking the steps we described earlier in this chapter—educating yourself, researching the field, listening to the experts. A number of potential sources for information on how to obtain capital have been listed in the appendix, pages 244–47, for your convenience.

MANAGING YOUR BUSINESS

Map out a budgeting system. With the aid of your accountant or bookkeeper, outline the costs of overhead, utilities, equipment, merchandise, labor, advertising, postage, filing fees, professional advice, telephone services, insurance, business machines and computers, furniture, rent and salaries. If you plan to have one or more employees, you will have to train them and provide an overall set of *personnel policies*. You should be aware that employees come under wage and hour laws, unemployment compensation and Social Security laws. They also require insurance. For up-to-date information go to your accountant, bookkeeper, insurance agent or the Department of Labor.

You will also have to formulate a *merchandising plan* if you are in the business of selling a product. Who will you buy your wholesale materials from, and how much will you pay? How will you control the size and quality of your inventory, and what guidelines will you use for competitive pricing? For the answers, write to the national association for the industry in which you're involved—the National Retail Merchants Association if you're starting a clothing store, for example. If all else fails, contact the Small Business Administration to find out where you can get the information you need.

A *marketing and advertising* scheme is also essential for the success of a business. Set up a realistic advertising budget, then determine what will deliver the most business for the least cost: direct mail, magazines, newspapers, radio, television, handbills or a combination of these methods.

Following is the Success Over Sixty checklist, created to help you decide if you should go into business for yourself.

Making the Decision

1. Do I have the experience?
2. Have I enough information to organize my own business?
3. Do I have a hobby that I can market?
4. Do I have the ability to work with and direct people?
5. Do I understand the risks inherent in my own business?
6. Can I maintain my present standard of living if I enter a business of my own?
7. Does the community need my service or product?
8. Will my service or product be needed in the future?

Researching the Market

1. Have I determined who will be my customers?
2. Do I know the income level of my customers?
3. Can I estimate the potential growth of my product?
4. Have I identified the competition?
5. Can I capitalize on my competition's weaknesses?
6. Is there room in the market for my service or product?
7. Will technology change my market?
8. Have I researched the successes and failures of similar businesses?
9. Have I protected my idea?
10. Is a good location available?

Type of Business

1. Should I form a proprietorship, partnership or corporation?
2. Should I buy a going business?
3. Should I start a business from scratch?
4. Do I have an attorney who will help me select the type of business I want?

Financial Planning

1. Do I have enough capital?
2. Do I have enough reserve?
3. Do I have sufficient bank connections and borrowing power?
4. Have I determined my rate of return on my investment?
5. Do I have a realistic growth plan?
6. How much business do I have to do to make a profit?
7. Have I studied the profit and loss statement of a similar business?
8. Do I need someone to share my investments?
9. Can I survive financially if the business fails?

Marketing My Product or Service

1. Do I have a marketable name?
2. Have I developed a good logo for my business cards, stationery and advertising?
3. Do I have an overall promotion plan?
4. Have I considered assembling a small board of experts who can help me?
5. Am I informed about advertising costs?
6. Do I know what media I will use in my advertising (direct mail, newspapers, magazines, radio, television)?
7. Do I have an advertising budget?

8. Do I need the help of an agency or advertising person?
9. Have I protected my idea with a copyright or a patent?
10. Can I get local publicity for my business?

Controlling My Business

1. Do I need a bookkeeper or accountant to set up my books?
2. Can I afford to put my company on a computer?
3. Can I keep track of my inventory?
4. Have I prepared a budget?
5. Do I have expense control in my business?
6. Do I plan to set up a system of credit and collections?
7. Do I have a system for accounts payable?
8. Do I have a system for accounts receivable?

Merchandising My Product or Service

1. Do I have dependable suppliers?
2. Can I keep the costs of materials in line so as to be competitive and make a profit?
3. Can I establish credit with my suppliers?
4. Can I get discounts by purchasing quantities?
5. Will my suppliers give me extra time to pay?
6. On what terms can I purchase supplies?
7. Do I know my market (who, what, when and where to pay)?

Personnel Planning

1. Can I operate the business myself?
2. How many employees will I need?
3. Can I manage and lead personnel?
4. Am I capable of training personnel?

5. Do I understand employee health, wage, hour and age laws, and unemployment insurance?
6. Do I have an insurance plan for my business and employees?
7. Do I have an accountant or bookkeeper to guide me on employment regulations?

SHOULD YOU BUY A FRANCHISE?

Before answering this question, learn everything you can about them. A franchise entitles the holder to market particular products or services under a brand name or trademark. You, the franchisee, pay a fee and a percentage of the gross.

Over the past decade, more than a half-million franchises were sold throughout the U.S., accounting for nearly $300 billion worth of goods and services sold to Americans. Franchises reflected consumer demand for fast foods and brand name goods and services at every streetcorner and in every shopping mall. But because franchises have traditionally been on the cutting edge of the market, some run the risk of disappearing as quickly as the public tastes that spawned them. The operation that caters to a fad instead of a trend may be raking in millions one year and filing for bankruptcy the next. Miniature golf courses and trampoline franchises were hot not that long ago, but when the fads evaporated, so did millions of the investors' dollars.

Franchising has its advantages. The brand and name are already established; the company has an identity in the marketplace; and through the franchiser, you can establish immediate credit. Also, your leasing, insurance, training, merchandise, purchasing and statements of profit and loss are under the control of the franchiser. In addition, some of the research you have to do before opening your business is done for you, and the franchiser should also help you with advertising and promotion.

But franchising is not for everyone. It is easier to lose money than to make it at the franchise game, and retirees who think they can parlay their life savings into a fortune running a franchise they know nothing about are among the prime victims. Not all franchisers are reputable. Beware of franchisers who make it too easy for you to qualify, or who are only asking for up-front money. Most reputable franchisers will review you thoroughly before letting you buy the right to use their good name.

Even if the franchiser appears to be solid, you may be in a market that is already saturated with the goods or services he is selling. Or perhaps technology could wipe out the business altogether in the not-too-distant future. Franchises, as we have pointed out, are characterized by fast—but not necessarily stable—growth.

You shouldn't think of buying a franchise until you have enough capital at the minimum to cover your initial investment and sustain your operation through the first six months. When you enter into a franchise arrangement, make it in a business *you already know something about*. A twenty-five-year career as an executive with an electronics firm does not qualify you to run a Cut and Curl Beauty Salon unless you have had the necessary training. Ideally, this should be an evolution and not a departure from what you have done in the past.

Interestingly, the franchise industry has historically been dominated by older men. Colonel Sanders is an obvious example. So, too, is Ray Kroc, the man who founded the worldwide chain of restaurants called McDonald's. Kroc, who launched the drive-in, fast-food era that changed the face and eating habits of America did not strike gold—as in arches—until he was sixty.

For Kroc, it was a meandering road to success. Born in a Czech neighborhood on Chicago's South Side, he dropped out of school at fifteen to join the ambulance corps during World War I. Then, as a pianist, he played with a number of dance bands before switching to radio as musical director of Chicago's WGES. An attempt at selling Florida real estate followed, then an eleven-year stint as a salesman (he eventually rose to Midwestern sales manager) for what became the Lily-Tulip Cup Corporation.

Kroc struck out on his own in 1937, after buying the rights to a machine that could mix six malts at once, the "Multi-mixer." This gadget helped make Kroc comfortable, though not wildly rich. It was not until 1954 that he stumbled upon a thriving San Bernardino restaurant run by Maurice and Richard McDonald. By then, the McDonalds had seven of these bustling drive-ins and wanted to franchise others. Kroc leaped in, proposing an arrangement in which he would supervise the franchise operation, paying the brothers .5 percent of the total revenues.

Kroc bought out the McDonald brothers in 1961, and within three years his McDonald's Corporation included 657 outlets with a $129 million annual gross. Kroc was sixty-two at the time. A dozen years later, he stepped down as chief executive, though he remained a very active chairman for years. Still pulling the strings as he entered his eighties, Kroc could boast of creating nearly a $1 billion-a-year empire. He could also lay claim to his own baseball team, the San Diego Padres, which he bought in 1974 for a reported $10 million. Before his death in 1984 at age eighty-two, Kroc had also given millions to charity through the Kroc Foundation, which funds research into arthritis, diabetes and multiple sclerosis, and the Ronald McDonald Houses, which give seriously ill children a place to stay when they are receiving treatment away from home.

Into his ninth decade, Kroc still routinely checked up on the stores and rated them on the points the company holds dear: Q.S.C. & V.—Quality, Service, Cleanliness and Value.

In the directory, under "Sources Over Sixty," you will find a partial listing of franchises and their price ranges. A more complete listing can be obtained from the following sources:

The Franchise Annual
Info Press, Inc.
736 Center Street
Lewiston, NY 14092
Lists over 1,200 franchise headquarters

Directory of Franchising Organizations
Robot Industries, Inc.
103 Cooper Street
New York, NY 11702

International Franchise Association
7315 Wisconsin Avenue
Washington, DC 20014

It would also be useful to go to a good public library and read newspapers and trade periodicals for information on the franchise operation you have in mind. In this respect, the *Wall Street Journal* is a must, and you will be able to locate whatever they or other major publications have published on the businesses simply by referring to the *Reader's Guide to Periodical Literature*. For a copy of the *Franchise Opportu-*

nities Handbook, write to Superintendent of Documents, U.S. Government Printing Office, Washington, D.C. 20402. Also, talk to other franchisees, and visit their operations.

The Council of Better Business Bureaus has developed an invaluable checklist that can keep you from making serious errors. It can also help point the way to a franchise that can help make the future the most prosperous and satisfying time of your life.

Industry Background

1. Collect information on both the franchise and the type of product or service. Continue your search for several months using numerous independent sources.
2. Double and triple-check everything the company tells you with independent sources. Note whether you get the same answer to all questions listed below from several sources.
3. Keep a notebook. Take notes of all your conversations.

The Company

1. What is the corporate name? Are you paying your franchise fee to a separate corporation set up specifically to sell franchises or to the founding company turned franchiser? Beware of professional franchise salesmen who may be brought in to set up a franchise sales corporation and sell many franchises quickly. There may be no continuing relationship, and that long-term association is essential to success as a franchiser.
2. How long has the franchiser been in business? How many franchises has he sold in each of the last five years? Of these, how many are still operated by their original purchasers?

3. Who are the principals of the firm? What businesses were they associated with during the last ten years? Are the principals experienced in this kind of business service, or are they specialists at franchise sales?

4. What is the company's financial position? Get a copy of the annual report and certified financial statement. Check banking references, trade creditor references, and lines of credit with financial institutions. (Learn the necessary jargon by asking your banker for definitions in plain English. When a bank tells you the firm has a "medium four-figure balance, nonborrowing account": that means that the firm has between $3,000 and $7,000 in the bank and the bank does not extend credit. If the bank does not extend credit, why are you paying $9,000 in advance? Aren't you extending credit?) How long have these financial arrangements been operant?

5. What are the franchiser's plans for future development? Are they written? Do they appear reasonable in light of recent past expansion and management and financial resources?

6. Check the firm and the owners with your local Better Business Bureau. Don't be satisfied by the fact that the company has no complaints against it. That is only relevant if the company has been in business locally for several years.

7. Is the franchiser licensed in the state? As of the late 1970s, fifteen states required a franchiser to register with the state and provide a disclosure statement to potential franchisers. Get your lawyer to check the statutes in your state. If your state does not require licensing, check the provisions of the law in a state that does. But don't drop your guard and be lulled into a false sense of security simply because the franchiser is licensed. Licensing is not protection against fraud. Under a Federal Trade Commission franchising trade rule, you will be provided with information on potential franchisees. (But

like the Interstate Land Sales Disclosure Act, the FTC rule will not eliminate fraud and will do you no good if you fail to study carefully the disclosure statement.)

8. Find out how selective the company is in choosing franchisees. Ask to see names and addresses to back up the numbers. Many claim they are selective and that the qualifications are tough. But often the qualifications are not written and the main one seems to be ability to pay the up-front fee.

The Product or Service

1. What is the quality of the product or service? Shop comparatively as your future customers will. How does the franchiser's offering compare in quality to similar products or services?
2. Is it a staple, a fad, a luxury item? If it is a luxury item, are income levels right for it in your area? If it is a fad, will it be a bestseller long enough for you to get your money out plus a profit? If it is a staple, is there enough demand to justify your additional competition? If it is a seasonal item or service, will you be ready to tap the first major selling season shortly after you open?
3. How well is it selling now? In the recent past? Over the last several years? How long has it been on the market in your area?
4. Is it priced competitively and packaged attractively?
5. Where is your competition?
6. Would you, your family, friends, and associates buy the product on its merits?
7. Is the marketing territory well defined?
8. What are the provisions for territorial protection?
9. Is it large enough to offer big enough sales potential?
10. What are its growth possibilities?
11. What is its income level?
12. Are there fluctuations in income?

13. What is the competition in this area?
14. How are nearby franchisees doing?

The Contract

1. Does the contract include all claims, written and oral, by both parties?
2. Are benefits and obligations for both parties balanced?
3. Can it be renewed, terminated, or transferred? Under what conditions?
4. Under what conditions can the franchise be lost?
5. Is a certain size and kind of operation specified?
6. Is there an additional fixed payment each year?
7. Is there a percent of gross sales payment?
8. Must a certain amount of merchandise be purchased? From whom?
9. Is there an annual sales quota?
10. Can the franchisee return merchandise for credit?
11. Can the franchisee engage in other business activities?
12. Is there a franchise fee? Is it equitable?
13. Has your lawyer examined it? Does your lawyer know anything about franchising?

Continuing Assistance

1. Does the franchiser provide continuing assistance?
2. Is there training for franchisees and key employees?
3. Are manuals, sales kits, an accounting system supplied?
4. Does the franchiser select store locations? Is there a fee?
5. Does he handle lease arrangements?
6. Does he design store layout and displays?
7. Does he select opening inventory?
8. Does he provide inventory control methods?
9. Does he provide market surveys?

10. Does he help analyze financial statements?
11. Does he provide purchasing guides?

The value of this checklist for a potential franchise cannot be overestimated.

THE NEW COTTAGE INDUSTRIES

Beyond buying an existing business, starting a new one or purchasing a franchise operation, there is a fourth approach to being your own boss. Futurist Alvin Toffler foresees a "tremendous shift of work into homes, a trend that will have major impact on production and taxation systems, education, downtown real estate and suburbia." This shift to the home-based "cottage" industry is tailor-made for the independent-minded person over sixty.

Coralee Kern, for instance, was in her fifties when her physician told her she was too ill to go out and earn a living. "I was divorced and had two children at home," she recalls. "I had to do something." Coralee's solution was to open a domestic cleaning service from her home. She called it "Maid to Order," and it became an instant success. "I had researched my market, was well-organized, and I put in a lot of hard work."

So did Mary Rittenhouse, who at fifty-nine founded "Part-Time Parents," a babysitting service that employed women who had already raised their families and now needed the extra income and/or the indefinable sense of self-worth that comes from working for pay. The service soon expanded to provide care for invalids and semiinvalids. Rittenhouse ran the business well into her eighties.

Rittenhouse and Kern are just two of the hundreds of success stories now being lived by the new captains of cottage industry. Kern, in fact, has become something of a guru for this new breed of entrepreneur. She publishes a newsletter called *Mind Your Own Business at Home* in which she shares her cottage-industry tips with fellow home-based businessmen and women.

Kern has very definite ideas about how to be successful at "home work." She advises that you "plan your work and work your plan. Be self-disciplined; set aside time for your work and follow a set business schedule. Remember that you are at work and have no time for visiting with friends. Prepare a definite place to work. Always get up, get dressed for business and get to work. Be a professional and hire professionals. Get expert advice on taxes and business laws and go steady with your accountant."

As part of the separation of church and state that must exist between your home life and your home business, Kern insists that you install a separate business phone (one that no one else in the house is permitted to use for social purposes—enforce this rule!) and get an answering service. "And always have a backup person," she adds, "someone who knows your business so it *never* stops functioning."

Many services are now provided by such home-based cottage industries. Among them: babysitting, employment services, clothing alterations, photo developing, art and graphic design studios, messenger services, research surveys, real estate sales, hair styling, vinyl repair, upholstery, catering, gardening, machine shop repairs, taxi services, laundering, beauty care, yard sales, sewing, quilting and essentially any creative idea that is marketable.

Whatever you chose, you do not have to go it alone. Companies like Mary Kay cosmetics, Tupperware Home Products, Amway, Shaklee and Stanley Home Products offer the opportunity to get into business with a relatively small investment.

Whichever of the four routes you choose to take—buying

(or buying into) an existing business, starting one from scratch, purchasing a franchise or launching a home-based cottage industry—you will discover that being your own boss offers its own challenges and rewards. There is an element of limited risk, to be sure. It can be rough sailing, and your boat can be capsized by even a minor swell on the small-business high seas. Once you have weathered the storm—and with the proper preparation, *you will*—there are fewer satisfactions so great in life. Any successful independent businessperson will tell you the same thing: ''I wouldn't trade places with anyone.''

And as an over-sixty there is every reason for you to want to make it as the boss of your own operation. Certainly you have an advantage over more callow competitors. After spending twenty, thirty or forty years helping others prosper, you have a breadth of knowledge and depth of experience that cannot be duplicated. You know your own strengths and how to tap them, where the business opportunities are and how to seize them. Your Success Over Sixty is assured.

8 Sharing Over Sixty: The Rewards of Volunteerism

There is no higher religion than human service. To work for the common good is the gentlest creed.

—Albert Einstein

The volunteer spirit is alive and well in America.

—Ronald Reagan

A community leader, in a recent address to a large group of volunteers, went on and on about "the commonality of human service," the "viability of organizations" and the "peripheral benefits" of volunteerism. When he was finally through, a woman in her sixties stood up in the back of the room. "I don't know about commonality, viability or peripheral," she said, "but if you need someone to bake a cake . . ."

Ingrained in all the successful people we have interviewed is a belief in volunteerism. In return for what society has given them, these people feel a moral obligation to repay their debt with whatever talents and skills they have.

Kitty Carlisle, singing star of stage and screen, panelist on TV's long-running "To Tell the Truth," and widow of playwright Moss Hart, became involved in public service in her sixties. "The best thing that can happen to anyone is to be able to give back some of the good things they have had in life," says Carlisle, who since the mid-1970s has headed the New York State Arts Council. "I've been fortunate. An awful lot of good things happened to me, and I think the only thing that makes growing older worthwhile is to be able to give them back.''

In 1981, a survey conducted by the American Association of Retired Persons showed that 30 percent of all Americans over fifty-five were serving as volunteers. Of those who had not volunteered, 20 percent said they were interested in doing so.

Frank Pace is chairman and chief executive officer of the International Service Corps and founder of the National Executive Service Corps. He has held a number of government and corporate jobs, including director of the Bureau of Budget, secretary of the army under Harry Truman, president and chairman of the board of General Dynamics Corporation and chairman of the board of the Corporation for Public Broadcasting. He is also chairman of Ronald Reagan's Committee on Marshaling Human Resources, and serves on many business and charitable boards. At seventy-one, he is busier than ever, attracting the top corporations of America to back his organizations.

"All of us would agree that volunteering is a good thing to do," concedes Pace. "If someone asked us why, we'd probably answer because it's a way to help other people or because it's a way to solve problems. Both statements are true. Volunteering is a way to help other people to feel useful and to help solve many kinds of individual, community, and national problems. But there's another side to volunteering, a hidden side no one talks about. In fact, it's a very well-kept secret. Everyone who volunteers knows about it, even if no one will say so. The secret is *volunteering is good for the volunteer*."

Volunteering is good for the volunteer because of the contacts it provides with other people—the companionship, the friendship, the fellowship of working with others toward a common goal. Both the housewife and the newly retired corporate executive who no longer goes to the office every day share a sense of isolation from the outside world that volunteering can eliminate.

Volunteering offers a way to exercise the skills, talents and experience gained through a lifetime of working with a corporation, being a housewife, serving in the government or in the military. It also offers an excellent opportunity to pursue goals and delve into areas of personal interest. The computer programmer who spent thirty years in a cubicle may find she can now use her long-dormant athletic ability to teach and coach a girls' soccer team. The accountant facing retirement may at last find an outlet for his passion for art by serving as a tour guide at a local museum.

Volunteering offers a chance to learn new skills as well. Many mothers can attest that the skills acquired through years of volunteering—organizing, managing and fund-raising, for example—were exactly the skills that got them hired for a paid position once their children were grown. A career government worker, in turn, can capitalize on his familiarity with government regulations, accounting and management procedures, putting all this hard knowledge to work for nonprofit agencies.

Volunteering is a form of continuing education. Working on a rescue squad, one learns the latest emergency medical techniques, working on an election campaign deepens our understanding of how the political process works. Staffing an emergency "hot line" makes us experts at counseling and human relations, and serving on a school board can keep us in touch with the ever-changing field of education. Volunteerism truly is a path to lifelong learning.

Volunteer work can also ease the transition to a new community. We live in a mobile society, but moving can be tough; in many ways, it means starting all over again. What better way to get to know new people in your new community than by getting involved in a local project? Most important, once you volunteer, you begin to claim power over your own life.

Says Pace, "It's time to let people know that volunteer work is and can be a significant part of their life experience which deserves to be taken seriously, to be protected and strengthened. Volunteerism is not just a means of getting things done—it is in itself a valuable, enriching experience."

Using the experience and techniques he gained during his eighteen years with the International Executives Service Corp (a nonprofit organization founded by David Rockefeller in 1964 which helps private enterprise in developing countries increase productivity and sales), Pace has brought management consulting assistance to other nonprofit organizations. Pace delivers to his clients, on a volunteer basis, the services of men and women who actually led and directed the most prestigious business enterprises in America. For example, of the first forty-three volunteer executives assigned to I.E.S.C. projects, thirty-three were senior vice-presidents, presidents, CEOs and/or chairmen of their companies.

Today, as testimony to the basic need for retired executive volunteers, there are service corps in Boston, Chicago, Dallas, Denver, Detroit, Indianapolis, New York City, (which serves the northeast corridor of Massachusetts, Connecticut, New Jersey and Washington), Philadelphia, Rochester, San Francisco and Tampa.

One of the first organizations to receive management consultant assistance from the service corps was the Outward Bound Survival Program. Pace and his vice-president, Phil Ewald, who had gone through the program when he was in his midfifties, were asked to put together an executive team to help Outward Bound solve some of the basic problems that threatened the group's existence.

Outward Bound started in England after Kurt Hahn, a Jewish refugee from Nazi Germany, got together with Lawrence Holt, a member of a Liverpool shipping family, in the early 1940s. Holt had been lord mayor of Liverpool and was deeply involved in volunteerism. He devoted a great deal of time to improving working conditions for dockers and miners and did a lot of volunteer work on behalf of boys clubs and dockside missions.

During the war, German submarines began to attack British ships and it became shockingly clear that the younger sailors in both the merchant and Royal Navy were far less capable of surviving a torpedoing than the old-time sailors. Large steel ships with sophisticated equipment had shielded them from the ravages of the sea, so they hadn't had to develop the skills necessary to navigate lifeboats and rafts in a war situation. More important, they lacked the will to survive in the face of extreme hardships. The younger sailors were without the toughness and resourcefulness of the older, more experienced sailors, so Hahn and Holt brought the experienced seamen and the novices together. As a direct result of this cooperative effort, thousands of lives had been saved by the end of the war. Since then, nearly three-quarters of a million people of all ages have signed up with Outward Bound, seeking the challenges of river, mountain and desert expeditions.

In the early 1980s, Outward Bound was having management and public relations difficulties and enlisted the help of the National Executive Service Corps. Phil Ewald put together a top executive team consisting of Marion Heiskell, a retired *New York Times* executive, Howard W. Blauvelt, retired chairman of Conoco, Inc., and Charles A. Anderson, retired president of the Stanford Research Institute. These three executives, all in their sixties, went through Outward Bound training, visited and studied all of the Outward Bound programs. As a result of their recommendations, a number of corporations signed up their employees for Outward Bound programs.

One of these corporations was Host International Restaurants. Along with twenty-nine of his managers, Host Vice-President Vince Kikugawa spent three weeks at the Colorado Outward Bound School. What Kikugawa had in mind was a wilderness learning experience testing his managers' capacity for planning, consensus and teamwork—all basic requirements for running a profitable corporation. The group arrived wearing red baseball caps emblazoned with a snow-capped mountain logo and the slogan "In Search of Excellence," taken from the title of the recent best-seller about America's best-run companies. The philosophy behind Outward Bound's Executive Wilderness Program is unique: by learning to communicate while white-water rafting or mountain climbing, the executive learns to transcend the business environment that so often fosters isolation, adverse competition and territoriality. Corporations like Denver Aerospace (a division of Martin Marietta) and Adolph Coors Company can attest to the validity of this program.

Outward Bound offers proof positive that nonprofit organizations can offer much to the corporate community—and vice versa. The rewards of the pro bono world are special indeed —a fact all very much appreciated by hundreds of the nation's top business leaders.

J. Henry Smith retired as chairman of the board and CEO of the Equitable Life Insurance Company in 1975 at age sixty-five. In addition to continuing as a director of Equitable, he has served on the boards of the Chase Manhattan Bank and Uniroyal, Inc. Not surprisingly, the N.E.S.C. chose Smith to engineer a merger between the New York Chamber of Commerce and the Economic Development Council. This was a delicate situation. Both groups were powerful independent forces in the New York area, but they often duplicated each others' efforts. Smith, working gratis, formed a committee to unite the two organizations. Today, thanks to Smith's efforts, they are the strongest single voice representing New York's business community.

Pace and Ewald also tapped their pool of retirees in the National Executive Service Corps to develop leadership training programs. In the late 1970s, N.E.S.C. became an operating partner for the Greensboro, North Carolina-based Center for Creative Leadership, which is supported by 135 U.S. corporations and the Smith Richardson Foundation. Together, N.E.S.C. volunteers are working with the center to promote leadership training courses for credit at twenty-five leading U.S. universities (including Princeton, Dartmouth, Columbia and M.I.T.), and fifteen thousand secondary schools. These leadership training courses combine academic theory with the pragmatic experience of retired businessmen and businesswomen. For the first time, business tyros and aspiring MBAs can draw on that corporate memory bank.

What motivates senior executives to share their expertise in this manner? "The most important element in all of our careers, both before sixty and after, was that we associated with people of outstanding ability and fine character," explains Curtis Frank, former president of Dun and Bradstreet. "The only major difference for most of us was that we were engaged in profit-making before retirement and in charitable activities after. At all stages, we love what we are doing. That is the answer to Success Over Sixty."

"Corporate responsibility is more than a social obligation," says Sears President Archie Bol. "It is a necessary commitment *in our own interest*. Monetary contributions alone, no matter how large, will no longer suffice. Corporations will have to exert their influence, and their people must become *personally* involved."

Toward that end, companies are taking on group projects,

giving employees time off to volunteer for community service activities, loaning personnel for fundraising projects and, in some cases, granting social service leaves of up to a year for community health, youth and welfare assignments.

Corporations are also recognizing that their retired workers represent a particularly important pool of talent for community services and agencies. Therefore, as part of preretirement counseling, many companies now outline the volunteer opportunities available to their employees. By supporting these programs, the corporation can open doors for their retirees.

One manager with an urban utility company in California dreaded the prospect of "frittering away" his sixties until he learned at a preretirement seminar given by his company that there was a pressing need for volunteers to drive handicapped people in his neighborhood to local stores. A year later, he estimates that he has driven more than one hundred people a total of 80,000 miles. "The best part," he says, "is the people you meet."

A midlevel supervisor with a moderate-sized appliance manufacturer did not realize there was a shortage of "Big Brothers" until he read about the Big Brothers program in the preretirement literature provided him by his employer; in the three years since, he has become a Big Brother to several boys in his community. And a computer typist with one of the country's biggest magazine publishers reports that life for her at sixty-six is "more rewarding than ever" since she began teaching her typing skills to underprivileged kids—an opportunity she says she "never would have known about" had it not been for the company counselor who talked to her two months before she was due to retire. In each of these cases, the corporation contributed financial backing for the volunteer organization to which the retiring employee was directed. Thus the contribution of the corporation itself is twofold: it provides the necessary funding to keep valuable community services operating, and it also channels into these volunteer agencies the expertise and energy of its retiring employees. General Electric, Time, Inc., Levi-Strauss and Johnson and Johnson are just a few of the many corporations making this twofold commitment to volunteerism.

For many employees, however, there is no such guidance. Ethel Christianson is only one of thousands who discovered volunteer opportunities for herself. Christianson spent her entire professional career as an administrator with the U.M.C.A. in Kansas, Pennsylvania, Oklahoma and New York. Since her retirement in 1968, she has devoted her life to the welfare of the elderly.

As volunteer president of the Health Support Council for Capitol Hill Seniors, she works with a board and an advisory committee to provide transportation, medical care and shopping assistance for older people who want to live independently in their homes. As chairwoman of a task force on Social Security for the Colorado delegation to the Washington Conference on Aging, she lobbied vigorously to keep the Social Security trust fund intact. By 1984, she was developing a seniors' hot line for information, guidance and help. Her advice to older citizens: remain politically active, vote regularly and learn the techniques of lobbying. "Get out and do things," she urges. "Do not sit home and turn the dial on the television set."

Actress-volunteer Virginia Gregg explains, "Just because a person is sixty or sixty-five does not mean that he should become a 'taker' and forget about others. A truly successful person over sixty shares the experience of a lifetime with others."

For many years, Gregg has worked with the deaf and made recordings for the blind; she also writes over 500 letters a year for older people at home. Her next-door neighbor is a ninety-year-old woman with whom she spends a great deal of time. Gregg takes her grocery shopping and helps her with her errands. "To sit one's life out," says Gregg, "would be deadly."

Marion Jeffries, now head of the nonprofit Second Careers Program in Los Angeles, spent most of her life as a wife, mother and volunteer worker in the community. Her current career was spawned when she was a hospital volunteer in the 1940s. Jeffries' years of pro bono work qualified her for a paid position in the hospital field, and in 1961 she was approached by fellow board members at Resthaven Psychiatric Hospital to take over the agency's public relations and volunteer program. One example of SCP's work is their placement of a retired engineer as a volunteer in a school for the handicapped where he adapts tools and wheelchairs to the needs of individual students.

Few have cut so wide a swath as Howard Samuels, who made his fortune by inventing Baggies and then marketing them and other products through his Kordite Corporation. In addition to his extensive involvement in business and public affairs, Samuels, now in his midsixties, has devoted himself to a wide range of civic activities. He not only chairs the State of Israel Bonds for New York City and serves as senior vice-president of the American Jewish Congress, but he also travels widely as one of the principal spokespersons for the Anti-Defamation League. He is also a member of the cabinet of the Federation of Jewish Philanthropies/United Jewish Appeal, and in 1975 and 1976 he led their fund-raising drive as mobilization chairman. As national chairman of Cities-In-Schools, Inc., a nonprofit organization, Samuels seeks to develop fresh approaches to the problems of urban education. As a director of the Blackfoot Indian Company, he uses his influence in the private sector to secure jobs for those living on the Blackfoot reservation.

How old is too old to be a volunteer? In late 1983, a number of men and women were paid tribute at a benefit dinner dance for the United Hospital Fund, the oldest federated charity in the nation. These individuals had two things in common: each was a leading volunteer in his or her community, and each was over ninety.

"I'm going to keep on to the fullest extent that my physical and mental capacities will allow," says Vienna-born Emil Baar, a former New York State Supreme Court Justice who at ninety-three goes to his office in the World Trade Center every day. He was a county commander of the American Legion, instrumental in starting the Gold Star Mothers of America in World War II. He was also active in the Big Brothers of America and the American Hebrew Congregations. "They'll have," he winks, "to carry me out feet first."

A 1907 graduate of Smith College, Hortense Hirsch was ninety-six at the time of the benefit. A trustee of Manhattan's Mount Sinai Hospital and a member of the executive committee of the division of voluntary programs of the United Hospital Fund of New York, Hirsch admits she never knows how she's going to feel tomorrow. "But I do what I can when I can. This work is still very important to me."

It is also still important to Louise Thompson, ninety-three, who has over ten thousand hours of service to her credit as a director of Flushing Hospital in Queens and president of its women's auxiliary for the past thirty-one years. What does her volunteer work entail? Well, in one month in the fall of 1983 she made 150 articles for the hospital's linen supply, including baby capes, bassinet sheets, tray covers and draw sheets, and cut several times that number of items for volunteers who make use of the seven sewing machines she keeps in her home.

Writing letters is what Mary Linder, ninety-two, enjoys

most—and does best: "It makes me feel as if I'm touching people's lives directly." She recently wrote forty on behalf of the United Hospital Fund, fifty for the Guild for the Blind and seventy-five for the UJA federation, all in a matter of three weeks. "I feel so badly that people who have leisure time," says Linder, "don't give some of it to charity."

Margaret Nourse, ninety, has been making that time available since World War I, when she was an occupational therapist aid with the U.S. Army. When she returned to civilian life, she taught sewing classes at a Manhattan church, then applied her therapist training as a volunteer in local hospitals. "I was always interested in doing something," she says, "and in my day women didn't always run for paying jobs." Nourse is on the board of the New York Eye and Ear Infirmary and attends the opera, the ballet and the Philharmonic whenever she can. She also keeps a close eye on a few big contributors to her favorite charities. "I know another organization has tried to get one of them," she smiles, "but as long as I'm alive they won't get that one."

For each of these remarkable over-nineties, volunteerism has been anything but a sacrifice; it has kept them sharp, vital, involved. "I came to this country as a boy and acquired a sense of its values," explains Baar. "I set out to repay part of my debt, and have gotten so much more in return. I was glad to do it, and I'm still glad to do it—for my own good as much as anything."

In 1979, two organizations, the National Center for Voluntary Action (NCVA) and the National Information Center for Volunteerism, merged to form "Volunteer: The National Center for Citizen Involvement." Volunteer, with George Romney as its chairman, has since established more than 300 action centers across the country. These centers furnish corporations and individuals with information concerning specific community needs—and what volunteers can do to fill those needs.

When you volunteer, chances are you'll get more than you'll give. You serve others, yes, but you also make new friends and learn new skills and develop new interests that can sometimes lead to paid jobs, a second career.

Once you have made the decision to volunteer, be sure and take the same time and care in finding a volunteer job that you would devote to finding a paid position. Don't rush into this with an "I'll do anything you give me" attitude. You have special abilities and specific interests; it would only be cheating yourself and your community not to put them to the fullest possible use. That means looking around for the volunteer job you are best suited for. Where do you go for this information? Look in the telephone book under Community Chest, United Way, United Funds, United Appeal, the Community Service Council, the Health and Welfare Council, and so on. These clearinghouses will direct you to the specific nonprofit agencies that can make the best use of your help. You can, particularly if you live in a small town or rural area, write ACTION, Washington, D.C. 20525, or contact the Cooperative Extension Service, the education arm of the United States Department of Agriculture. The Extension Service has more than 3,000 branch offices nationwide, usually located in the county seat. You'll find the names and addresses of other agencies and organizations—as well as a list of volunteer opportunities and what they entail—under "Sharing Over Sixty" in the directory.

"The great use of life," said the philosopher William James, "is to use it for something that will outlast it." Volunteer work offers you a way in which you can, whatever your age, make a difference—and reap a great deal of personal satisfaction in the bargain. The same lifetime of experience that makes you ripe for a second career or may qualify you to own your own business is the lifetime of experience that makes you especially valuable as a volunteer. By pinpointing precisely how your skills can be most effectively employed gratis, you will enrich your neighbors' lives and, not incidentally, your own.

9 *Healthy Body*

Age doesn't matter, unless you're cheese.
—Billie Burke

You've heard it a million times, but now more than ever your health is your most precious possession. Without it, you will be hampered in your quest for Success Over Sixty. With it, you will be equipped for the challenge. But before you make any changes in your diet or start exercising, be sure to get a complete physical examination and clear your plans with your doctor.

To add years to your life and life to years, you must start watching what you eat and embark on a program of regular exercise. That is, if you haven't already.

A proper diet of food and exercise targeted to our special needs as over-sixties can reduce our susceptibility to illness, give us the strength to bounce back from physical and emotional setbacks, even slow down the aging process and increase our longevity.

If you are an over-sixty who is just 10 percent overweight, you have a one-third greater chance of dying prematurely from heart disease, high blood pressure or diabetes. If you are 20 percent overweight, you are one-and-a-half times more likely to die prematurely.

If you want to stay healthy, keep your fat consumption down to 30 percent of your total calorie intake (as compared to the 50 percent common in most diets today), which probably means a sharp reduction in meat and dairy products, a shift from beef and pork to poultry, fish and veal. You will also be better off replacing saturated fats with unsaturated fats, i.e., substituting margarine for butter and using vegetable oil for all your cooking. Sugar and salt must be cut drastically. The average American consumes ten times more salt than he needs and fully ninety pounds of sugar per year.

In addition, make sure to get enough whole grains and fresh fruits and vegetables. Eat regular meals; this makes it easier to keep track of what and how much you're eating. Limit your alcohol intake to two mixed drinks a day, and reduce your caffeine consumption. We know caffeine can make us confused and irritable, but researchers are looking into the possibility that this drug might have even more damaging long-range effects on our bodies, so cut back to no more than one or two cups of coffee, tea (tea leaves contain twice as much caffeine as coffee) and soft drinks per day.

You do have to watch for a few things that probably won't concern a younger person. For one thing, you should be taking in fewer calories because your body can run on less fuel. For a man over sixty, 2,300 calories per day should be the optimum (compared to 3,000 for a thirty-year-old male) and women over fifty should probably hold the line around 2,000 calories per day. But in curbing your calories, don't go on one of those nasty crash diets. When you diet too quickly, weight loss comes from muscle, bone and blood cells, as well as fat cells; so diet gradually and you'll lose only the fat.

As for vitamins and minerals you need the same ones you did when you were younger—particularly potassium, phosphorus, iodine, iron and calcium (you actually need *less* vitamin D). The best source of these vitamins and minerals is the food we eat. Dairy products, meats (particularly liver), fish, bread and cereals, green leafy and dark yellow vegetables, citrus fruits, vegetable oils and a small amount of iodized salt can provide you with virtually all the necessary requirements. How do you know you're getting enough? Fortunately, the FDA now requires that U.S. recommended daily allowances (RDAs) be listed on all food labels. These tell you the RDA of carbohydrates, protein, calories, vitamins A and C, riboflavin, niacin, calcium, thiamine and iron in each package. Just add them up to make sure that you are getting 100 percent of each nutrient in your daily diet.

The following diet developed by the Southern Illinois University Medical School is one of the best for the over-sixty group.

DAILY SERVING GUIDE

Milk Group

1 Serving = 1 cup milk or yogurt. May substitute ⅓ cup nonfat dry milk, 1½ oz. cheese, 2 cups cottage cheese or 1¾ cups ice cream.

Meat-Meat Alternative

2 Servings - All age groups
1 Serving = 2-3 oz. fish, poultry or meat; 1 cup cooked dried beans, peas, lentils; 4 T peanut butter; 2 oz. cheese or 2 eggs. Meats should be broiled, baked, roasted, boiled or stewed without added fat. If vegetables are sole source of protein, appropriate combinations are necessary to achieve adequate protein intake. Consult reliable reference for combinations.

Vegetable-Fruit Group

4 or more servings daily
1 Serving = ½ cup or one portion such as ½ banana, ½ grapefruit, or 1 small piece of any other fruit. Low-calorie vegetables include asparagus, beets, broccoli, Brussels sprouts, cabbage, carrots, cauliflower, celery, cucumber, eggplant, endive, greens (all kinds), lettuce (all varieties), mushrooms, okra, green pepper, radishes,

TARGET FOR A HEALTHY DIET
Aim for the Center

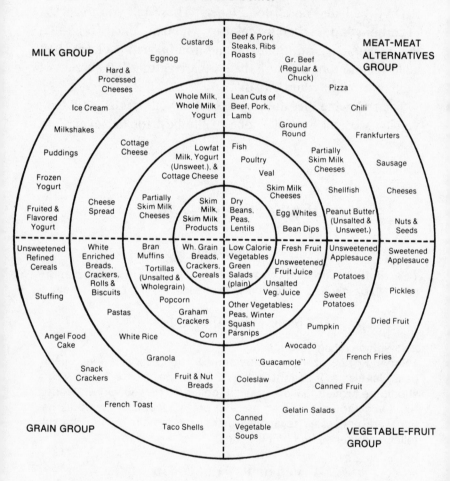

Karen G. Little, M.S.R.D.
Department of Family Practice
Southern Illinois University School of Medicine

rhubarb, string beans, summer squash, tomatoes, tomato juice, turnips, zucchini.

Grain Group

4 or more servings daily
1 Serving = 1 slice bread or 1 biscuit, roll, muffin or 1 oz. ready-to-eat cereal or ½ cup cooked cereal, rice, pasta products or corn. Wheat germ (¼ c.), bulgur, brown rice and oats are included in the center of the target as whole grains.

Others

Extras - These supply mainly calories and are unnecessary for a balanced diet. Includes Fats (margarine, butter, oils, bacon, sour cream, cream cheese, salad dressings, etc.), Sweets (sugars, honey, syrups, cookies, cakes, pies, soft drinks, candy, etc.), Refined carbohydrates (unenriched breads, snack chips, pastries, doughnuts, etc.) and Alcoholic Beverages (beer, wine, liquor).

Recommended Snacks
Raw vegetables (listed above), fresh fruit, unsweetened fruit and vegetable juice, decaffeinated tea and coffee, skim milk, plain lowfat yogurt.

Seasonings
Herbs and spices, parsley, onion and garlic powder, celery seed, pepper, lemon, lime, vanilla, etc.

EXERCISE OVER SIXTY

Diet alone won't give you the healthy body you want, so one of the cornerstones of Success Over Sixty is exercise. No one knows this better than Albert Myers. Not only does Myers run five miles every morning, compete in racquetball tournaments, play tennis, swim and ski—he recently took up windsurfing!

Myers argues that our bodies work on much the same principle as our automobiles: as long as they are properly maintained, cars and people can function efficiently years beyond what is considered the norm. In England and Europe it is not unusual for cars to be driven until they have several hundred thousand miles on them. Yet in the U.S., we have been conditioned to believe that a car is ready for the junk heap at 100,000 miles. Europeans obviously believe in preventive maintenance to a degree that we don't.

How much mileage is left in you depends on how you approach yourself mentally and physically. "So many people 'rust out' before they 'wear out' because they fail to realize that the human body was made to be used for as long as a person lives," says Dr. Robert E. Wear, exercise physiologist at the University of New Hampshire. By keeping the parts of your body moving, you will not only stay on the road, you will zoom down the fast lane.

If Europeans seem to know how to get more out of their automobiles, Asian cultures do the same for their citizens. In China, millions of older people can be seen in the parks and public squares doing their Tai Chi and martial arts exercises, and in Japan all ages are encouraged to participate in fitness programs. In the U.S., however, sedentary men and women, many only in their forties or fifties, complain that it is too late for them to start an active physical regimen. No matter what they do now, these people moan, it won't be enough to undo the damage.

Not so. Take the California octogenarian who began attending exercise classes at seventy-nine and now, three years later, is "pumping iron." She has a seventy-six-year-old boyfriend and says that "love and exercise" make her look like a woman in her late fifties. And then there is Sam Dorman, at seventy-two the world senior Olympics champion. And Milton Jaffee, our seventy-nine-year-old millionaire clothing-executive-turned-ski instructor.

Duncan Maclean, a man with a great deal of mileage on

him, won a silver medal at the 1975 World Veterans Olympics in Canada when he ran twenty meters in forty-five seconds. He was ninety years old. Maclean's ambition: to run one hundred meters on his hundredth birthday.

George Allen, a former surgeon general of the United States and head of the President's Council on Physical Fitness, points out that about 75 percent of the factors that influence health are heredity and behavior. We can't choose our genes, but we can change our behavior.

A report issued by the Council on Physical Fitness Conference on Aging pointed out that many over-sixties harbor the misconceptions that their need for exercise diminishes with time, that they risk a heart attack or injury if they exercise too vigorously and that—if they exercise at all—sporadic activity will suffice. In fact, a major study conducted by Dr. Leslie Brelow of UCLA showed that by observing five simple health practices—not smoking, using alcohol in moderation, eating a proper diet, and getting the proper amount of sleep and *exercise*—a forty-five-year-old can expect to live ten or eleven years longer than one who doesn't monitor his habits. Women who observe the same health practices can expect to live seven years longer.

At age eighty-one, Dr. Thomas K. Cureton, Jr., was ranked All-American Masters No. 1 swimmer in his age group (eighty to eighty-four) for 1983. "It isn't necessary for older individuals to train three hours a day to improve their physical condition," says Cureton. "But thirty minutes of vigorous walking, swimming, some stretching exercises and sensible calisthenics will help them a great deal."

Cureton knows whereof he speaks; he is a pioneer in the field of sports medicine. In 1944, he founded the Physical Fitness Research Laboratory at the University of Illinois, where he was a professor for thirty years. His fitness methods have been implemented in over 600 U.M.C.A.s in the U.S.A.

As a professor of physical education, he has trained more than 20,000 physicians, trainers and educators in sports medicine, including such top authorities as Dr. Henry Montoye, Charles Tupton and James Skinner—all past presidents of the American College of Sportsmedicine—and William Orban, who originated the Canadian Air Force fitness program.

Another top American exercise physiologist is Dr. David Bruce Dill, who, in his nineties, is the oldest research scientist supported by the National Health Institutes. For a study that he is conducting at the University of Nevada Desert Research Center, Dill gave himself and fifty volunteers over the age of sixty stress tests. Those who passed were sent on three one-hour walks around a track while being monitored. The results show that older persons actually do much better than younger ones. Taking advantage of opportunities to remain physically active, older people can perform extraordinarily well, even in desert conditions.

In a study done by U.S.C.'s Dr. Herbert A. DeVries, a class of seventy-year-old men joined a one-year exercise program. They ended up with bodily reactions of men thirty years younger. No one comprehends this phenomenon more fully than Dr. George Sheehan, the cardiologist who took up running late in life and became the marathoner's guru. "I got lucky," says Dr. Sheehan, whose books include *Dr. Sheehan on Running* and *Running and Being*. "My days used to be filled with nothing. Life is *so* good now."

Clara Golden Frazer, a retired real estate broker living in the California town of Hermosa Beach, recalls the day in 1980 when she returned from a trip to Europe mentally and physically exhausted. "A friend of mine took me to the Manhattan Athletic Club for Women," she says, "and it completely changed my life." Fraser has been working out ever since. She exercises three days a week, lifts weights, pedals on an exercycle, swims and winds down with yoga and in the Jacuzzi. "I haven't seen a physician except to say hello in three years," she smiles. "I feel great emotionally and physically. And I just got my driver's license renewed!"

But surely a woman in her eighties must feel some limitation. "I can do anything any thirty-five-year-old woman can do," declares Frazer. "My philosophy is to always look ahead to tomorrow—to live today—and to learn from yesterday." What of the women or men, for that matter, who panic at reaching forty? "All they need is a little exercise and some love in their lives," she says. "Our bodies are marvelous machines and with a little care and maintenance, they heal themselves."

With her doctor's blessing, Mavis Lindgren, who had been subject to terrible chest colds all her life, started running. She was sixty-two, and though she started very tentatively, she soon worked her way up to five miles a day. In the ten years since she started running Mavis has not had a single cold and has been sick only once—a bout with the flu that lasted for a single day. When she started running, her pulse rate was between 72 and 76. Today it is between 52 and 56—the pulse rate of a person of fine aerobic fitness. In the summer of 1983 Mavis ran the Pike's Peak Marathon eighty-seven minutes faster than she had the previous year. The world record holder for her age group, her time was four hours, twenty-three minutes. Clara Frazer and Lindgren may make exercise sound like a panacea. The truth is that, for most of us, it is.

Just ask that paragon of fitness over sixty, Jack LaLanne. Way back in the fifties, long before Richard Simmons and Jane Fonda, LaLanne, who turned seventy in 1984, was spreading the exercise gospel on his own television show. Three decades and more than 120 health spas later, LaLanne's dimensions are just what they've been for the past half-century: chest, forty-seven inches; biceps, sixteen-and-a-half inches; neck, seventeen inches; waist, twenty-seven-and-a-half inches; hips, thirty-five inches; thighs, twenty-three inches; weight, one hundred and sixty pounds.

LaLanne has performed a remarkable series of birthday feats to promote his nutrition and exercise philosophy. The day he turned forty, he swam the length of the Golden Gate Bridge underwater, wearing 140 pounds of scuba gear. He covered the two miles in forty-five minutes. A red balloon, bobbing on the surface of the bay, marked his location. The next year he swam the two miles from Alcatraz to San Francisco's Fisherman's Wharf. Just to add a little sport, he wore handcuffs. At forty-two, LaLanne set a world record for pushups: 1,033 pumped off on his TV show. It took him twenty-three minutes.

To mark his sixtieth birthday, LaLanne repeated his Alcatraz swim, this time handcuffed *and* shackled at the ankles and towing a 1,000 pound boat. For the Bicentennial, the sixty-two-year-old marvel swam one-and-a-half miles in Long Beach Harbor, handcuffed, shackled and towing thirteen boats (for each of the thirteen colonies) containing seventy-six kids in life jackets. A frog-kicking LaLanne towed the 25,000-pound flotilla for one hour, eighteen minutes and twenty-four seconds. When he finished, his pulse rate was only seventy-six beats compared to sixty, which is a normal rate for someone who is resting. "Strength," he says, "is energy."

As he entered his seventies, LaLanne was pouring his prodigious energies into writing a new series of fitness books, speaking on the lecture circuit and running the marketing campaign for his private-formula food supplements.

Jack's wife Elaine, fifty-nine, is his biggest booster. She works out faithfully, is an ardent golfer and swims every day. Her license plates read EXERCIZ, his REDUCE.

You don't have to look far beyond the avalanche of health,

diet and beauty books, TV exercise programs and the running boom to see that America is in the midst of an exercise revolution. A recent Gallup Poll found that 59 percent of the adult U.S. population regularly engages in some form of physical exercise, compared to the 1961 figure of only 24 percent. Exercise, along with the decrease in smoking, cholesterol and fat intake, is one reason for the sharp decline in heart attack deaths over the past decade. Yet many of us still have not joined the revolution because we cling to myths that persist about exercise. Myths such as

Exercising makes me tired. At the outset of any exercise program, you will be exhausted as your lungs, muscles and circulatory system begin to adjust to the demands being made on them. As your body gets into better shape, you will gain energy and a sense of well-being. The stamina you develop as a result of regular exercise pays added dividends: you tire less easily during the day, but find it easier to relax at night. The reason for this is that by exercising you have been able to "burn off" some of the emotional stress that can lead to irritability and insomnia.

I don't have the time. You've seen "Pumping Iron," and you know in your heart that if you are really going to get into shape, you will have to devote three or four hours a day to sweating off those pounds in a gym. Not true. All you need to set aside is twenty minutes three times a week—*one hour per week*—for a moderate exercise regimen that will, over time, improve your endurance, flexibility, muscle tone and general health.

I'm too old. The fitness movement, on the surface, appears to be a youth-oriented one, judging by magazine covers and television commercials. But regardless of age, any reasonably healthy person can start an exercise program tailored to his or her own fitness level—and millions of over-sixties are doing just that.

I'm not athletic. Many people have never considered themselves jocks and are adamantly uninterested in sports. But jogging, walking, stretching, swimming, bicycling and aerobics are just a few of the excellent forms of exercise that require little athletic ability.

You can start today on a supervised program and add a dimension to your life you never believed possible.

Again, it is essential that you first get your physician's approval. If you have an overweight, sedentary doctor who smokes, we suggest you get a second opinion. If you go to a Y.M.C.A. health club, the trained personnel there will gather detailed information on your health and present physical activities, then recommend a program tailored to your individual needs.

The Aspen Fitness Institute is just one of the many excellent sports medicine and fitness centers that have sprung up around the country. One of the programs the institute recommends was devised by Dr. Covert Bailey. He outlines a new path to health and fitness through nutrition and aerobics, with sports like tennis, skiing and racquetball thrown in for "dessert"—pure fun.

The word "aerobic" comes from the Latin *aero,* for "air." The muscles need oxygen to function, and their need for oxygen increases dramatically when we work them. We can measure how hard a muscle is working by how much oxygen it is burning. Bailey contrasts endurance exercises that fit aerobic definition (running, cross-country skiing, jumping rope, cycling, rowing, swimming) with nonaerobic exercises that either involve relatively short bursts of energy (tennis, downhill skiing, calisthenics, handball, racquetball, sprinting, weight-lifting) or are too low in intensity (golf, bowling).

Dr. Lawrence Morehouse, himself in his seventies, outlines a fitness program that people in reasonably good health can use to improve their performance as workers, athletes, executives, dancers and lovers in a relatively short period of time. Dr. Morehouse invented the bicycle ergometer, which measures the metabolic and cardiovascular response to exertion during stress tests. When the astronauts on the space shuttle orbit the earth, they exercise on a machine he invented, according to a system he devised.

According to Morehouse, your physiological age is extremely sensitive to the amount of use you make of your body. At a calendar age of sixty, you could be functioning like a seventy-year-old owing to a sedentary life-style, or you could be going like a significantly younger person because you are active. Conversely, if you are sixty and functioning as if you were seventy, within months you can be well on your way to functioning like a forty-year-old.

There are, of course, some functions that may have deteriorated with age, such as vision and hearing, that are not going to be restored by increased use (though they can almost always be compensated for by glasses and hearing aids), but most others—especially flexibility, strength and endurance— will respond markedly in a relatively short period of time. This kind of rejuvenation is neither strenuous nor time-consuming. Each day you are slightly more active than you were the day before. Each day you make a slight improvement in the quality of your activity.

Begin by gradually intensifying the ordinary activities of your regular daily life: stand more, bend more, stretch more, walk more. Once you are in touch with the fact that your daily activities can improve your physical performance, you are ready to move into the Success Over Sixty exercise program which can:

1. Provide a safety valve for stress
2. Rid you of unwanted pounds
3. Lower your blood pressure and blood sugar
4. Help alleviate headaches, ulcers, arthritis, insomnia, nervous tension, indigestion, diabetes, heart conditions
5. Replace intramuscular fat with lean muscle, leading to more efficient utilization of calories
6. Increase energy and stamina
7. Lead to more restful sleep
8. Improve appearance, resulting in a positive self-image and outlook in life
9. Lessen the need for drugs, coffee, tea, alcohol, tobacco, sugar
10. Result in more enjoyable sex

Whatever form of exercise you select, be sure to precede each workout with a fifteen-minute warm-up period of stretching exercises and to follow each workout with a fifteen-minute cool-down period. The warm-up is necessary to prevent joint problems and cardiovascular difficulties. It also increases blood flow and hence heightens the oxygen supply to the muscles, helping them to function more efficiently and to stave off injury. Bob Anderson's *Stretching . . . for Everyday Fitness* provides a superbly illustrated guide to precisely the right warm-up exercises for your particular endeavor. Runners, for example, must stretch hamstrings, calves, inner thighs and lower back. Tennis players should do the above, as well as stretch muscles in the neck, shoulders and upper back.

Similar stretching exercises are usually employed during the fifteen-minute cool-down. A gradual tapering off after strenuous exercise is essential, because if you stop abruptly, your blood remains concentrated in your muscles, not your brain. You may become dizzy, or pass out. A sudden stop after a vigorous workout could even impair the circulation to your heart—and trigger a coronary.

If you've never been particularly sports-minded, you may have a difficult time deciding what to do between the warm-up and the cool-down. For purposes of cardiovascular conditioning, you might consider starting off with the fifteen-to-twenty-minute jog-walk regimen developed by Dr. Herbert A. DeVries, director of the exercise laboratory at the University of Southern California's Andrus Gerontology Center. You start out with an equal number of walking and running steps (fifty running steps followed by fifty walking steps, the sequence repeated five times). You do this three times a week, and over a period of ten weeks you gradually increase the ratio of running to walking until you are mostly running. If it becomes too strenuous, you just cut back on the running and increase the walking. The best overall alternative to DeVries' jog-walk regimen is swimming, which utilizes and strengthens the arms, legs, back and abdominal muscles, increases lung capacity, conditions the heart and burns up calories.

Even if you can't pursue a vigorous exercise program, there is plenty you can do in the course of an average day to improve your fitness. Bonnie Pruden, seventy-one-year-old head of the Institute for Physical Fitness and a pioneer in the field, suggests a number of relatively mild activities for the house-bound. Pruden's "Ten-Penny Trick" involves putting ten pennies on the floor, picking up each penny and one-by-one placing each on the highest shelf you have. Then, you reach up for each penny, retrieve it, and place it back on the floor. In addition to stretching the back and shoulders, Pruden's Ten-Penny Trick strengthens the thigh muscles. Or you might try Pruden's "Rock Trick." Keep a two-pound rock by

SUCCESS OVER SIXTY EXERCISE CHART

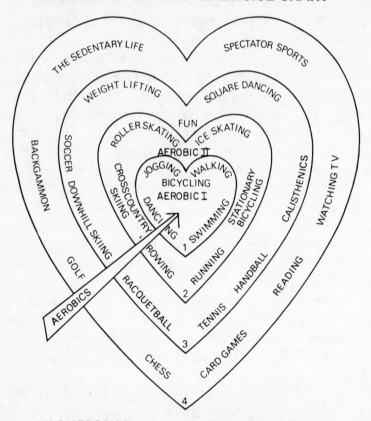

1,2. AEROBICS

Pick your own exercise. The center is best for the over 60's but the second heart of aerobics is just as good. It's your choice —aim for the center and Improve your Heart and Lung Condition.

3. ACTIVE SPORTS

Calisthenics and weight lifting for stretching, flexibility, balance, muscle tone, strength and stamina. Then have fun with your favorite sport—Tennis, Downhill Skiing—whatever.

4. THE SEDENTARY LIFE

Games you can pursue that are enjoyable but have little or no value in a Fitness Program.

Look Better—Feel Better—Do Better

the telephone, and every time you use the phone hold the rock in your free hand and swing it over your head and down to your side. After doing this a dozen times with one hand, switch to the other hand and repeat the process. Of course, these activities are not sufficiently strenuous for cardiac conditioning, but they can do much to tone your body—and to lift your spirits.

Many forward-thinking companies are discovering that paying attention to the fitness of their workers can pay big dividends in keeping those employees healthy and productive into their sixties and beyond.

Xerox has a $3.5 million-dollar fitness and recreation center at its training complex in Virginia. General Foods' health and fitness program extends to 50,000 employees in thirty locations. Pepsico has had a fitness program for more than twenty years. The company's campuslike headquarters in suburban Purchase, New York, has exercise and sports facilities for all employees. Senior executives use an exercise room equipped with jump ropes, exercise bikes, stall bars, a universal gym and an electric treadmill. Encircling the Pepsico complex is a road marked at quarter-mile intervals for cyclists and joggers. A Maxwell House plant in New Jersey, lacking inside space, sends its employees to a nearby Y.M.C.A.

This corporate commitment to fitness comes straight from the top. In a recent survey of more than two hundred CEOs, it was found that 60 percent take part in daily exercise programs of thirty minutes or more, that 66 percent do not smoke (of these, 63 percent used to) and that 70 percent have a complete physical examination each year.

When we first met Lee Iacocca, he was still president of the Ford Motor Company. Then in his mid-fifties, he had just had a paddleball court constructed in his backyard. Now the head of Chrysler Corporation, Iacocca still keeps trim by playing a daily game with his daughters.

David Rockefeller preferred a different daily workout. Right up until the day he stepped down at age sixty-five as head of the Chase Manhattan Bank to pursue his many other interests, Rockefeller reserved a portion of each day for the rowing machine in the company gym. "It clears away the cobwebs," he said. As he enters his seventies, Rockefeller still exercises daily. The message from the people who run America's businesses is clear: even if you've "made it" you won't "keep it" without paying attention to your health.

SEX OVER SIXTY

"Sex," proclaims George Burns, "is fun after eighty, after ninety—and after lunch." At eighty, Bob Hope agrees that sex remains an important part of life. The only catch: "These days I get motion sickness."

In its 1984 report, *Love, Sex and Aging,* the Consumers Union polled more than 4,000 men and women aged fifty to ninety-three and discovered that the majority of respondents —whether married or unmarried, male or female—lead happy and sexually active lives. A large number also reported that the "overall quality" of sex in their lives has improved over time.

In their book, *The Pleasure Bond,* researchers Masters and Johnson established beyond doubt that sexuality does not decline with age so long as a reasonably good state of health is maintained. Moreover, Dr. Masters points out that a certain "mental atrophy" sets in once we opt out of sexual life. Here the old axiom, "Use it or lose it," really does apply.

Still, mature people are often caught in the crossfire of their own guilt and the misguided expectations of the young—particularly their own children. Brought up in an age still fraught with Victorian hangups, many people now over sixty feel, as we observed earlier, that it's time to call it quits in the bedroom. "I don't," one sixty-eight-year-old attorney told us, "want to be thought of as some dirty old man. By the time you get to a certain age, it just isn't dignified."

Dignified? "At the core of these nagging doubts," says Dr. Alex Comfort, "is the fear that somehow we will disappoint our children if we remain sexual beings." After all, most of us resist the notion that our parents ever did something so crass as to have sexual intercourse. Ours, we have managed to convince ourselves, was an immaculate conception. If we find it impossible to picture our parents in the act, that is one thing. But to deny our mothers and fathers—and eventually ourselves—a sexual existence is nothing short of foolish.

"Affection, warmth and sexuality do not have to deteriorate with age and may, in fact, increase," says noted gerontologist Robert N. Butler, author of the Pulitzer-prizewinning *Why Survive? Being Old in America*. "Sex in later life is sex for its own sake: pleasure, release, communication, shared intimacy. Except for older men married to younger women, it is no longer associated with child-bearing and the creation of families," Butler continues. "This freedom can be exhilarating, especially for those who have literally never had the time until now to think about and get to know themselves and each other."

If all this seems a slight departure from the thrust of *Success Over Sixty*—that is, how to embark on new careers and prolong our lives as vital members of our communities—we must stress that sex over sixty is important for many reasons beyond the sheer pleasure of it. As we get older, sex is important because it:

• *Boosts self-image, self-esteem and self-confidence.* If we know that others still find us desirable, we are likely to value ourselves more highly; we feel more attractive, more likeable, more *loveable*. It's hard to beat sex as a source of positive reinforcement.

• *Reduces anxiety.* About losing loved ones, about our own mortality. Sexual closeness provides a unique feeling of security; we are less likely to worry about things when we are physically intimate with someone.

• *Makes us feel vital.* If we function well sexually, our confidence in our bodies is bolstered. Medical authorities agree that an upbeat attitude about life is a potent weapon against age-related illness.

• *Affirms our power over our own lives.* Lovemaking infuses both partners—whatever their age—with a sense of control and authority that the age-old old-age myths are designed to rob us of.

Although he made a smooth transition from working at a New York City law firm to running his own flower shop in Connecticut when he was in his early sixties, Edward Thornton was plunged into a pit of despair upon the death of his wife in 1978. Unable to pull himself out of his depression, Thornton began closing his shop for days at a time while he stayed at home sleeping, or staring vacantly at the TV. Within a year of the time his wife died, Thornton had let his business affairs slide drastically. Bankruptcy seemed imminent.

Thornton now says it wasn't just the grief over his wife's death that almost destroyed him. "It was the feeling," he says, "that love and sex were over for me forever. I thought

I was too old to ever have that kind of life-affirming relationship with another person again." In 1980, at the urging of his friends, Thornton began dating. He also started to take a renewed interest in his business affairs. The flower business was blooming once again by the time Thornton married for the second time in 1983. He was seventy-one, his bride, sixty-three.

More than ever before, you possess the potential for heightening the pleasures of love and sex. Your perceptions are sharper, your appreciation of the preciousness of life keener. And as in all other areas of your life, *experience* counts here, too. "Perhaps only in the later years can life with its various possibilities shape itself into something approximating a human work of art," says Dr. Butler. "And perhaps only in later life, when personality reaches its final stages of development, can lovemaking and sex achieve the fullest possible growth. Sex does not merely exist after sixty; it holds the possibility of becoming greater than it ever was."

Much the same can be said for your general state of physical well-being. No one is denying that there are changes in the body that come with age, *but it is never too late* to halt those changes in their tracks and, in fact, to reverse them. With a little preventive maintenance, i.e., a sensible diet and an appropriate exercise program, you can feel fitter than you have in years. Dr. Ernst Wynder, president of the American Health Foundation, says the goal of every individual should be to "die young as late in life as possible." The likelihood of this happening is really up to you, but one thing is certain: the physical and psychological benefits of a good diet and the right exercise will improve the quality of life—your life—no matter if you are eight or eighty-eight.

10 Healthy Mind

As long as you are curious, you defeat age.
—Burt Lancaster

The coffee has been poured and the cognac served. Promptly at 8:00 P.M., Kathryn Forman's guests sit down, as they have done for more than thirty years, to discuss one of the things in life they love most, books. On this occasion, the dozen men and women (average age, sixty-seven) have gathered in Mrs. Forman's elegant Sands Point, Long Island, home to discuss James Joyce's *Ulysses*. At different times, the subject has been Plato's *Republic,* Dickens's *David Copperfield,* Tolstoy's *War and Peace* and Fielding's *Tom Jones.*

This is one of America's longest running Great Books clubs, formed after self-described "philosopher-at-large" Mortimer J. Adler established the Great Books Foundation at the University of Chicago in 1947. In 1952, the foundation started publishing and selling to the clubs complete sets of the Great Books. Along with thousands of other bookworms across the country, the Sands Point group began getting together every two weeks to talk over the literary masterworks on their carefully selected reading list.

Mrs. Forman, now seventy-seven, has taken the Great Books' nine-hour leadership training course so that she can ask the kinds of Socratic questions that best stimulate discussion. Helen Williams, another charter member of the group, takes over when poetry is discussed, while Ernest Graf, head of Ben Kahn furs in New York, leads the group when talk turns to the existentialists. "When you're in business," says Graf, who joined the Sands Point group not long after its inception, "this kind of mental exercise is important. It's also a discipline. Where else would I read Aristotle or Spinoza or Maimonides? It gives you substance."

Abel Just, a retired lawyer in his seventies, is typical of his fellow group members in his exuberance. "*Ulysses* abounds with religious and literary allusions," says Just, "and every time I find one I get a thrill of discovery." Such enthusiasm is doubly appreciated by Silvia Kaye, an English professor at Nassau Community College who joined the Great Books club recently. "The big difference between my literature classes and this," she said, "is that not only has everyone read the assignment but they *wanted* to read the assignment." For the group's older members, this may be the first time in their lives that they have actually had the time and the opportunity to fully indulge their passion for reading. Helen Williams bought her copy of *Ulysses* in 1934—"and," she beams, "I finally finished it last month!"

Kathryn Forman's Great Books club offers incontrovertible proof that you're never too old to learn. So do the third-century B.C. Roman orator Cato the Elder and the very-much-alive-and-kicking journalist I. F. Stone, both of whom began studying ancient Greek in their eighties.

"The brain is the one organ we depend on to last," said gerontologist Edgar J. Munter. "Even at eighty your brain can learn at the speed of a thirteen-year-old's—and that's damn fast!" Indeed, recent studies belie the old saw that you "can't teach an old dog new tricks." Heredity, environment and early conditioning certainly affect our capacity to learn in our fifties, sixties, and beyond. But there is evidence that by continuing to use our senses, we keep them sharp. In many cases, the ability to reason has been shown actually to *increase* with age.

Unfortunately, the individual who believes that his brain has atrophied because he has reached a certain age turns that myth into a self-fulfilling prophecy. He doesn't believe he is capable of learning anymore, so he doesn't try.

This is not a problem for you. After all, you probably wouldn't be reading this book if you weren't open to new ideas. And like the members of the Sands Point Great Books club, you are doubtless learning for the pure joy of it. Your numbers are growing. Today, one out of every eight adults—many fifty-five or older—is participating in some sort of adult education. Many are women who, after raising their children, have returned to college for that degree that will qualify them for the career they long ago put on hold (enrollments among women in the fifty-and-over age group went up 30 percent during the past five years). There is also the retired attorney who went back to school to pursue a degree in archeology, a former executive who at sixty-six earned his MBA and then went to work as a consultant to shipping firms, a manufacturer who returned to his alma mater to earn his master's degree in economics, a research assistant for a publishing company who earned a degree in theology at sixty and a secretary who, after thirty-five years with the same firm, enrolled in college and earned a bachelor's degree in art history.

Whether they are motivated by the practical desire to educate themselves for a second career or by the exciting realization that they can finally study the things they never had time for when they were younger, the over-sixties are demanding new learning options. And they are getting them. *Learning exchanges,* for example, are springing up all over the country for the express purpose of bringing like-minded people together. These exchanges offer instruction in everything from TV repair to Russian literature. The faculty of a typical learning exchange is usually comprised of knowledge-able community volunteers, and although no formal teaching credentials are required, the caliber of the instructors is often first-rate. Your local bank president, for instance, may sign up with a learning exchange to teach a course on personal finance, or the city editor of your local newspaper teach a journalism class. "Learning exchanges and community infor-mation networks can lead beyond promoting individual growth," says Ron Gross, author of the bestselling books, *The Lifelong Learner* and *The Independent Scholar*. "Groups can take form out of shared interests discovered through the exchange, often focused on problems and issues facing a com-munity or a certain group within the community. Such dia-logues can, in turn, lead to coalition-building to effect social change."

A new breed of professional in the education field—the *educational broker*—has evolved in recent years to link up the individual with the right program. A good example is the Regional Learning Service of Central New York, a voluntary nonprofit organization that assists adults looking for a degree, training for a second career or just studying for the fun of it. At the Regional Learning Service, counselors provide solid advice on establishing goals and locating and pursuing the right program. Another excellent regional clearinghouse for information about educational opportunities is the Educa-tional Information and Referral Service in Atlanta.

Not everyone with responsibilities and daily demands can schedule formal adult education or college courses for contin-uing lifelong learning, but all of us have the time to choose for ourselves what we want to learn through *independent study*. Ron Gross points out that new frontiers in the sciences and the humanities were first explored by "amateurs" like Charles Darwin and Sigmund Freud, and he praises the inde-

pendent scholar for whom "learning is a joy, not a job."
People like:

• Retired executive Joseph F. Burke of Staten Island, New
York. Burke devotes several hours a day to his pioneering
research on diatoms—unicellular plants that are found
throughout the world's ocean beds.
• Esther Kelly Watson, who credits her "hankering for history" with keeping her from "living in my own immediate
past." At eighty-four, she published a history of the West-
minster Presbyterian Church, a book honored as a significant
addition to the history of her native city of Portland, Oregon.
• Norman Macbeth, a retired lawyer and semi-invalid who,
in an idle moment, picked up a volume of essays commemo-
rating the centennial of Darwin's *The Origin of Species.*
"That was the beginning of my biological studies," he recalls.
In the next three years, he read widely on the subject of
evolution. As a result, Macbeth noticed some startling contra-
dictions between what everyone understood biologists to believe about evolution and what leading experts actually said.
At this point, his curiosity was sufficiently piqued so that he
immersed himself in all the available scientific literature. He
then wrote a book called *Darwin Retired,* arguing that classi-
cal Darwinism is dead. The book was praised by leading scientists and scholars, including British historian Sir Karl
Popper and Harvard professor of biology Ernst Mayr.

Unencumbered by conventional notions, the amateur—
particularly the older amateur—is free to draw on his broad
experience, observations and imagination. What came first,
of course, was curiosity. As one noted author and editor in
his mid-sixties told us, "The only way to keep ahead of the
game is to stay a little bit naive."

For the over-sixty learner, there are numerous alternatives
to be found between the "amateur" and formal approaches

to education. To begin with, more and more colleges and universities are allowing you to audit classes at little or no cost, to take short-term "minicourses," to attend classes on weekends or in the evenings. In addition, the Adult Education Association lists in its pamphlet more than 3,500 agencies—libraries, schools, churches, arts centers, learning groups, museums, and so on—that offer programs specifically geared for students over fifty. Whether you just want to take some French classes to enhance your upcoming vacation, or study for your Ph.D. so you can hang out your shingle, there is a whole stimulating world of learning opportunities out there waiting for you.

Even if you are not seeking credit toward a degree, you may wish to check out the opportunities offered by your local college. Call the campus public affairs office and ask for a schedule of activities. Why not attend one or more of the lectures, plays, conferences, concerts and exhibits that appeal to you? There you will certainly meet lifelong learners like yourself.

You might also be interested in programs offered by the schools of continuing education operated by many colleges. Fees for these schools are usually a fraction of those charged for credit courses. And since the adjunct faculties are often business, professional and community leaders, the experience constitutes what Ronald Gross calls "the lifelong learner's best academic buy."

Many of these same institutions offer excellent correspondence courses. This is a particularly inexpensive way to learn (usually under $20 per credit hour), and you can make your own study hours. Generally, you are assigned twenty-five lessons involving one or more textbooks. A brief quiz is sent along after each lesson, graded by the instructor and returned to you within a week. There is a final exam, and, if you are fortunate, you will get feedback from the individual who marks it. Remember, the quality of correspondence courses varies widely, so take time to shop around.

You might also be interested in looking into one of the accredited private correspondence schools, some of which offer better designed, more sophisticated (hence costlier) mail order curricula than the unaccredited programs. The best source for private correspondence schools is the National Home Study Council, 1601 18th Street, N.W., Washington, D.C. 20009.

Many correspondence courses include taped cassettes. You need not, however, enroll in a correspondence course to take full advantage of the cassette curriculum. The best source for this is the Center for Cassette Studies (University Microfilms, 300 North Zeeb Road, Ann Arbor, Michigan 48106). The center's free catalogue lists thousands of tapes available on twenty-three subjects.

The Tape Rental Library, Inc., P.O. Box 2107, South Vineland, New Jersey 08360, will rent you tapes on every business endeavor from real estate to advertising and insurance. Taped management seminars are another staple of the rental library, which, for an annual fee of $95, allows you to borrow two tapes at a time. Cassettes offer a particularly convenient and effective way to study that foreign language you never had time for when you were younger—and to practice your pronunciation in, as they say, the privacy of your own home.

In Chapter 6, we talked about the importance of networking in determining and pursuing the correct career for you. You can also plug into an intellectual network, a switchboard that connects people (from less than a dozen to thousands) who share your interest in a particular topic or issue such as chess, gardening or the nuclear freeze.

A simple way to connect with one of these networks is to subscribe to a periodical that covers your particular area of interest. If an article intrigues you, write and ask the author to steer you to other articles and books on the topic. More often than not, he or she will be pleased to oblige. A retired advertising sales executive, for example, became interested in solar energy, and began subscribing to the newsletter *Alternate Sources of Energy*. He wrote to one of the newsletter's contributors, who then supplied him with further information on workshops, seminars and source materials. While many of these newsletters have tiny readerships and are highly idiosyncratic (*Worm-Runners Digest* is one good example), a number have achieved considerable distinction. Among them: Henry Geiger's *Manas,* which is filled with reflective essays on sociology, and I. F. Stone's radical political *Weekly*.

One clear advantage of these networks is that you can plug in without ever leaving home. Many over-sixties, however, want to share personally the adventure with their fellow life-long learners. One way is to join the millions who have banded together to form learning groups. Thousands of such informal groups exist in the form of women's associations, investors' clubs, singles' clubs, encounter groups, hobby groups and the like. If you cannot find the group that fits your particular need, launch one of your own. For instance, if you want to start your own investment club, Ronald Gross suggests you write to the National Association of Investment Clubs, P.O. Box 220, Royal Oak, Michigan 48068, which will provide you with free brochures and publications. So will any financial advisory service or brokerage house you write to directly. You can locate them merely by looking through the financial pages of your local newspaper.

Structuring your own learning group is usually a relatively simple process. Give your group a straightforward name and then look for members among your friends and neighbors. If you need or want to look further, post notices on billboards, or get an article about your group published in the local paper. You'll probably start out meeting at members' homes and should probably select someone to serve as chairman, though the looser the structure and the more relaxed the atmosphere the better. Someone should also be responsible for taking notes during each session, and having them typed up and distributed to the members. A brief rundown of the topics discussed and references used will prove invaluable in giving the group direction.

"Society must acknowledge the principle," says Mortimer Adler, "that every human being throughout his life should aspire to become an educated person." That pursuit of knowledge can be fun. You may want to consider one of the "Back-to-College Vacations for Grownups" being offered by such colleges as Stanford, Harvard, Brown, Cornell, and the universities of California, Michigan, Oregon and Oklahoma. These programs offer both alumni and new students the chance to combine education with tennis, golf, music, swimming and dance. The tuition for these seven-day, seven-night "vacation colleges" is comparatively low, and you usually get an air-conditioned room (double occupancy) in a college dormitory, linen service, use of all the school's recreation facilities, welcoming parties, field trips and courses often taught by leading authors, scientists and educators.

Educational cruises and tours have become increasingly popular in recent years. For instance, the National Audubon Society, the Smithsonian Institution and the National Geographic Society all sponsor frequent guided trips for their members, ranging from one-day excursions to wildlife sanctuaries to transcontinental expeditions.

Boston-based Elderhostel, Inc. is a nonprofit organization that conducts overseas study programs specifically designed for women and men over sixty. Last year, 3,665 "elderhostelers" studied abroad. Of these, 90 percent were retired and most were seasoned travelers. One-quarter were teachers, and the rest former librarians, doctors, lawyers, social workers, bankers and corporate managers. The overseas program is an extension of Elderhostel's domestic program, which places an estimated 70,000 over-sixties for one to three weeks of intensive study at schools and colleges throughout the United States and Canada.

Elderhostel's overseas program costs around $700 for air-fare, ground travel, and tuition, room and board for a week. For this $700, the elderhosteler can study Thomas Hardy in the author's native Dorset or prowl the Roman ruins. Irene Goodman, a retired executive with the New York City Housing Authority, last year at seventy-one traveled to France to study French history. A retired Uniroyal executive interested in world affairs got a firsthand glimpse of some of Scandinavia's pressing social and political problems, while a retired physician went to Germany to immerse himself in Goethe. This year, Israel has been added to the list of countries where elderhostelers will be able to travel. Although Elderhostel does not advertise, it receives 100,000 unsolicited requests for catalogues each year.

Of course, there are plenty of exciting possibilities for the life-long learner right on our home turf. Fairhaven College, in Bellingham, Washington, for example, offers a program called "Bridging the Gap Between Generations" to encourage inter-mingling of all age groups on campus, while at New York's Syracuse University a dormitory is connected to a retirement community so the two groups can get to know one another and the young can draw on the experience of their elders.

In Bucks County, Pennsylvania, the five hundred students at the coeducational George School draw on the wisdom and expertise of a roughly equal number of retirees who live in nearby Pennswood Village. The average age of a Pennswood resident is seventy-nine, and among the retirement community's population are engineers, doctors, bankers, lawyers, educators and civil servants. Many say they were attracted to Pennswood because of its academic setting—and because it gave them the opportunity to continue to learn while sharing their experience with students at the George School.

Robert Hilkert, a retired first vice-president of the Federal Reserve Bank in Philadelphia, moved to Pennswood because it was "a forward-looking place, not an old folks' home." Hilbert, who plays the cello with the George School orchestra, chairs the Pennswood committee that plans joint activities with the school. The committee arranged a dinner party, for example, in which six prelaw students were paired with six retired lawyers, several of whom had been partners in some of the biggest firms in the country. Many students are matched on the basis of common interests with Pennswood residents. Mark Bigelow, sixteen, was matched with Bertha Greenbaum, seventy-three, because they shared an interest in politics and current affairs. Both say they owe much of their present understanding of the world to one another.

There are no limits to your capacity to learn, to grow. Education is not something that starts at age five and stops when you finish school. It need not happen in a lecture hall or a classroom. "The lifelong learner," explains Ron Gross, "is liberated from these superstitions about education—and therefore free to pursue his or her growth in an infinite variety of ways." Among the towering minds who fully appreciated this fact were longshoreman philosopher Eric Hoffer, anthropologist Richard Leakey, architect and visionary Buckminster Fuller, Polaroid founder Edwin Land and Winston Churchill, none of whom earned a university degree, yet all of whom soaked up knowledge long after achieving preeminence in their chosen fields. Marin and Indian Valley College in Kentfield, California, boasts an emeritus college with a slogan that speaks to the wishes and desires of all Success Over Sixty candidates: "Knowledge, Wisdom, and Experience cannot be Retired; Dynamic Learning and Creative Leisure can be Lifelong Adventures."

11 *Epilogue*

You stand on the threshold. Ahead stretch twenty years or more of opportunity and challenge—a time when you will be free to release the powers of your mind and spirit, and in so doing discover a fresh sense of purpose and fulfillment.

The possibilities are limitless. "Human beings," says Dr. Robert Butler, "need the freedom to invent and reinvent themselves a number of times throughout their lives. By loosening up we enlarge the value of the gift of life." You will have to take control of your life, and that's all right too; just because you've blown out a certain number of candles on the cake, doesn't mean you should stop being the master of your own destiny. That "freedom to reinvent yourself" can only be won through a conscious decision.

The elements necessary for achieving Success Over Sixty are the same ones required for success at any age: change, curiosity, communication, confidence and commitment. Whether or not you ever had the time to stop and think about it, the Five Cs were what propelled you through life. And they will continue to do so. Rather than retire, you will simply chart a new course and *refire* those engines that have served you so well.

Risk is an inevitable part of this journey. But we are no strangers to it; daily we risk our resources, our energies, and our pride. We face the added risks involved in starting out again because we are not about to sit back and let events overtake us.

We have a powerful ally in those corporations that are recognizing our right to remain in the mainstream for as long as we choose. The Success Over Sixty Top Ten companies are not only abolishing mandatory retirement altogether, they are devising comprehensive preretirement counseling programs and pioneering such exciting new policies as phased and "rehearsal" retirement, part-time work for employees in their sixties, seventies and eighties, rehiring retirees full-time, retraining senior employees for transfer to more challenging jobs within the corporation, paying tuition costs for those approaching retirement age to launch them on second careers, and prohibiting age-related discrimination against job-seekers.

Scores of corporations are following suit in changing the rules, but business alone cannot solve the broader social problem. We must not be satisfied until we have obliterated the ageist myths. Unproductive? Sexless? Cranky, difficult, forgetful? The job of disabusing everyone of these onerous stereotypes is the responsibility of each of us.

So, too, is the responsibility for bringing about real change in our lives. We all possess the power to be creative, and we can harness that power. Success Over Sixty has shown you how to find that precious time in your schedule for creative thinking by using our Creative Living chart in Chapter 5, and then how to give birth to new ideas through such techniques as brainstorming, intellectual "prospecting" and networking.

Once you have mastered the art of creative thinking, you will have some hard decisions to make about where to go from here with your life. Chapter 6, *Making the Most of What You*

Already Know: Matching Experience with a New Career,
helps illuminate the way. The Party Exercise and Transferable Skills Chart are just two of the tools offered in Chapter 6
for helping you determine what jobs you are best suited to
and best qualified for. Whether you choose to embark on a
second career or stick with the career you are in, Success
Over Sixty has told you how to make the best use of your
experience and contacts, how to prepare a resumé, and how
to handle an interview so that you will land the position you
want.

If you want to run your own business, Success Over Sixty
provides the first comprehensive program designed for the
over-sixty entrepreneur by a highly successful entrepreneur
over sixty. For the first time, here is a comprehensive rundown of the most potentially profitable opportunities for the
independent businessperson in your age group, as well as inside information essential to your making it as your own boss.

In its own way, nothing is more satisfying than volunteer
work. Although the need for your time, skill and compassion
has never been greater, you may have hesitated because you
were not certain where to go to offer your services. *Success
Over Sixty*'s "Sharing Over Sixty" section points you toward
those areas where you can do the most good and can reap
immense personal rewards in the process.

After launching that second (or third or fourth) career, you
owe it to yourself to take care of yourself. That means paying
particularly close attention to your diet, and keeping that
body in shape through a regular program of exercise. After
all, it's got to serve you well for many years to come.

Just as you have chosen to be a part of the fitness revolution, you may also want to join the revolution in adult education. Certainly, there have never been more choices available
to the lifelong learner. You may wish to return to college,
become one of Ron Gross's "independent scholars," join a

learning group, or take off on one of the many "learning vacations" now being offered. Learning Exchanges and educational brokers have sprung up around the country to help you sort out all the options. Drawing on what you have learned here, you will achieve the balance in life necessary for Success Over Sixty—the right proportion of work, fitness, leisure, education. And sex!

Politically, you are perhaps the single most important group in the nation; people over fifty-five cast more votes than any other segment of the population. You are also emerging as a potent force in the marketplace, and that is only logical. After all, today there are more consumers your age than there are teenagers. There is strength in numbers, but the ultimate responsibility for Success Over Sixty rests with the individual. You have made the very personal choice to be liberated from conventional retirement—a life-style that might be right for others, but not challenging or rewarding enough for you. It is a choice you have made gladly, for you know now that all that has gone before pales in comparison to the adventure that lies ahead.

SOURCES OVER SIXTY

CONTENTS

The Success Over Sixty Institute

Box 3095
Aspen, CO 81611

Career Information

The National Executive Service Corps
622 Third Avenue
New York, NY 10017

The International Executive Service Corps
622 Third Avenue
New York, NY 10017

Mature Temps (14 offices nationwide)
1750 K Street, N.W.
Washington, DC 20006

New Career Opportunities, Inc.
625 North Maryland Avenue
Room 207
Glendale, CA 91206

Second Careers Program
611 South Oxford Street
Los Angeles, CA 90005

Work in America Institute
700 White Plains Road
Scarsdale, NY 10583

Help for Entrepreneurs

GENERAL

Small Business Administration
1441 L Street, N.W.
Washington, DC 20416

The Center for Entrepreneurial Management
311 Main Street
Worcester, MA 01608

CREDIT INFORMATION

The National Credit Union Administration
1776 Sixth Street, N.W.
Washington, DC 20006

SCORE
Small Business Administration
1441 L Street, N.W.
Washington, DC 20416

EDUCATION

Colleges with entrepreneurial and free enterprise chairs and
programs:

American International College, Springfield, MA
Appalachian State University, Boone, NC
Augusta College, Augusta, GA
Babson Institute, Babson Park, MA
Baylor University, Waco, TX
Birmingham Southern College, Birmingham, AL
Brescia College, Owensboro, KY
John Carroll University, Cleveland, OH
Georgia State University, Atlanta, GA
Harding College, Searcy, AK
Kent State University, Kent, OH
Lambuth College, Jackson, TN
Loyola University, Chicago, IL
North Georgia College, Dahlonega, GA
Northeast Louisiana State College, Monroe, LA
Ohio State University, Columbus, OH
George Peabody College, Nashville, TN
Southwest Baptist College, Bolivar, MO
Texas A & M University, College Station, TX
Texas Christian University, Fort Worth, TX
University of Akron, Akron, OH
University of Indiana, Bloomington, IA
University of Oklahoma, Norman, OK
University of Tennessee, Chattanooga, TN

University of Texas, Austin, TX
University of Wisconsin, Madison, WN
Washington University, St. Louis, MO
Wharton School, University of Pennsylvania, Philadelphia, PA
Wichita State University, Wichita, KA

SEMINARS

The Country Business Brokers
225 Main Street
Brattleboro, VT 05301

The Entrepreneurship Institute
90 East Wilson Bridge Road
Suite 247
Worthington, OH 43085

Marshall Thurber Enterprises
1700 Montgomery
Suite 230
San Francisco, CA 94111

LEGAL ASSISTANCE

American Bar Association
1155 East 60th Street
Chicago, IL 60637

PERIODICALS

The Business Owner
50 Jericho Turnpike
Jericho, NY 11758

Venture Magazine
35 West 45th Street
New York, NY 10037

Entrepreneur Magazine
631 Wilshire Boulevard
Santa Monica, CA 90401

PATENTS AND TRADEMARKS

Patent and Copyright Information
Copyright Office
101 Independence Avenue, S.E.
Room 401
Washington, DC 20559

HOW TO GET A PATENT BOOKLET

Consumer Information Center
Department 126E
Pueblo, CO 81009

The United States Trademark Association
6 East 45th Street
New York, NY 10017

TAX INFORMATION

Tax Guide to Small Businesses
I.R.S. Publication 334
The U.S. Printing Office
North Capitol and H Streets
Washington, DC 20401

WOMEN ENTREPRENEURS

Advocates for Women
414 Mason Street
San Francisco, CA 94102

American Women's Economic Development Corp.
(AWED)
1270 Avenue of the Americas
New York, NY 10020

National Association of Women Business Owners
500 N. Michigan—Suite 1400
Chicago, IL 60611

A List of Profitable Businesses

Here is a list of recommended businesses for over-sixties, courtesy of the American Entrepreneurs Association:

ANIMAL-ORIENTED BUSINESSES

Pet shop
Pet hotel and grooming service
Aquarium and tropical fish store

APPAREL BUSINESSES

Costume jewelry and earring shop
Women's apparel shop
Men's apparel shop
Children's apparel shop
Shoe store
Consignment used clothing store

AUTOMOTIVE BUSINESSES

Thirty-minute tune-up shop
Do-it-yourself auto repair shop
Muffler shop
Auto parking service
Auto painting shop
Self-service gas station
Car wash
Vinyl repair service
Rent-a-used-car agency
Auto parts store
Sheepskin seat-cover shop

CRAFT BUSINESSES

Art show promoting
Custom rug-making
Hot tub manufacturing and sales
Handicrafts co-op gallery

Candle shop
Do-it-yourself framing shop
Balloon bouquet service

EDUCATION-ORIENTED BUSINESSES

Bartender/waitress trade school
Teacher's agency
Home tutoring service

SERVICES TO THE HOME

Window-washing service
Tool and equipment rental service
Furniture stripping service
Carpet cleaning service
Kitchen cabinet facelifting
Maid service
Pay-TV service
Lawn care service
Firewood business
Food and party catering service
Wallpapering service
Porcelain refinishing service

FAST FOOD BUSINESSES

Pizzeria
Mobile restaurant/sandwich truck
Hot dog/hamburger stand
Frozen yogurt shop
Chocolate chip cookie shop
Donut shop
Pasta shops

HOME-BASED BUSINESSES

Mail-order business
Flea market and swap meet promoting
Import and export

HOME FURNISHINGS

Furniture store
Bedding store
Paint and wallpaper store
Furniture rental store
Oriental rug store and auction house
Waterbed store
Consignment used furniture store

ENERGY-RELATED BUSINESSES

Energy-loss prevention business
Insulation contracting business
Used paper collection and recycling
Solar sales and installation service

MISCELLANEOUS RETAIL BUSINESSES

Plant shop
Antiques business
Computer store
Gift shop/boutique
Pipe shop
Discount fabric shop
Gourmet cookware shop
Flower shop
Phone store
Bridal shop
Optical shop
Religious gift shop

EMPLOYMENT SERVICES

Employment agency
Temporary help service
Executive recruiting service

MISCELLANEOUS SERVICE BUSINESSES

Dry-cleaning shop
Miniwarehouse
Day-care center
Digital watch-repair service
Private mailbox service
Security patrol service
Coin laundry
Locksmith shop

PERSONAL SERVICES

Roommate-finding service
Cosmetics shop
Family hair salon
Sun-tanning center
Dating service

PHOTOGRAPHY-ORIENTED BUSINESSES

Antique photo shop
Photocopy shop
Videotaping service
One-hour photo-processing lab

RECREATION AND ENTERTAINMENT BUSINESSES

Pinball and electronic game arcade
Hobby shop
Travel agency
Video store/videocassette rentals

RETAIL FOOD AND SPIRITS

Cheese, wine and gourmet food shop
Liquor store
Bake shop
Health food store

Convenience food store
Candy store
Coffee and tea shop

SELF-IMPROVEMENT BUSINESSES

Smoke-enders clinic
Weight control clinic
Physical fitness center
Aerobic dance studio

SERVICES TO BUSINESSES

Instant print shop
Secretarial service
Telephone-answering service
Collection agency
Advertising agency
Limousine service
Coupon mailer service
Typesetting service
Financial broker

STREET VENDING BUSINESSES

Balloon vending
Flower vending
Popcorn vending
Ice cream vending
Hot dog vending

SPORTS BUSINESSES

Ski shop
Tennis and racquetball club
Athletic shoe store
Bicycle shop
Roller skate rental shop
Roller skating rink and skateboard park
Windsurfing equipment shop

Backpacking shop
Moped shop

UNUSUAL BUSINESSES

Contest promoting
Seminar promoting
Burglar alarm sales
Christmas ornament shop
Christmas tree lot
Safe deposit box rental center
Sunken golf ball recovery

Franchises

FRANCHISE LISTINGS

The Franchise Annual
Info Press Inc.
736 Center Street
Lewiston, NY 14902

Directory of Franchising Organizations
Pilot Industries
103 Cooper Street
New York, NY 11702

FRANCHISE OPPORTUNITIES (EXAMPLES)

(Where figures are available, they are estimates)

ACCOUNTING AND TAX SERVICES

Axion Tax and Accounting Service
6575 East 22nd Street
Tucson, AZ 85710

Binex Automated Business Systems, Inc.
3120 "O" Street
Sacramento, CA 95816
(an estimated investment of $8,500)

Econotax, Inc.
1211 Ellis Avenue
Jackson, MI 39203
(an estimated investment of $10,000–$12,000)

H & R Block, Inc.
4410 Main Street
Kansas City, MO 64111
(refundable deposit: $300–$500)

Tax Man, Inc.
639 Massachusetts Avenue
Cambridge, MA 02139
(estimated investment: $5,000)

ADVERTISING

American Advertising Distributors
234 South Extension Road
Mesa, AZ 85202
(estimated investment: $20,000–$50,000)

Graphics One, Inc.
3220 South Susan Street
Santa Ana, CA 92704
(estimated investment: $15,000–$25,000)

Trimark
184 Quigley Boulevard
New Castle, DE 19720
(co-op direct mail ad service—estimated investment: $15,000)

AUTOMOTIVE SERVICES AND PRODUCTS

AAMCO Automatic Transmissions, Inc.
408 East Fourth Street
Bridgeport, PA 19405
(estimated investment: $35,000)

Lee Myles Transmission Service
59–24 Maurice Avenue
Maspeth, NY 11378

Maico Products, Inc.
361 Fairview Avenue
Barberton, OH 44203
(estimated investment: $4,000–$5,000)

Midas International Corp.
222 South Riverside Plaza
Chicago, IL 44203
(need $120,000 plus working capital)

National Auto Service Centers
1605 South Missouri Avenue
Clearwater, FL 33516
(estimated investment: $45,000)

Perma Shine, Inc.
1380 Speers Road
Oakville, Ontario
Canada
(estimated investment: $12,500)

Uniroyal Tire
1230 Avenue of the Americas
New York, NY 10020
(estimated investment: $7,500 minimum)

Ziebart Auto Truck Rustproofing
1290 East Maple Road
Troy, MI 48084
(estimated investment: $45,000–$55,000)

AUTO RENTALS

Airways Rent-A-Car Systems, Inc.
433 Airport Boulevard
Burlingame, CA 94010

Budget Rent-A-Car Corporation of America
35 East Wacker Drive
Chicago, IL 60601

Econo-Car International, Inc.
300 Sevilla Avenue
Coral Gables, FL 33134

Rent-A-Wreck
10889 Wilshire Boulevard
Los Angeles, CA 90024
(estimated investment: $50,000 minimum)

Thrifty Rent-A-Car System
2400 North Sheridan Road
Tulsa, OK 74115

BEAUTY SALONS AND COSMETICS

Cut and Curl
125 South Service Road
(L.I. Expressway)
Jericho, NY 17753
(estimated investment: $50,000 and up)

Great Expectations
125 South Service Road
(L.I. Expressway)
Jericho, NY 11753
(estimated investment: $6,000 and up)

Vivian Woodard Cosmetics
14621 Titus Street
Panorama City, CA 91402

BUILDING SERVICES AND PRODUCTS

Cradle Drain Corp.
2200 West Harper
Poplar Bluff, MO 63901

Crain Chemical Co., Inc.
2630 Andjon Street
Dallas, TX 75220

Crossland Laboratories, Inc.
10009 East Toledo Road
Blissfield, MI 49228

Independent Home Builders of America, Inc.
302 West 5400 South
Salt Lake City, UT 84107
(estimated investment: $10,000 minimum)

Timber Lodge, Inc.
1309 Swift Avenue
North Kansas City, MO 64116

Whirl-Spa Inc.
5320 N.E. 10th Terrace
Fort Lauderdale, FL 33309
(estimated investment: $5,000 minimum)

BUSINESS SERVICES

American Dynamics Corp.
Box 11
Cathedral Station
New York, NY 10025
(estimated investment: $350–$1,000)

Business Consultants of America
222 Munson Road
Wolcott, CT 06716
(estimated investment: $15,500)

Business Data Services, Inc.
Post Office Box 16685
Jackson, MI 39216
(estimated investment: $19,500)

Commercial Services Co.
2699 Lee Road
Winter Park, FL 32789
(estimated investment: $18,000)

Creative Capital Corp.
6922 Hollywood Boulevard
Hollywood, CA 90028
(estimated investment: $18,000)

Corporate Finance Associates
22 Perimeter Park Drive
Atlanta, GA 30341
(estimated investment: $25,000)

J.P. Dolan Associates, Inc.
Post Office Box 125
Glenolden, PA 19036
(estimated investment: $15,000)

Exchange Enterprises International
222 South Mill Avenue
Tempe, AZ 85281
(estimated investment: $35,000)

General Business Services, Inc.
51 Monroe Street
Rockville, MD 20850
(estimated investment: $21,500)

Law Research Service, Inc.
Post Office Box 125
Scarsdale, NY 10583

Liberty Leasing Company, Inc.
221 North LaSalle Street
Chicago, IL 60601

Marcoin Business Management Services
1924 Cliff Valley Way, N.E.
Atlanta, GA 30329
(estimated investment: $20,000–$25,000)

Medipower
Division of the Mackenzie Corp.
Post Office Box 613
Bellaire, TX 77401
(estimated investment: $1,000)

Simplified Business Services, Inc.
100 Presidential Boulevard
Bala Cynwyd, PA 19004
(estimated investment: under $2,500)

Small Business Advisors, Inc.–Whitehall Systems
1437A Broadway
Hewlett, NY 11557
(estimated investment: $14,500)

Typing Tigers
Post Office Box 613
Bellaire, TX 77401

Western Appraisers
Division of West/App Inc.
Post Office Box 851
Fair Oaks, CA 95628
(estimated investment: $15,000)

CANDY STORES

Calico Cottage Candies, Inc.
393 Sagamore Avenue
Mineola, NY 11501

Corn Cabin Co.
Box 1209
Carmel, CA 93921

Karmelkorn Shoppes, Inc.
101 31st Avenue
Rock Island, IL 61201

Lone Star Candy Manufacturing Company of Texas, Inc.
2227 North Main Street
Forth Worth, TX 76106
(estimated investment: $7,500 and up)

CARPET AND UPHOLSTERY CLEANING

Carpet-Genie Systems, Inc.
Post Office Box 724144
Atlanta, GA 30339
(estimated investment: $15,500)

Duraclean International
2151 Waukegan Road
Deerfield, IL 60015
(estimated investment: $5,500)

Fiber Care Corporation of America
4542 Roger B. Chaffee Drive
Grand Rapids, MI 49508
(estimated investment: $20,000–$30,000)

Servicemaster Industries, Inc.
2300 Warrenville Road
Downers Grove, IL 60515
(estimated investment: $14,500)

Steamatic, Inc.
1601 109th Street
Grand Prairie, TX 75050
(estimated investment: $9,000–$35,000)

CAR WASHES

Automation Equipment, Inc.
Post Office Box 3208
Tulsa, OK 74101
(estimated investment: $1,500–$50,000)

Cook Machinery Co., Inc.
4301 South Fitzhugh Avenue
Dallas, TX 75226
(estimated investment: $10,000–$20,000)

E.P.I., Inc.
Box 543
Longboat Key, FL 33548
(estimated investment: $40,000)

Hydro-Sonic Systems, Inc.
5136 Richmond Road
Bedford Heights, OH 44146

Jiffiwash, Inc.
Post Office Box 2489

San Francisco, CA 94126
(estimated investment: $5,000–$20,000)

Sherman Car Wash Equipment Co.
600 West Broad Street
Palmyra, NJ 08065

CLEANING SERVICES

Americlean National Service Corp.
19 Hemlock Road
Boxford, MA 01921
(estimated investment: $3,000–$8,000)

General Sewer Service
Post Office Box 83
Iselin, NJ 08830
(estimated investment: $12,500)

The Maids International
5015 Underwood Avenue
Omaha, NB 68132
(estimated investment: $15,000)

Master-Kleen—Dynamic Machinery Corp.
12350 South Belcher Road
Largo, FL 33543
(estimated investment: $6,000)

Power Vac, Inc.
500 Graves Boulevard
Salina, KS 67401
(estimated investment: $30,000)

Servicemaster Industries, Inc.
2300 Warrensville Road
Downers Grove, IL 60515
(estimated investment: $14,000)

Servpro Industries, Inc.
11357 Pyrites Way
Post Office Box 5001

Rancho Cordova, CA 95670
(estimated investment: $33,000)

CREDIT AND COLLECTION

Audit Controls, Inc.
87 N.E. 44th Street
Fort Lauderdale, FL 33334
(estimated investment: $150 for collection letter service/$2,500
  for establishing agency)

Credit Service International, Inc.
2025 Canal Street
New Orleans, LA 70112
(estimated investment: $2,850)

Dixon Commercial Investigators, Inc.
736 Center Street
Lewiston, NY 14092
(estimated investment: $5,000)

DONUT SHOPS

Dunkin' Donuts of America, Inc.
Post Office Box 317
Randolph, MA 02368
(estimated investment: $16,000–$36,000 plus working capital)

Mister Donut of America, Inc.
1200 Multifoods Building
Minneapolis, MN 55402
(estimated investment: $50,000 excluding land and building)

Tastee Donuts, Inc.
Post Office Box 2708
Rocky Mount, NC 27801
(estimated investment: $36,000)

EMPLOYMENT AGENCIES AND PERSONNEL

AAA Employment Franchise, Inc.
400-83rd Avenue North
St. Petersburg, FL 33702

ACME Personnel Service
Post Office Box 14466
Opportunity, WA 99214
(estimated investment: $9,500–$19,500)

Automated Personnel International, Inc.
350 Fifth Avenue
New York, NY 10001

Fanning Enterprises, Inc.
180 Broadway
New York, NY 10038

Fortune Franchise Corporation
505 Fifth Avenue
New York, NY 10017
(estimated investment: $40,000 and up)

Hartman Temporary Personnel
3550 Biscayne Boulevard
Miami, FL 33137
(estimated investment: $25,000)

Management Recruiters International, Inc.
1015 Euclid Avenue
Cleveland, OH 44115
(estimated investment: $27,000–$58,000)

Manpower, Inc.
5301 North Ironwood Road
Milwaukee, WI 53201
(estimated investment: $50,000)

Personnel Pool
303 S.E. 17th Street
Fort Lauderdale, FL 33316
(estimated investment: $70,000–$100,000)

Snelling and Snelling, Inc.
4000 South Tamiami Trail
Sarasota, FL 33581
(estimated investment: $20,000–$60,000)

Staff Builders Temporary Personnel
122 East 42nd Street
New York, NY 10017
(estimated investment: $25,000–$40,000)

Timesavers Temporary Personnel Service
1296 Lawrence Station Road
Sunnyvale, CA 94086
(estimated investment: $38,000)

Uniforce Temporary Services
1335 Jericho Turnpike
New Hyde Park, NY 11040
(estimated investment: $50,000)

ENTERTAINMENT

Entertainment Industries, Inc.
6430 Sunset Boulevard
Hollywood, CA 90028
(estimated investment: $18,000–$165,000)

Fun Services, Inc.
221 East Cullerton Street
Chicago, IL 60616
(estimated investment: $20,000 and up)

T.V. Focus, Inc.
One Anderson Avenue
Fairview, NJ 07022
(estimated investment: $3,500)

T.V. Tempo, Inc.
387 Old Commerce Road
Athens, GA 30607
(estimated investment: $14,500)

FIRE AND THEFT PREVENTION

Arrow Investigation and Security Service, Inc.
483 78th Street
Brooklyn, NY 11209
(estimated investment: $7,500)

Defensive Instruments, Inc.
925 Penn Avenue
Pittsburgh, PA 15222

Everguard Fire Alarm Company, Inc.
19th Street and Indiana Avenue
Philadelphia, PA 19132

Photo-Scan International
3221 Carter Avenue
Marina del Rey, CA 90291
(estimated investment: $25,000)

Video Guard, Inc.
South 312 Post
Spokane, WA 99204
(estimated investment: $10,000–$20,000)

FOOD—DRIVE-IN, CARRY-OUT RESTAURANTS

A & W Restaurants, Inc.
2240 Welsch Industrial Center "A"
St. Louis, MO 63141
(estimated investment: $450,000)

Arby's Systems, Inc.
3565 Piedmont Road, N.E.
Atlanta, GA 30305
(estimated investment: $100,000)

Bagel Nosh, Inc.
110 East 73rd Street
New York, NY 10021
(estimated investment: $120,000)

Black Angus Systems, Inc.
13001 Northeast 14th Avenue
North Miami, FL 33161
(estimated investment: $175,000)

Bonanza International, Inc.
8350 North Central Expressway
Dallas, TX 75206

Bun & Burger International Inc.
41 East 42nd Street
New York, NY 10017
(estimated investment: $50,000 and up)

Burger Chef Systems, Inc.
Post Office Box 927
College Park Pyramids
Indianapolis, IN 46206
(estimated investment: $150,000)

Burger King Corp.
Post Office Box 520783
Biscayne Facility
Miami, FL 33152

Copper Penny Family Restaurants
4001 Warner Boulevard
Burbank, CA 91503
(estimated investment: $25,000)

Country Kitchen International, Inc.
7800 Metro Parkway
Minneapolis, MN 55420
(estimated investment: $53,000)

Der Wienerschnitzel International, Inc.
4440 Von Karman Avenue
Newport Beach, CA 92660
(estimated investment: $50,000–$150,000)

Farrell's Ice Cream Parlor Restaurant
Marriott Drive
Washington, DC 20058
(estimated investment: $125,000)

Fosters Freeze International
2400 Marconi Avenue
Sacramento, CA 95821

Ground Round Restaurants
222 Forbes Road
Braintree, Massachusetts 02184
(estimated investment: $900,000)

Hardee's Food Systems, Inc.
Post Office Box 1619
Rocky Mount, NC 27801
(estimated investment: $200,000 plus building and land)

Howard Johnson's Restaurants
200 Forbes Road
Braintree, MA 02184
(estimated investment: $1,000,000)

International Blimpie Corp.
1414 Avenue of the Americas
New York, NY 10019
(estimated investment: $80,000–$90,000 cash)

International House of Pancakes
6837 Lankershim Boulevard, N.
Hollywood, CA 91605
(estimated investment: $45,000 plus land, building and equip-
   ment)

Jack in the Box
Division of Foodmaker, Inc.
9330 Balbao Avenue
San Diego, CA 92112
(estimated investment: $95,000)

Kentucky Fried Chicken Corp.
Post Office Box 32070
Louisville, KY 40232

The Little King Restaurant Corp.
11811 "I" Street
Omaha, NB 68137

Long John Silver's Seafood Shoppes
Post Office Box 11988
Lexington, KY 40579

Lum's Restaurant Corp.
8420 N.W. 53rd Terrace
Miami, FL 33166
(estimated investment: $100,000

McDonald's Corp.
One McDonald's Plaza
Oak Brook, IL 60521
(estimated investment: $300,000 and up)

Nathan's Famous, Inc.
1515 Broadway
New York, NY 10036

The Orange Bowl Corp.
227 N.E. 17th Street
Miami, FL 33132
(estimated investment: $110,000–$130,000)

Orange Julius of America
2850 Ocean Park Boulevard
Santa Monica, CA 90405
(estimated investment: $85,000–$125,000)

Pepe's Inc.—Pepe's Mexican Restaurants
1325 West 15th Street
Chicago, IL 60608
(estimated investment: $75,000–$150,000)

Pizza Time Theatre, Inc.
1213 Innsbruck Drive
Sunnyvale, Ca 94086
(estimated investment: $300,000 and up)

The Round Table Franchise Corp.
601 Montgomery Street
San Francisco, CA 94111
(estimated investment: $220,000–$240,000)

Roy Rogers Restaurants
One Marriott Drive
Washington, DC 20058
(estimated investment: $200,000)

Shakey's Inc.
3600 First International Building
Dallas, TX 75270
(estimated investment: $50,000 cash, $250,000 net worth)

Sizzler Family Steak Houses
12731 West Jefferson Boulevard
Los Angeles, CA 90066
(estimated investment: $100,000 cash; net worth $600,000–
   $650,000)

The Straw Hat Restaurant Corp.
6400 Village Parkway
Dublin, CA 94566
(estimated investment: $115,000)

Stuckey's Inc.
4501 Circle 75 Parkway
Atlanta, GA 30339

Swensen's Ice Cream Co.
2408 East Arizona Biltmore Circle
Phoenix, AZ 85016
(estimated investment: $160,000–$400,000)

Taco Bell Corp.
16808 Armstrong Avenue
Irvine, CA 92714
(estimated investment: $150,000)

Wendy's International, Inc.
4288 West Dublin-Granville Road
Dublin, OH 43017
(estimated investment: $500,000 and up)

Wiener King Corp.
Post Office Box 3548
Charlotte, NC 28235
(estimated investment: $30,000–$50,000)

Wuv's International, Inc.
5500–4 Northwest 21st Terrace
Fort Lauderdale, FL 33309
(estimated investment: $50,000–$75,000)

FOOD STORES

Alpen Pantry, Inc.
950 South Tamiami Trail
Sarasota, FL 33577
(estimated investment: $57,000)

Grandma Love's Cookies and Co.
The Cookie Store
387 Old Commerce Road
Athens, GA 30607
(estimated investment: $70,000)

Hickory Farms of Ohio
300 Holland Road
Maumee, OH 43537
(estimated investment: $180,000)

Quik Stop Markets, Inc.
Post Office Box 5745
Fremont, CA 94538
(estimated investment: $25,000 plus inventory)

The Southland Corp.
2828 North Haskell Avenue
Dallas, TX 75204
(estimated investment: $32,500 and up)

Swiss Colony Stores, Inc.
One Alpine Lane
Monroe, WI 53566
(estimated investment: $100,000 plus leasehold improvements)

Tiffany's Bakeries, Inc.
4950 West Kennedy Boulevard

Tampa, FL 33609
(estimated investment: $40,000)

HEALTH AIDS AND SERVICES

Aerobic Fitness and Diet Center
1026 South Powell Road
Independence, MO 64050
(estimated investment: $15,000 and up)

Elaine Powers Figure Salons, Inc.
105 West Michigan Street
Milwaukee, WI 53203
(estimated investment: $50,000)

Gloria Stevens Figure Salons
10 Forbes Road
Braintree, MA 02184
(estimated investment: $50,000)

Lean-Line, Inc.
151 New World Way
South Plainfield, NJ 07080

Personnel Finders (d.b.a. Nursefinders)
1400 North Cooper
Arlington, TX 76011
(estimated investment: $70,000–$140,000)

Physicians Weight Loss Centers of America, Inc.
30 Springside Drive
Akron, OH 44313
(estimated investment: $32,000)

SPA Development Associates, Ltd.
16720 Northeast 6th Avenue
North Miami Beach, FL 33162
(estimated investment: $150,000)

Venus De Milo
1600 Dove Street
Newport Beach, CA 92660
(estimated investment: $43,500–$48,000)

Woman's World Health Spas
210–216 Dexter Avenue
Watertown, MA 02172
(estimated investment: $20,000–$25,000)

ICE CREAM STORES

Baskin-Robbins Ice Cream Co.
21 Baskin-Robbins Place
Glendale, CA 91201
(estimated investment: $65,000–$75,000)

Carvel Corp.
201 Saw Mill River Road
Yonkers, NY 10701
(estimated investment: $50,000)

International Dairy Queen
Box 35286
Minneapolis, MI 55435
(estimated investment: $40,000)

McWilly's Enterprises
Post Office Box 5769
Sarasota, FL 33579
(estimated investment: $75,000)

Mister Softee, Inc.
901 East Clements Bridge Road
Runnemede, NJ 08078
(estimated investment: $12,000)

Polar Bear Ice Cream Co.
400 South Zang Boulevard
Dallas, TX 75208

INDUSTRIAL PRODUCTS AND EQUIPMENT

Chem-Mark International
820 West Chapman
Orange, CA 92668
(estimated investment: $18,000)

Mac Tools, Inc.
Post Office Box 370
Washington Court House, OH 43160
(estimated investment: $25,000)

Remaco, Inc.
200 Park Avenue
Northvale, NJ 07647
(estimated investment: $1,000)

Snap-on-Tools Corp.
2801–80th Street
Kenosha, WI 53140
(estimated investment: $20,000–$40,000)

Tepco, Inc.
3609 Marquis Drive
Garland, TX 75042
(estimated investment: $25,000)

LAUNDRY AND DRY CLEANING STORES

Betty Brice International, Inc.
2243 Bryn Mawr Avenue
Philadelphia, PA 19131
(estimated investment: $25,000)

Comet International, Inc.
178 North County Road
Palm Beach, FL 33480
(estimated investment: $15,000)

General Electric
Appliance Park
API-231
Louisville, KY 40225

London Equipment Co.
2243 Bryn Mawr Avenue
Philadelphia, PA 19131
(estimated investment: $25,000 minimum)

The Maytag Co.
(Commercial Laundry Division)
403 West 4th Street North
Newton, IA 50208

Wascomat/Wascoclean
461 Doughty Boulevard
Inwood, NY 11696

LAWN CARE SERVICES

Lawn Doctor, Inc.
142 Highway 34
Matawan, NJ 07747
(estimated investment: $15,000)

Lawn King, Inc.
Three Edison Place
Fairfield, New Jersey 07006
(estimated investment: $70,000)

Spring-Green Lawn Care Corp.
Post Office Box 908
Naperville, Illinois 60540
(estimated investment: $10,000–$50,000)

Superlawns, Inc.
17032 Briardale Road
Rockville, MD 20855
(estimated investment: $20,000 plus working capital)

MEN'S AND WOMEN'S CLOTHING AND SPECIALTY SHOPS

Formal Wear Service
639 V.F.W. Parkway
Route 1
Chestnut Hill, MA 02167
(estimated investment: $65,000 minimum)

Jilene, Inc.
800 Miramonte Drive
Santa Barbara, CA 93109
(estimated investment: $35,000 and up)

Just Plants
201 North Wells Street
Chicago, IL 60606
(estimated investment: $80,000–$135,000)

Lady Madonna Management Corp.
36 East 31st Street
New York, NY 10016
(estimated investment: $45,000 and up)

Modern Bridal Shoppes, Inc.
600 Route 130 North
Cinnaminson, NJ 08077
(estimated investment: $14,000–$35,000)

Wrangler Wranch Dealer Division
Blue Bell, Inc.
335 Church Court
Greensboro, NC 27401

MOTELS

Days Inns of America
2751 Buford Highway, N.E.
Atlanta, GA 30324
(estimated investment: $600,000)

Holiday Inns, Inc.
3796 Lamar Avenue
Memphis, TN 38118
(estimated investment: in excess of $1,500,000)

Howard Johnson's Motor Lodges
220 Forbes Road
Braintree, MA 02184
(estimated investment: $2,500,000 approximately)

Quality Inns
10750 Columbia Pike
Silver Spring, MD 20901
(estimated investment: land plus $275,000–$325,000)

Ramada Inns, Inc.
3838 East Van Buren Street
Phoenix AZ 85008

Red Carpet Inns of America, Inc.
2032 Hillview Street
Sarasota, FL 33579

Rodeway Inns International, Inc.
2525 Stemmons Freeway
Dallas, TX 75207

Sheraton Inns, Inc.
60 State Street
Boston, MA 02109
(estimated investment: $3,500,000–$5,000,000)

Super 8 Motels, Inc.
224 Sixth Avenue, S.E.
Aberdeen, SD 57401
(estimated investment: $100,000–$200,000)

Travelodge International, Inc.
250 Travelodge Drive
El Cajon, CA 92090
(estimated investment: $1,000,000 minimum)

Treadway Inns and Resorts
140 Market Street
Paterson, NJ 07505
(estimated investment: $1,000,000)

PET STORES AND SERVICES

Docktor Pet Centers, Inc.
Dundee Park
Andover, MA 01810
(estimated investment: $130,000–$150,000)

Petland, Inc.
195 North Hickory Street
Post Office Box 1606
Chillicothe, OH 45601
(estimated investment: $15,000–$35,000)

Puppy Palace Enterprises, Inc.
927 East Terra Lane
O'Fallon, MO 63366
(estimated investment: $25,000–$50,000)

PRINTING SERVICES

Alphagraphics, Inc.
845 East Broadway
Tucson, AZ 85719
(estimated investment: $35,000–$60,000)

Business Cards Tomorrow, Inc.
3000 N.E. 30th Place
Fort Lauderdale, FL 33306

Kwik-Kopy Corp.
5225 Hollister
Houston, TX 77040
(estimated investment: $76,000)

Postal Instant Press
8201 Beverly Boulevard
Los Angeles, CA 90048
(estimated investment: $56,000 plus working capital)

Printmasters, Inc.
655 Deep Valley Drive
Rolling Hills Estates, CA 90274
(estimated investment: $49,500)

Speedy Printing Centers, Inc.
30700 Telegraph Road
Birmingham, MI 48010
(estimated investment: $40,000 includes working capital)

RENTAL SERVICES

A to Z Rental Centers, Inc.
3550 Cedar Avenue South
Minneapolis MN 55407
(estimated investment: $8,500–$80,000)

Nation-Wide General Rental Centers, Inc.
1408-B Miamisburg-Centerville Road
Dayton, OH 45459
(estimated investment: $25,000–$85,000)

Taylor Rental Corp.
570 Cottage Street
Springfield, MA 01104
(estimated investment: $55,000–$65,000)

United Rent-All, Inc.
2042 Armacost Avenue, W.
Los Angeles, CA 90025
(estimated investment: $150,000–$200,000)

RETAIL STORES

American Vision Centers, Inc.
138–49 78th Avenue
Flushing, NY 11367
(estimated investment: $25,000)

Bathique International, Inc.
161 Norris Drive
Rochester, NY 14610
(estimated investment: $35,000–$75,000)

The Book Rack
2703 East Commercial Boulevard
Fort Lauderdale, FL 33308
(estimated investment: $6,000)

Carpeteria, Inc.
1122 North Vine Street
Hollywood, CA 90038
(estimated investment: $75,000–$200,000)

Coast to Coast Stores
Post Office Box 80
Minneapolis, MN 55440
(estimated investment: $70,000–$150,000)

Computerland Corp.
30985 Santana Street
Hayward, CA 94544
(estimated investment: $60,000–$165,000)

Conroy's Inc.
11260 Playa Court
Culver City, CA 90230
(estimated investment: $90,000)

G. Fried Carpetland, Inc.
800 Old Country Road
Westbury, NY 11590
(estimated investment: $20,000)

Lewis of London, Inc.
72–17 Austin Street
Forest Hills, NY 11375
(estimated investment: varies)

The Love Shops
2428 Gravel Drive
Fort Worth, TX 76140
(estimated investment: $75,000–$90,000)

National Video, Inc.
7325 N.E. 55th Avenue
Portland, OR 97218
(estimated investment: $54,900–$95,000)

Nettle Creek Industries
Peacock Road
Richmond, IN 47374
(estimated investment: $45,000)

Pearle Vision Centers
2534 Royal Lane
Dallas, TX 75205
(estimated investment: $30,000–$60,000)

Pier 1 Imports, Inc.
2520 West Freeway
Fort Worth, TX 76102
(estimated investment: $90,000–$110,000)

Rasco Stores
Division of Gamble-Skogmo, Inc.
2777 North Ontario Street
Burbank, CA 91504
(estimated investment: $75,000)

Riviera Convertibles, Inc.
3876 South Santa Fe Avenue
Los Angeles, CA 90058
(estimated investment: $100,000)

Scandia Down Corp.
1040 Industry Drive
Seattle, WA 98188
(estimated investment: $15,000)

Searle Optical Inc.
2534 Royal Lane
Dallas, TX 75205
(estimated investment: $30,000–$60,000)

Spring Crest Co.
505 West Lambert Road
Brea, CA 92621
(estimated investment: $35,000)

Stretch & Sew, Inc.
Post Office Box 185
Eugene, OR 97440
(estimated investment: $55,000–$88,000)

The Tinder Box International, Ltd.
Post Office Box 830
Santa Monica, CA 90406
(estimated investment: $20,000–$50,000)

Videa Van On Wheels, Inc.
2809 Eglinton Avenue, East
Scarborough, Ontario
Canada M1J 2E1
(estimated investment: $30,000)

Western Auto Supply Co.
2107 Grand Avenue
Kansas City, MO 64108
(estimated investment: $60,000)

Barbizon School of Modeling & Fashion
3 East 54th Street
New York, NY 10022
(estimated investment: $25,000–$50,000)

Child Enrichment Centers
6 Passaic Street
Hackensack, NJ 07601
(estimated investment: $60,000)

Evelyn Wood Reading Dynamics, Inc.
155 Bovet Road
San Mateo, CA 94402

International Computer Training Centers, Inc
3644 East McDowell Road
Phoenix, AZ 85008
(estimated investment: $30,000–$70,000)

John Robert Powers School System
9 Newbury Street
Boston, MA 02116
(estimated investment: $25,000)

Patricia Stevens International, Inc.
Post Office Box 31818
Omaha, NB 68131
(estimated investment: $25,000)

Robert Fiance System, Inc.
404 Fifth Avenue
New York, NY 10018
(estimated investment: $75,000–$150,000)

SPORTS AND RECREATION

The Athlete's Foot Marketing Associates, Inc.
601 Grant Street

Pittsburgh, PA 15219
(estimated investment: $90,000)

The Athletic Attic, Inc.
Post Office Box 14503
Gainesville, FL 32604
(estimated investment: varies)

Forty Love Tennis Shoppe, Inc.
26 Fashion Island
Newport Beach, CA 92660
(estimated investment: $85,000–$130,000)

Holiday Inn Trav-L-Parks
3796 Lamar Avenue
Memphis, TN 38118
(estimated investment: $100,000 plus)

Kampgrounds of America
Post Office Box 30558
Billings, MT 59114
(estimated investment: $65,000 and up)

Putt-Putt Golf Courses of America
Post Office Box 35327
Fayetteville, NC 28303
(estimated investment: $50,000–$150,000)

Sylvan Pools
Route 611
Doylestown, PA 18901

United Safari International, Inc.
Post Office Box 11528
Knoxville, TN 37919
(estimated investment: $50,000–$100,000)

Warehouse Sports & Recreation
637 East Main Street
Mesa, AZ 85203
(estimated investment: $15,000)

TRAVEL

Fugazy International Travel
67 Whitney Avenue
New Haven, CT 06510
(estimated investment: $60,000)

International Tours, Inc.
5001 East 68th Street
Tulsa, OK 74136

Travel Travel, Inc.
679 Encinitas Boulevard
Encinitas, CA 92024
(estimated investment: $55,000)

Vacation America Travel Network
555 Fifth Avenue
New York, NY 10017
(estimated investment: $35,000–$50,000)

VENDING MACHINES

Canteen Corp.
1430 Merchandise Mart
Chicago, IL 60654

Ford Gum & Machine Co., Inc.
(Division of Automatic Service Co.)
Newton & Hoag Streets
Akron, NY 14001
(estimated investment: $5,000–$30,000)

Mechanical Servants, Inc.
4615 North Clifton Avenue
Chicago, IL 60640
(estimated investment: $5,000 minimum)

WATER SOFTENERS

Culligan USA
Division of Culligan Int. Co.

One Culligan Parkway
Northbrook, IL 60062
(estimated investment: $25,000 and up)

Rainsoft Water Conditioning
1225 East Greenleaf Avenue
Elk Grove, IL 60007
(estimated investment: $15,000 minimum)

Rayne Corporation
121 East Mason Street
Santa Barbara, CA 93102
(estimated investment: $40,000–$100,000)

Water Purification Systems, Inc.
1465 S.W. 21st Avenue
Fort Lauderdale, FL 33312
(estimated investment: $10,000 and up)

Sharing Over Sixty

GENERAL

Association of Volunteer Bureaus
420 Bank Street
Norfolk, VA 23501

Call for Action, Inc.
575 Lexington Avenue
New York, NY 10022

Commission on Voluntary Service and Action
Room 1700A
475 Riverside Drive
New York, NY 10027

Goodwill Industries of America, Inc.
9200 Wisconsin Avenue, N.W.
Washington, DC 20014

United Way of America
801 North Fairfax Street
Alexandria, VA 22314

GOVERNMENT VOLUNTEER SOURCES

Action
Action Recruiting Office
812 Connecticut Avenue, N.W.
Washington, DC 20525
(includes Active Executives, Foster Grandparents, Older
Americans, Retired Senior Volunteer and Senior Compan-
ions programs)

The Peace Corps
806 Connecticut Avenue, N.W.
Washington, DC 20525

Service Corps for Retired Executives
(SCORE)
1129 20th Street, N.W.
Washington, DC 20416

VISTA
(Volunteers in Service to America)
806 Connecticut Avenue, N.W.
Washington, DC 20525

VOLUNTEER: National Center for Citizen Involvement
1111 North 19th Street
Arlington, VA 22209

MEMBERSHIP ORGANIZATIONS

American Association of Retired Persons
National Retired Teachers Association
(AARP-NRTA)
215 Long Beach Boulevard
Long Beach, CA 90801

The Gray Panthers
3700 Chestnut Street
Philadelphia, PA 19104

VOLUNTEER OPPORTUNITIES

BUSINESS AND ADMINISTRATION

You could help with:
   Bookkeeping/accounting
   Employment counseling
   Grant writing
   Personnel
   Shorthand
   Typing

Typical Opportunities:

   Research analyst. Fund-raising agencies for scholarships for minority colleges need research analysts, CPAs and people to recruit other volunteers.

   Job developer/counselor. Agencies that work with women reentering the job market need volunteers to help clients in all aspects of job search and placement. Persons with a background in personnel work are especially desired.

CIVIC AND CULTURAL

You could help with:
   Gift shop
   Fund raising
   Gardening
   Hosting
   Public relations
   Public speaking
   Research
   Story-telling
   Tours
   Weaving
   Wood carving

Typical Opportunities:

Building botanists. Botanical organizations need volunteers in several areas: graphic artists, history researchers, nature instructors for children, volunteers for their greenhouses, and help in the research department.

Walk through history. Needed: part-time guides to conduct tours through landmark buildings.

COUNSELING AND CASEWORK

You could help with:
- Alcoholism
- Child abuse families
- Delinquency
- Drug abusers
- Emotional problems
- Ex-offenders
- Mother-to-mother counseling
- Rape victims
- Stress situations

Typical Opportunities:

Counselor/friend. After-care centers need peer counselors to work one-to-one with persons with emotional problems. There are also needs for hobby specialists, and for people to take residents on outings, plan parties, and generally help them return to the mainstream of living independently.

CRISIS INTERVENTION

You could help with:
- Drug overdoses
- Emotional crises
- Family problems
- Potential runaways
- Rape counseling
- Suicide prevention
- Telephone communication for the deaf
- V.D. information

Typical Opportunities:

Women in crisis. Not-for-profit agencies that need telephone coun-selors to do intake and follow-up of rape victims, battered women and children. They are also in the market for volunteers interested in legislation on lobbying.

Drug hot line. Drug organizations working primarily in preventive education need hot-line workers who provide callers with informa-tion on items and quality of current street drugs. Other volunteers may assist in the in-school drug education programs. They also need clerical and maintenance help.

DAYTIME

You could help with:
> Child-care/day-care centers
> Clerical services
> Counseling
> Crisis work
> Driving
> Food services (Meals on Wheels)
> Friendships
> Health care
> Special interests
> Teacher's responsibilities

Typical Opportunities:

Classroom aid. Special schools for children with learning problems need volunteers to work as classroom teachers' aides, camp coun-selors, children's and research library assistants. This might prove to be an interesting volunteer assignment for persons interested in a possible career in this field.

Upgrade skills. Almost every not-for-profit agency is looking for persons with office and clerical skills. This could prove to be an excellent opportunity for people who are reentering the job market in this field to practice and upgrade their skills before going back to work.

COMPANIONSHIP/FRIENDSHIP

You could help with:
> Children from one-parent homes

Children in residential institutions
Disabled
Elderly
Isolated adults
Nursing home residents
Retarded

Typical Opportunities:

Visitors. There are hundreds of convalescent hospitals and board-and-care homes that need volunteer help. Every resident needs someone who cares, but many men and women are short on relatives and friends. Volunteers are needed to make visits, to talk with them, to play cards or checkers, read and write lettters—just to be a friend.

Big brother/big sister. There's a large group of young boys and girls from one-parent families who would be greatly benefited by having a substitute big brother or sister—who could take up the slack left by the missing parent. You can work out your own program with your little brother or sister. Sporting events, fishing, shopping trips or just visiting and being interested.

GROUP PROJECTS

You could help with:

Crafts
Driving
Entertainment
Making special appliances for the handicapped
Neighborhood and agency clean-up and paint-up
Minor maintenance
Recreation
Sewing
Sports
Visiting

Typical Opportunities:

Group project. One organization that is interested in the conservation of the forests and landscapes of Southern California has developed a strand of smog trees, which they plant in areas where native growth has been killed or damaged by smog. They are also

290 SUCCESS OVER SIXTY

very active in replanting seedlings in mountain areas that have been destroyed by fires. Groups are needed to help with the tree plantings, and in helping maintain the nursery and its thousands of seedlings.

Adopt-a-group. Mental health agencies need groups to adopt residential care homes, or wards in state hospitals. These groups provide parties on special occasions, group outings, trips to points of interest, and bring into some lonely lives a touch of the outside world.

HEALTH CARE

You could help with:
    Blood mobiles
    Clerical work
    Escorting hospital patients
    Friendly visiting
    General hospital services
    Gift shop
    Hospital information desk
    Immunization registration
    Public speaking
    Transporting blood
    Transporting patients

Typical Opportunities:

Health information. Busy mid-city hospitals need volunteers to answer calls from people requesting medical information, and insert prerecorded tapes into special machines. No medical knowledge is required, and training in phone answering and how to insert tapes is provided.

Bilingual volunteers. Almost every hospital and health clinic needs volunteers who speak a second language. Some need help with intake and receptionist duties; some need interpreters for doctors and nurses; others need patient visitors to cheer up the sick by conversing with them in their native language.

LEADERSHIP DEVELOPMENT

You could help with:
    Camp counseling

Campfire
Scouting
YMCA/YWCA

Typical Opportunities:

Program assistants. Neighborhood centers often have a shortage of personnel for their youth programs. Consequently, some youngsters are prevented from participating in programs from which they would derive great benefit. You can help by supervising field trips, teaching special-interest groups, helping with homework, or refereeing sports activities. After school hours.

Adult advisors. Branches of one national agency that works with girls and women of all ages needs volunteers to act as sponsors of teenage groups. Typical responsibilities would be chaperoning girls on short, local trips; acting as advisor or counselor, and supervising activities. After school hours.

MENTAL HEALTH

You could help with:
Playing table games
Psychological testing and observation
Sports
Teaching a craft
Tutoring

Typical Opportunities:

Social rehabilitation. Social and vocational rehabilitation services for young adult psychiatric outpatients, both pre- and posthospitalized, need volunteers with special counseling and testing skills, or with arts, crafts or hobby skills. Volunteers are also needed to help with basic living skills, such as how to use the bus, money management, and how to go shopping. Day-to-day living is taken for granted by the vast majority of the population, but it can be a frightening experience for those recovering from a mental breakdown.

Hospital aides. Volunteers are needed in many psychiatric hospitals to help the professional staff work with emotionally disturbed children. This volunteer opportunity provides an excellent training ground for retirees who wish to determine if working in the mental health field is what they really want to do.

MINOR MAINTENANCE

You could help with:
    Carpentry
    Electrical work
    General handyman services
    Painting
    Plumbing

Typical Opportunities:

Carpenters and painters. One wildlife sanctuary, for example, needs carpenters to help maintain buildings; a thrift shop needs someone to refinish donated furniture; a city recreation department needs painters to keep playground equipment in good condition; a nonprofit theater group needs carpenters and painters with emphasis on set construction and scene painting.

Gardeners. Many convalescent and board-and-care homes need gardeners for their grounds, as well as "green thumbers" to work with the residents in helping them learn to grow their own indoor plants. For the highly skilled, agencies need nursery managers, horticulturists, and farming instructors.

SPECIAL INTERESTS

You could help with:
    Barbering
    Car mechanics
    Cards
    Ceramics
    Chess/checkers
    Driving
    Environmental programs
    Hair styling
    Interior decorating
    Magic
    Musical arts
    Needlepoint

Painting
Photography
Pottery
Stamp collecting
Woodworking

Typical Opportunities:

Audio-visual aides. Youth-serving agencies need people to teach photography; hospitals need video-tape operators, many convalescent hospitals need projectionists, and there are many requests for people who are photography buffs who would bring their own slides of vacations, trips or special interests to show patients.

Drivers. In large metropolitan areas where public transportation is inconvenient, drivers are needed for the blind, the physically handicapped, patients who have a doctor's appointment or receive therapy, to deliver hot meals to the housebound, for immigrants and refugees who are unfamiliar with the cities and their complexities. Youth agencies need bus drivers to take youngsters on outings. In some instances there is reimbursement for expenses.

SPORTS AND RECREATION

You could help with:
Basketball
Baseball
Boxing
Dancing
Football
Karate
Soccer
Swimming
Volleyball

Typical Opportunities:

Recreational assistants. Many agencies who work with physically and mentally handicapped children and adults need instructors and aides in swimming, physical fitness and dance—folk and square, modern, ballet and, yes, even belly dancing.

Coaches. Nearly every agency that works with young people has an on-going need for coaches and officials for the sport of the season, be it baseball, softball, football, soccer, volleyball or tennis. Agencies and the special Olympics programs, which sponsor track and field events for physically and mentally handicapped children, need teenagers and adults to help with all aspects of the program.

TUTORING AND EDUCATION

You could help with:
    Auto mechanics
    Cooking
    Math
    Office procedures
    Reading
    Science
    Sewing
    Typing

Typical Opportunities:

Tutors/teachers. Non-English-speaking people from preschoolers to senior citizens need help in learning to read and write. School-age children need tutoring help in special fields, such as math and science. Immigrants and refugees need bilingual tutors to teach them not only English, but how to figure out American money, bus routes and grocery shopping.

Special needs. People trained in ESL (English as a second language) are also in demand, as are those trained in deaf signing and Braille. Other special requests are for cake decorating, ethnic cooking, good grooming and beauty, sheet metal and machine shop.

Sports Over Sixty

SOURCES FOR HEALTH AND FITNESS

American Association of Fitness
Directors in Business and Industry
P.O. Box 2000
Leesburg, VA 22073

Fitness Systems, Inc.
505 Flower Street

Post Office Box 71606
Arco Plaza
Los Angeles, CA 90071

The President's Council on Physical Fitness and Sports
Washington, DC 20001

Senior Sports International Association
5225 Wilshire Boulevard
Suite 302
Los Angeles, CA 90036

Schooling Over Sixty

SELECTED LIST OF EDUCATIONAL SOURCES

Adult Education Association of America
810 18th Street, N.W.
Washington, DC 20006

American Association for Higher Education
1 DuPont Circle
Washington, DC 20036

Capital Higher Education Service
275 Windsor Street
Hartford, CT 06120

Center for Open Learning
Alabama Consortium for the Development of Higher Education
306 North Main Street
Deomopolis, AL 36736

Educational Information and Referral Service
3393 Peachtree Road, N.E.
Atlanta, GA 30326

Educational Opportunity Center Program
18 Tremont Street
Boston, MA 02149

The Independent Scholarship Project
17 Myrtle Drive

Great Neck, NY 10021

Independent Study by Correspondence
Pennsylvania State University
3 Shields Building
University Park, PA 16802

Institutes for Lifetime Learning
American Association of Retired Persons
1346 Connecticut Avenue, N.W.
Suite 601
Washington, DC 20036

The National Council on Aging
600 Maryland Avenue, S.W.
Washington, DC 20009

The National University Extension Association
Suite 360
DuPont Circle, N.W.
Washington, DC 20009

New Jersey Education Consortium
228 Alexander Street
Princeton, NJ 08540

Pennsylvania Adult Counseling Program
Department of Education
Box 911
Harrisburg, PA 17126

Regional Learning Service of Central New York
405 Oak Street
Syracuse, NY 13203

School for New Learning
DePaul University
23 East Jackson Boulevard
Chicago, IL 60604

BIBLIOGRAPHY

Albert, Kenneth, J., *How to Pick the Right Small Business Opportunity,* New York: McGraw Hill, 1977.

Allen, Kerry Kenn, *Worker Volunteering: A New Resource for the 1980s,* New York: Amacon, 1980.

Anderson, Robert, *Stretching for Everyday Fitness,* New York: Random House, 1980.

Argusico, Victor M., *Learning in the Later Years,* New York: Academic Press, 1978.

Areti, S., *Creativity—The Magic Synthesis,* New York: Basic, 1976.

Ashley, Sally, *Connecting,* New York: Avon Books, 1982.

Bailey, Covert, *Fit or Fat,* Boston: Houghton Mifflin Co., 1978.

Barrow, Georgia M. and Smith, Patricia H., *Aging, Ageism, and Society,* St. Paul, Minn.: West Publishing Co., 1979.

Biegel, Leonard, *The Best Years Catalogue,* New York: G. P. Putnam, 1978.

Blanchard, K. and S. Johnson, *The One Minute Manager,* New York: William Morrow, 1982.

Bolles, R. N., *The Three Boxes of Life,* Berkeley: Ten Speed Press, 1978.

———, *What Color Is Your Parachute?* Berkeley: Ten Speed Press, 1983.

———, and John C. Crystal, *Where Do I Go from Here with My Life?* Berkeley: Ten Speed Press, 1980.

Buckley, Joe, *The Retirement Handbook,* New York: Harper and Row, 1977.

Burns, George, *How to Live to Be 100,* New York: G. P. Putnam, 1983.

Butler, R. and Lewis, Myra, "Age-ism—A Form of Bigotry," *The Gerontologist,* 1969.

Butler, R. and Lewis, Myra, *Sex After Sixty,* New York: Harper & Row, 1976.

Butler, R., *Why Survive?* New York: Harper & Row, 1976.

Cavett, Robert, *Success with People Through Human Engineering and Motivation,* Chicago: Success Unlimited, 1969.

Comfort, Alex, *A Good Age,* New York: Simon & Schuster, 1976.

Cooper, Kenneth, M.D., *New Aerobics,* New York: Bantam Books, 1970.

Cowley, Malcolm, *The View from 80,* New York: Viking/Penguin, 1982.

Cox, Harold, *Aging* (3d ed.), Guilford: Conn.: Dushkin Publishing, 1983.

De Beauvoir, Simone, *The Coming of Age,* New York: G. P. Putnam, 1972.

DeVries, Herbert, *Report on Jogging and Exercise for Older People,* Washington, D.C.: U.S. Administration on Aging, H.E.W., 1968.

———, *Vigor Regained,* Englewood Cliffs, N.J.: Prentice Hall, 1974.
Downs, Hugh, *Thirty Dirty Lies About Age,* Niles, Ill.: Argus Communications, 1979.

Feinstein, Lloyd L. and Linda Kline, *Career Changing,* Boston: Little, Brown, 1982.

Foner, Anee and Karen Schwab, *Aging and Retirement,* Monterey, Cal.: Brooks-Cole, 1981.

Generations, San Francisco: Western Gerontological Society, 1982.

Greene, Gardner (Mentor), *How to Start and Manage Your Own Business,* New York: New American Library, 1983.

Goldstein, Jerome, *In Business for Yourself,* New York: Charles Scribner's Sons, 1982.

Gore, Irene, *Add Years to Your Life and Life to Your Years,* New York: Stein & Day, 1973.

Gross, Henry, *Financing for Small and Medium Size Businesses,* Englewood Cliffs, N.J.: Prentice Hall, Inc., 1969.

Gross, Ronald, *The Independent Handbook,* New York: Addison Wesley, 1982.

———, *The Lifelong Learner,* New York: Simon & Schuster, 1979.
———, *The New Old,* Garden City, N.Y.: Doubleday, 1978.

Gumpert, P. E. and Tummons, J. A., *The Insiders' Guide to Small Business Resources,* Garden City, N.Y.: Doubleday, 1982.

Haldane, Bernard, *How to Make a Habit of Success,* New York: Prentice Hall, 1960.

Hallberg, Edmund, *The Grey Itch,* New York: Warner, 1978.

Harris, L., *The Myth and Reality of Aging in America,* Washington, D.C.: National Council on Aging, 1975.

Holz, Loretta, *How to Sell Your Arts and Crafts,* New York: Charles Scribner's Sons, 1977.

Jacobson, Beverly and Reinhold, *Young Programs for Older Workers,* New York: Van Nostrand Reinhold & Co., 1980.

Jessup and Chips, *The Women's Guide to Starting a Business,* New York: Holt, Rinehart and Winston, 1976.

Joffe, Gerardo, *How You Too Can Make at Least One Million in the Mail Order Business,* San Francisco, Advance Books, 1979.

Jorgensen, James, *The Graying of America: Retirement and Why You Can't Afford It,* New York: McGraw Hill, 1981.

Kastenbaum, Robert, *Growing Old,* Willenstad, Curacoa: Multimedia Publications, Inc., 1979.

Kent, Paul, *The Life Extension Revolution,* New York: William Morrow, 1980.

Kessler, Julia Braun, *Getting Even with Getting Old,* Chicago: Nelson Hall, 1980.

Knoff, *Successful Aging,* New York: Viking Press, 1975.

Kroc, Ray, *Grinding It Out,* New York: Berkeley, 1977.

Lasser, J. K., *How to Run a Small Business,* New York: McGraw Hill, 1974.

Le Shan, Eda, *Eda Le Shan on Living Your Life,* New York: Harper & Row, 1982.

Lester, Mary, *A Women's Guide to Starting a Small Business,* New York: Pilot Books, 1981.

Levesey, Herbert B., *Second Chance,* New York: New American Library, 1977.

Lugeman, Joseph, *Success Forces,* Chicago: Contemporary Books, 1980.

McKenzie, Sheila, *Aging and Old Age,* Glenview, Ill.: Scott Foresman and Co., 1980.

Mancuso, J. R. and Philip, J. Fox, *Four Hundred Things You Must Know Before Starting a Business,* Englewood Cliffs, N.J.: Prentice Hall, 1980.

Mancuso, J. R., *How to Start, Finance and Manage Your Own Business,* Englewood Cliffs, N.J.: Prentice Hall—Spectrum, 1982.

Mangold, Maxwell J., *How to Buy a Small Business,* New York: Pilot, 1976.

Maslow, A. H., *The Farther Reaches of Human Nature,* New York: Viking Press, 1971.

Masters, William and Virginia Johnson, *Human Sexual Response,* Boston: Little, Brown, 1966.

May, Rollo, *The Courage to Create,* New York: W. W. Norton, 1975.

Morehouse, Larry and Leonard Gross, *Maximum Performance,* New York: Simon & Schuster, 1977.

Moskowitz, Milton, Michael Katz, and Robert Levering, *Everybody's Business Scoreboard,* San Francisco: Harper & Row, 1983.

Nasbitt, John, *Megatrends,* New York: Warner Books, 1982.

Nayer, Harriet H., *Leadership for Volunteering,* New York: Dryden Associates, 1976.

Neesenberg, Gerard, *The Art of Creative Thinking,* New York: Simon & Schuster, 1982.

Neugarten, Bernice, "The Young Old," *Chicago University Magazine,* Autumn, 1975.

Nicholas, Ted, *How to Form Your Own Corporation Without a Lawyer for Under $50.00,* Wilmington, Del.: Enterprise, 1983.

Norton, *Creative Ability,* New York: Bantam, 1976.

Null, Gary, *Profitable Part-Time Home Based Businesses,* New York: Pilot, 1974.

Peale, Norman Vincent, *Enthusiasm Makes the Difference,* New York: Fawcett-Crest, 1967.

Percy, Charles, *Growing Old in the Country of the Young,* New York: McGraw Hill, 1974.

Peters, Thomas J. and Robert H. Watermann, Jr., *In Search of Excellence,* New York: Harper & Row, 1982.

Pickford, Gaylan, *Always a Woman,* New York: Bantam Books, 1982.

Porter, Sylvia, *Sylvia Porter's Money Book,* New York: Doubleday, 1975.

Quadagno, Jill S., *Aging, the Individual and Society,* New York: St. Martin's Press, 1980.

Radin, Robert J., *Full Potential,* New York: McGraw Hill, 1983.

Raudsephy, Eugene, *How Creative Are You?* Princeton, N.J.: Princeton Creative Research, Inc., 1978.

Rosow, Jerome M. and Robert Zager, *V.P., The Future of Older Workers in America,* Scarsdale, N.Y.: Work Institute, 1980.

Rubin, I., *Sexual Life After Sixty,* New York: Basic Books, 1975.

Salmans, Sandra, "Persisting Joys of 30 Years in a Club of Book-worms," *New York Times,* November 2, 1983.

Sheber, Sharon and Judith Schroder, *How to Make Money at Home,* New York, Wallaby Books, 1982.

Sheehy, Gail, *Passages,* New York: E. P. Dutton, 1976.

———, *Pathfinders,* New York: William Morrow, 1981.

Small Business Bibliography, SBA, Washington, D.C.: Government Printing Office.

Stoleewek, Toni, *Back to Work, Ladies,* New York: Pilot Books, 1967.

Tate, C. E. et al., *The Complete Guide to Your Own Business,* Homewood, Ill.: Sow Jones Irwin, 1976.

Taylor, John R., *How to Start and Succeed in a Business of Your Own,* New York: Reston, 1978.

Thompson, Frances Coombs, *The New York Times Guide to Continuing Education in America,* New York: Quadrangle Books, 1972.

Toffler, Alvin, *Future Shock,* New York: Random House, 1970.

———, *The Third Wave,* New York: Random House, 1980.

Troll, L. E., J. Israel, and K. Israel, *Looking Ahead,* Englewood Cliffs, N.J.: Prentice Hall—Spectrum, 1977.

White, Richard, *The Entrepreneur's Manual,* Radnor, Pa.: Chilton Book Company, 1976.

Willing, Jules Z., *The Lively Mind,* New York: William Morrow, 1982.

———, *The Reality of Retirement,* New York: William Morrow, 1982.

Winston, Sandra, *The Entrepreneurial Woman,* New York: Newsweek Books, 1983.

Winston, Stephanie, *Getting Organized,* New York: Warner Books, 1978.

Winter, Ruth, *Ageless Aging,* New York: Crown, 1973.

Films

The Art of Age, L.S.B. Productions, California

Arthur & Lillie, Pyramid Films, Santa Monica, California

Now Is Forever, Film Dynamics, Los Angeles, California

Claude Pepper, Committee on Aging, House of Representatives, Washington, D.C.

Picasso Is 90, CBS Films, New York

ABOUT THE AUTHORS

Albert Myers is President of the Success Over Sixty Institute. In his pre-sixties life Myers graduated from the University of Illinois, was a Lieutenant Colonel in the Air Force, and was President and CEO of Myers Brothers Department Stores. In his post-sixties life he has been a successful entrepreneur, a business consultant, an inventor, a columnist, a lecturer, the recipient of the Copley First Citizen Award for Volunteerism, and an avid sportsman. He divides his time between Aspen, Colorado, Springfield, Illinois, and Los Angeles, California.

Christoper P. Andersen is a senior editor at *People* magazine, and the author of four books. He has also been a staff writer and correspondent for *Time* magazine. He lives in New York City.

THE SUCCESS OVER SIXTY INSTITUTE

Albert Myers is President of the Success Over Sixty Institute, a national organization created to develop plans for coping with problems faced by men and women approaching retirement age.

It seeks to establish guidelines with major corporations of America to help older corporate employees and individuals lead active, productive and useful lives in their sixties and after.

If you are interested in receiving further information about corporate preretirement programs, attending the Success Over Sixty Seminars, organizing and becoming a member of a local Success Over Sixty chapter or receiving the Success Over Sixty Newsletter, please write to Albert M. Myers, President, Success Over Sixty Institute, Box 3095, Aspen, Colorado 81611.